China in One Village

China in One Village

*The Story of One Town
and the Changing World*

Liang Hong

Translated by Emily Goedde

VERSO
London • New York

First published in English by Verso 2021
Translation © Emily Goedde 2021
Translation of the Preface and Afterword © Natascha Bruce 2021
Originally published as 中国在梁庄 © 江苏人民出版社, 2010

Published with support from the China
Translation and Publishing House

1 3 5 7 9 10 8 6 4 2

Verso
UK: 6 Meard Street, London W1F 0EG
US: 20 Jay Street, Suite 1010, Brooklyn, NY 11201
versobooks.com

Verso is the imprint of New Left Books

ISBN-13: 978-1-83976-177-5
ISBN-13: 978-1-83976-556-8 (EXPORT)
ISBN-13: 978-1-83976-178-2 (UK EBK)
ISBN-13: 978-1-83976-179-9 (US EBK)

British Library Cataloguing in Publication Data
A catalogue record for this book is
available from the British Library

Library of Congress Cataloging-in-Publication Data
Library of Congress Control Number: 2021930158

Typeset in Sabon by Biblichor Ltd, Edinburgh
Printed and bound by CPI Group (UK) Ltd, Croydon CR0 4YY

Contents

Preface

A decade ago, I took a train trip from my home in Beijing to a far-flung corner of China, a village in rural Henan Province. Originally, I merely intended to write a travel diary of a trip to Liang Village, the community where I was born and grew up. But by the time the book was published, followed a few years later by a second book, it contained things that were called sociological "field investigations" and anthropological "oral histories." The books sold hundreds of thousands of copies and kickstarted a trend in contemporary Chinese "literary non-fiction."[1] All the major newspapers and media outlets ran articles and interviews about them, leading to ongoing discussions on themes such as "What's next for the countryside?" "Occupied hometowns!" and "Big country, small people." Since then, *China in One Village* has become required reading for sociology and anthropology majors in universities around the country.[2]

---

1 In 2009, *People's Literature* [*Renmin Wenxue*] magazine started a column called "Non-Fiction" ("Feixugou"). In 2010, it ran pieces including "Liang Village" by Liang Hong, "China: In the Absence of a Remedy" by Murong Xuecun, and "Southern Dictionary" by Xiao Xiangfeng, sparking widespread conversations and debates. As a result, literary non-fiction articles began to feature in large numbers on literary, news media, and social-media platforms, establishing the genre as both a literary phenomenon and a lasting trend.

2 Published in China as *Zhongguo zai Liangzhuang* by Jiangsu Art Publishing House, October 2010 and *Chu Liangzhuang Ji* by Flower City Publishing House, April 2013. As is common practice in Chinese literary non-fiction, "Liang Village" is a made-up name, and characters and relationships described in the book have been altered to protect privacy.

I had absolutely no idea that it would provoke such a huge reaction, and I've given a lot of thought to the reasons for this. Inadvertently, the book seems to have touched on a very fundamental concern, which has nevertheless been consistently overlooked: In rapidly developing, increasingly urbanized China, what *is* happening in the countryside? After all, this "countryside" is where the majority of Chinese people come from. Concern for its uncertain fate lurks within us all. Society is developing too fast—we don't go home for a year, and when we do familiar roads and trees have vanished; two or three years, and the river behind the village has gone. Our villages are increasingly deserted, many left almost in ruins. This has led to a sense of "psychological homelessness" and a deep, steadily building sorrow. I wrote *China in One Village* on behalf of everyone affected by this. On behalf of us all, I raise the questions: What on earth is going on in the Chinese countryside? What on earth is happening to my home?

Another reason for the reaction is surely the style in which I wrote the book: as though on the scene. From the start, I wanted to convey a sense of immediacy—for a reader to come with me to the fields around Liang Village, then to come with me inside villager such-and-such's home, sit down, look into their eyes, make conversation, listen to their stories. I wanted each reader to feel as if they were back in their own village, meeting the villagers there, seeing their own rivers and little streams. There's an intrinsic universality to that experience. Later, while I was traveling for research, whenever I spoke about the book people always wanted to talk to me about their own villages and what had happened to them; never about Liang Village. This is important to keep in mind.

Even readers born in cities have been deeply moved by *China in One Village*. Some have written me letters about it or posted essays online. It's made me think that the so-called native soil experience of our agricultural civilization still lingers deep in the soul of every Chinese person. It's a kind of collective subconscious, at the root of our experience of the world.

But no matter how readers understand this book, how scholars and officials choose to interpret it, or how many academic disciplines happen to be touched upon inside it, I will always insist that it is literature, first and foremost. Because, ultimately, it is about people. It describes the complex fabric of contemporary Chinese society and tells the story of our lives. It relies on emotion, rather than using the language of logic and reason to produce an account of social norms and community attributes.

And so, while reading this book, I hope you will keep an open heart. Regardless of the genre, regardless of where the story is from, you and I are in this together—we're on a train, setting off on a journey to Liang Village. In a remote corner of this vast land we call China, a village, a community, and a river await. They are waiting for you to walk on in.

1

Where Is Liang Village?

Return to Rang County

Last night I hardly slept. The jolting train kept my son, three years and two months old, from sleeping soundly. The slightest discomfort had him swinging his arms, tossing and turning. To keep him from falling out of the bunk, I lay at his feet and put my legs around him, but he, in his dreams, kept pushing them away. In the end I sat up, turned on the little lamp at the head of the bed, and read the book I had brought with me: *The Outermost House: A Year of Life on the Great Beach of Cape Cod* by the American naturalist Henry Beston. Beston wrote this collection of essays after spending a season on an isolated stretch of the Cape Cod coast. There he was in direct contact with the majestic ocean, all kinds of seabirds, unpredictable weather, and the omnipresent perils of the sea. You can sense the richness, precision, and deep love with which his gaze took everything in. The natural world and humankind became one:

> Whatever attitude to human existence you fashion for yourself, know that it is valid only if it be the shadow of an attitude to Nature. A human life, so often likened to a spectacle upon a stage, is more justly a ritual. The ancient values of dignity, beauty, and poetry which sustain it are of Nature's inspiration; they are born of the mystery and beauty of the world. Do no dishonor to the earth lest you

dishonor the spirit of man. Hold your hands out over the earth as over a flame. To all who love her, who open to her the doors of their veins, she gives of her strength, sustaining them with her own measureless tremor of dark life.

Life's meaning and the true nature of human existence only take form when joined with the natural world. You are insignificant. You are also immense. And you become eternal, for humankind is only one part of the whole.

I lift the curtain. The train is speeding through the night's hazy glow, and the plains recede rapidly. Between the trees, houses come and go in silence. You can hear the night breathing faintly. On the eve of my trip home, I am filled with yearning. My village, my loved ones, my little stream, and that big tree in the middle of the stream where, when I was young, I carved my name. To me its scenery is both majestic and conducive to the same kinds of solemn reflection.

In the early morning, the train slowly makes its way toward the county seat, and when I see the bridge I know we've arrived at Rang County. This is the first stop on my journey. Once, on this bridge, I saw the most beautiful moon in the whole world. It was nearly dark, and the moon had already risen in the sky. Its color was a strange, light yellow, like fine Xuan rice paper, and its round elegance was set off by a wisp of cloud across it. Like youthful melancholy, it had a subtlety that was hard to convey. I was thirteen that year, and it was both my first time at the county seat and my first time seeing a train, yet my first impression of the city, the one that has remained with me, is that moon. I had come to the city to meet my eldest sister, but as I searched for her workplace in the darkness, in the city's crisscrossing streets, I had started to panic. In fact, I was so terrified that I hadn't even dared ask directions, for the people walking leisurely by me had an air about them that made me unwilling to approach them. I paced back and forth in front of a building for quite a while, wanting to go in and ask directions.

I had a vague sense that I was close to where she worked, or perhaps that this was actually the place, but I couldn't bring myself to ask. Now I realize that the city, even just a small county seat, had impressed upon that young country child a distinct difference in social class.

Rang County was once very significant in "deer hunts on the central plains," that is, historical attempts to overthrow the throne. Time and time again, fierce wars and natural disasters nearly wiped out the people of Rang County. But advantages in geography and climate, as well as ease in transportation, meant that immigrants quickly arrived to fill in any population gaps. According to historical records, in the fifteenth year of King Zhaoxiang of Qin's reign (281 BCE), "disobedient followers" were relocated to Rang County. During the Tang Dynasty, in the tenth year of Emperor Xuanzong's reign (722 CE), "Hu barbarians" (non-Han Chinese) from six cities in Hequ County, more than 50,000 people, were moved to Xu, Ru, Tang, Rang, and other areas.

Among migrations, the one involving the largest number of people happened during the second year of the reign of Emperor Zhu Yuanzhang (1369 CE) in the Ming Dynasty. People were moved from Shanxi, Jiangxi, Fujian, and other provinces to Rang County. People in Rang County who claim Hongtong County in Shanxi as their ancestral home arrived at this time. Now Rang County is 2,360 square kilometers or about 900 square miles. It has 28 townships (offices and administrative divisions) and 579 individual administrative villages, with a total of approximately 1,560,000 people and 2,440,000 square *mu* of arable land (1 *mu* = 666.5 square meters, so about 627 square miles of farmland).

Rang County is primarily agricultural; it is known as a "grain basket." Rich in wheat, cotton, tobacco, chili peppers, and peanuts, it's nationally significant for the production and manufacturing of goods such as grain, cattle, and export tobacco. It is also an important site for cotton and sesame production.

Nevertheless, large-scale industry is almost nonexistent, and there has been no development of industrial infrastructure. This means that it has been at a disadvantage throughout the many waves of "reform and opening up." The government's general assessment of Rang County is this: an economy that's undeveloped; customs that are conservative; points of view that are backward.

Finally the train comes to a stop. Outside the window, my relatives make an impressive group: Father, Eldest Sister, Second Sister, Third Sister, and Little Sister's entire family; more than a dozen people. When the train door opens, my son, who had been waiting anxiously at the door, suddenly starts to cry and doesn't want to get off. Pointing at the ground he says it's dirty—too dirty. Everyone bursts out laughing. It rained the night before, and the ground is damp. It's covered in mud, fruit peels wet from the rain, and bits of paper and trash, and flies are buzzing all around. My son is clearly a bit intimidated.

At noon, we all go to a restaurant to eat together. When I was a child, our family included Father, Mother, and seven of us sisters. Now we've expanded to a family of more than twenty. We can't all fit around a single table, so the kids—big and small—sit at the table next to us and make a racket with their nonstop laughter. To a stranger we must look like a happy family, or at least like a family that has emerged from a long period of poverty; we can now enjoy a proper meal together in a restaurant.

My son, in the midst of this rowdy scene, is skittish and apprehensive. He clings to me, not wanting to be put down. City kids these days aren't used to these big, noisy family gatherings.

As usual, in the evening, the family goes over to my younger sister's house. My father, elder sisters, and their husbands don't play their customary card game, "Fight the Landlord," a game that's been a favorite over the past seven or eight years—it's a common form of entertainment in most small northern towns. Instead, everybody sits together, talking about goings-on around

4

the village. My sisters married early and left home, eventually moving to the city. So for them this is a "homecoming" too, and their curiosity and excitement about village happenings is no less than my own.

There is one more reason that the family is excited: I'm finally able to come home to stay for a spell. Since the age of twenty, when I left to go to school, I've never been home for more than a short visit. Now I can finally stay for a while and live with them again.

Lost

The roads leading out of the city were built along the river, and one long section rises more than ten meters above river level. From your car, you can see down along the river, where excavators roar, piles upon piles of sand loom high, and industrial-sized transport trucks rush back and forth. It's a bustling construction scene. Yet the river itself, which only ten years ago flowed broad and smooth, is gone, and the river birds, which once circled above the water, have left without a trace.

The effects of thirty years of "reform and opening up" are most visible in the roads. New roads, wider roads, extend in all directions and cut the distances between villages, cities, and towns. While I was growing up, riding the bus into the city would take at least two hours, not including time spent waiting for the bus, and the ride was so bumpy you were in danger of banging your head painfully on the ceiling. People rode the bus very rarely; a two-kuai (or about twenty-five cents) one-way ticket represented living expenses for a family of six for a month. Students who went to the county teachers college would usually borrow a bicycle to come home. Two students would take turns carrying each other, as the ride home could take six hours. Your backside would inevitably be rubbed sore, but the students didn't care. Riding along the river, birds circled overhead, and

5

along the side of the road there were long irrigation canals, filled with deep, green grass and little, multicolored wild flowers that followed the rise and fall of the canals, stretching into the blue depths of the sky. The villages, set off in the trees along the roads, were quiet and modest, seemingly eternal.

But this, I know, is only my memory. Those eternal villages, when brought back to reality, are riddled with ills like this multi-lane expressway, crossing through the plains, as if proclaiming to all the world: modernization has arrived at the countryside's doorstep. But, as far as the villages are concerned, modernity is as distant as before, and perhaps even more so. At the beginning of the 2010s, the expressway had just been opened, and the local people still had no sense of road safety.

They walked on the road. They rode bikes and drove three-wheeled carts; they went against traffic; they crossed traffic. Occasionally the sky above the plains would ring with the ear-piercing sounds of horns and brakes. "My fellow villagers" were walking, cool as cucumbers, on the expressway, having cut a giant hole in the wire fence below. But no one walks on the road anymore. I guess they've finally learned.

They have learned they must return to their designated track. The cars speeding past have nothing to do with them—on the contrary, the cars only confirm their status as the "other" in this modernizing society. Never mind all the land the roads have occupied: Two villages that were once so close that villagers would drop by for a meal can now reach each other only by taking a detour of several miles. The roads have damaged the village ecology, but the harm done to this living organism has never registered, even remotely, with the policymakers who direct the construction process. No one thinks about the villagers' experiences, even though not so much as a drain is installed without reference to official data. The expressway, with its strong smell of asphalt and metal, is an immense scar on the plains beneath the sun.

The town of Wu gradually grows closer.

Our landing point is my elder brother's house, where he does business in Wu town. Wu is situated about forty kilometers northwest of the county seat. It was formerly one of Rang County's "four famous towns" and home to a bustling market. The main roads run through its center, in the shape of a cross. When I was young, it would become a veritable ocean of people on market days and especially during the temple fair in the spring. We would walk from the north end to the south, being jostled here and there. It seemed our feet couldn't stick to the ground. Cars could barely move an inch and though they honked to the high heavens, no one seemed to hear them. Certainly no one paid them any mind, immersed as they were in the noisy hustle and bustle.

At the north end is the Muslim Hui district. We passed by their houses every day on the way to school and saw them slaughtering sheep, holding funeral processions, or reading from the Quran. Their lifestyle has always seemed both strange and sacred to me. There are no factories, no businesses. Other than the necessary professions and government functionaries, most of the people work the land for their livelihood or do a little peddling now and then, selling or bartering grain, eggs, and fruit from their homes.

Now Wu has a central market and business district along the new road. Row after row of brand-new buildings line its sides, all built in the same slanted roof, European style, which appears both very modern and very out of place. The former main street, enclosed within the roads and construction rising up on the outskirts of town, is virtually empty and has fallen into disrepair. Even though the buildings and businesses are all still there, though the shopkeepers haven't changed, the transformation all around them has given the neglected buildings a sense of displacement—as if something's not quite right. This feeling of displacement is something I haven't gotten used to; every time I walk down the road, I have the strong sense that I am in some foreign land.

My brother and sister-in-law opened a small clinic in town, but my brother has also followed the times and does some business on the side, contracting land, opening a recreation hall, and, most recently, investing in real estate with some of his classmates. Despite initial setbacks, they seem to be doing well. This time the entrance to his home is piled high with sand, stones, and steel rods, and a cement truck is humming. He's planning to divide the house he bought into two and then sell one half to pay off the mortgage.

We stop only briefly before we go buy firecrackers and joss paper to take down to the village, where we'll pay homage at Grandfather and Third Great Uncle's graves. This is the first thing we do whenever we get home. Twenty years of expansion have almost joined Liang Village and the town of Wu together; my brother's house is only about 500 meters from the village. When I was young, I would go to the study hall at school in the evenings, and the trip home afterwards was the most terrifying experience of my life. The roads were empty, silent, and tenebrous, surrounded by tall white poplars, blowing wind and rustling leaves. The back of my neck would go ice-cold with fear, and this stretch of road, from the school to the village, seemed the most endless road in the world. Of course, there were better times, too, like when I was a teenager, and especially when the romance and wuxia writers Chiung Yao and Jin Yong were popular. I read everything of theirs I could get my hands on, as if possessed. Afterwards, on the night road, panicked and afraid, I would imagine a young man in white, riding in swiftly from afar, handsome and flushed, reaching for my hand with great tenderness as he offered to take me home.

But today it would be hard to believe that this was the village where I lived for twenty years, if it weren't for the fact that my family, my former home, and my relatives' graves are still there.

Grandfather and Third Great Uncle are buried behind our former home. We call this our "back courtyard," but the wall around it has collapsed, and the weeds reach up to our waists.

Sharp and clear, the sound of firecrackers crackle above us. There, in the sky over the village, the explosions startle the silent awake, perhaps connecting us with the souls on the other side. We kowtow and burn joss paper, and then Father rubs his eyes and says, "In 1960 your grandfather entered the communal nursing home. When he went in, he was in good health. He could speak; he could sing. He even carried a small chamber pot. Four days later they sent him back on a mat. He was dead, plumb starved to death." Every time we pay our respects, father tells this story as a matter of course. Even though I never met Grandfather, I have heard this tale so many times that I can see him in my mind. He is wearing a fitted black cap, and because he sold tofu, which he carried on a shoulder pole through the village all year round, he is bent at the waist. As he totters toward the old folks home, five *li* (about 1.5 miles) from the village, he's holding his bedding in one hand and a small chamber pot in the other.

Hearing the sound of the firecrackers, a few people from the village come out and regard me politely. They ask Father, "Guangzheng, which of your daughters is this? Is this your fourth daughter? How'd she get so fat?" I look at their faces, both familiar and unfamiliar, and in their expressions I sense the traces of the years. I realize: I, too, have undergone marked change.

To the right of the back courtyard is a newly built two-story house. Father says it belongs to Zhang Daokuan. Daokuan's siblings all left the village and went to college; only he remained. He doesn't speak well and isn't much good for labor. He married a pretty little devil from Sichuan with a fiery temper. She ran away from home a few times, and each time he dragged her back, but one day she left for good. Daokuan has suffered plenty, and now he's the village laughingstock.

Pushing back the knee-high weeds and shrubs, we come around to the front of our old home, where I lived for twenty years. The front, too, is filled with weeds and grasses, and one side of the caved-in kitchen has been turned into an ad hoc toilet. There are also signs that animals have been kept there. The front and back roofs of the main house both have large holes in them, and the foundation has started to lean a little. A few years ago my brother tried to fix things up, but because no one lives here, it quickly fell into disrepair again. On the exterior wall a poem my younger sister wrote at school is still faintly visible, complete with the wrong characters. Every year when we go back, we read it again, laughing together. Father forgot the key, so we can't go inside. Instead, Father and Elder Sister stand in front of the house and take a picture. The contrast between Daokuan's house and our own is shocking.

Mother's grave is in the public cemetery on the river slope behind the village. Looking out over it, it seems open and peaceful and filled with mist. It gives a sense of the eternity of life and nature. Every time I come here, my heart expands, not in sorrow, but with peace and solace. Here I feel I am at home. I have returned to life's beginnings—my mother is here—and my own final resting place will also be here. We burn joss paper, kowtow and set off firecrackers. I have my son kneel on the ground and follow me as I bow three times. I tell him, this is your maternal grandmother. He asks, "Who's she?" I say, "She's your Mama's Mama, the one closest to me." Then, as always, we sit beside the grave and chat about what's going on in the family.

Every time we come, my eldest sister repeats over and over, "If only Ma were still here, things would be so much better . . ."

Yes. "If only Ma were here." We've imagined it untold times; and it's become our constant dream—and sorrow. Looking at the grass on the grave, and the bits of firecracker, thinking back on Mother's life and our years of hardship, the idea of home and the significance of kinship always flash into my mind. What would our lives, our struggles, our successes, and our losses mean if it weren't for this, if it weren't for our hometown, which keeps us together, reveals our pasts and the traces of our former lives?

The Past

Today's plan is to "interview" Father. "Interview" sounds a little strange, as Father is always here with us, and his character and temperament could not be more familiar. As for his stories: how he was clever and quick-witted in his youth, how my maternal grandmother personally took a fancy to him, how marriage was proposed, how he went secretly to see Mother, how during the Cultural Revolution he was criticized and denounced and subject to "struggle sessions," how he constantly escaped, and so on and so forth. These stories I know, "more or less."

But it's still only "more or less." When I think of Father, think of everything about him, everything seems fragmented. Those vague and distant years will, along with our shared history, disappear with his passing. Seeing his tottering body, I always have the sense that it's already too late.

There is another reason to "interview" Father. He is the village's living encyclopedia. Seventy this year, he knows its history: the configurations, whereabouts, personalities, marriages, emotions—the connecting pulse—of three generations of villagers, as clear as day, as if he were listing off family treasures.

Father knows the postliberation power struggles and takeovers in the village well, because he was a participant. The difference is he draws his stories from those who were denounced and destroyed. He has always been known as a "busybody" or a "headache," a "thorn in the side" and a "troublemaker." He hasn't worked for the government a day in his life, but he has always sparred with officials. All of the family's misfortunes stem from this.

Liang Guangzheng. Seventy years old. Emaciated, with high cheekbones, sunken cheeks, and cloudy eyes. Stooped in a round-backed chair, his very outline is blurry, as he sits silently. Above, you can sense death's great shadow urging him on. But tenacity emanates from his weak old body, as well as the optimism and candor formed by a lifetime of suffering—qualities that tell us that this man will not go gently unto death.

Your grandfather (sixty-six years old) died in 1960 on the fourteenth day of the second month of spring. Your third great uncle died on the seventh day of the first month of the New Year. Your grandfather starved to death in a nursing home. At that time, the elderly, it didn't matter if they had children or not, if they had a home or not, all had to be put together in a nursing home; they were cared for collectively. When he went, your grandfather was a hale and hearty man. He carried his chamber pot in his hands, his quilt on his back. He was the healthiest of men. Four days later he had died of starvation.

At that time, I was at a camp in Heipozhou fixing the reservoir. We were traveling around all over the place; I guess you could say we were engineers. At that time everyone was starving and so disoriented that no one paid attention to anyone else. When I came back, I realized your uncle's body was so swollen with edema that it was shiny, and he had a large sore on his leg. He was so hungry he couldn't cry. My heart churned to see him like that, but it wasn't time for tears. First I had to find something to eat. As people used to say, "everyone was a thief, if you didn't steal you starved to death." Everything that didn't belong to the production team, even the leaves on the trees, had been eaten clean away. Actually, there weren't any leaves, because in 1958 all the trees had been cut down. In the rural areas there wasn't a single tree, everything that could be burned had already been burned for the steel-making. Everyone starving like ghosts; everywhere burned things.

Before 1960, there were more than 200 of us Liangs in Liang Village. In 1960 between sixty and seventy starved to death. Nearly every household had had someone die.

Liang Guangming was the village clerk then, but his house saw the most death: his father and mother and his sisters-in-law all starved. His second sister-in-law went to steal wheat in the middle of the night. They beat her and broke her leg, but he didn't do anything. After that, when she died, his niece didn't have anyone to take care of her, so she died too. He was a man without feeling. He gave everyone a hard time. He was the most aggressive in struggle sessions and hit the most brutally.

The most people died in the second month of 1960. Originally the daily per capita grain ration had been 4 *liang* (less than a cup). Then it was changed to 2.5 *liang*. It simply wasn't enough. Then Liu Shaoqi decreed a ration of 7 big *liang* (or 10 *liang*). Only after that did fewer people die. Grain was controlled by each production brigade's granary. It was all going bad, but they still wouldn't let people eat it. Liang Guangming watched without yielding. After the wheat harvest, more elderly people died: they'd been starving for so long that their intestines had thinned. If you ate a lot, you burst to death. The Wang family's crooked pagoda tree, do you remember it? It's at the turn where I left the main road to go work. During the great steel-making time, they dug a large pit for the smelting there. Later they buried people, piles of dead people. As their relatives burned the paper money, there would be wailing for father, wailing for mother, for the newborn child. So for many that Wang family place is taboo.

During the 1962 "Four Cleanups" (Mao's movement to cleanse politics, economy, organization, and ideology), we went through the formalities, but no one was purged. At home there was nothing to eat, nothing to drink, really nothing I could do, so I put some broken tobacco leaves in baskets that I balanced on a pole across my back, and went into the mountains to trade for food and firewood. People in the mountains liked to smoke. But I didn't think it through and went to another county and switched to a pushcart, and then that was confiscated by a "big work unit." At that time they permitted the transport of firewood, but you weren't allowed to trade for food. I cried the whole way home, my hands empty. Black night hung in the sky when I got back. Your ma didn't blame me though.

All these absurd public policies were in effect for a long time. They lasted as long as the Chairman was around. Back then they said production was high because they planted the grain thick. They said it was so thick rabbits couldn't even squeeze between the stalks. You knew it was a lie as soon as you heard it. If rabbits couldn't squeeze into the wheat, could it still bear grain? There would be a meeting to announce the output, and whoever reported first put the next one on the spot. Everyone had to one-up the guy before him. "No guts, no output," as people were always saying.

I've hated empty boasts since I was small, and I don't like make-work either. They were advocating dredging projects back then, so on the Western Slope we dredged Happiness Canal, apparently to find happiness. In fact it was just a dry ditch. We followed the Chairman's personal fantasies. At the slightest sound, everyone would get up and go. Idealism was the standard. Pots, bowls, ladles were all burned, iron and ore. It was all used up, not a trace of iron was left.

No matter what story he's telling, if it has to do with the "classics," Father always begins with Grandfather entering the nursing home. He speaks haltingly, but his memory is surprisingly good for seventy. He can still clearly recall the political slogans and policy directives from forty or fifty years ago. Somehow it's already noon, and my sister-in-law has urged us to eat several times, but Father is immersed in his memories; if he's said it before, it bears saying again. At lunch, one of the messier aspects of being home comes up: against our strong opposition, Father insists on adding a spoonful of hot sauce to his food, even though his stomach lining can't handle the irritation. Father says life means nothing if he can't eat hot sauce; he'd rather just kick the bucket and be done with it.

When I was young, vegetables and cooking oil were hard to come by, and everyone depended on chili peppers to get their food down. But by wintertime, the peppers would all be eaten, and no matter how hard we had economized, the daikon radishes, stored in sand, would be all gone, too.

Then Father would take dried peppers ground into powder and sprinkle them in his bowl. Even if he were eating bread he would break into a sweat. Lots of households in the village did this. Often local traditions are rooted in poverty.

After we finish lunch, Father wants to get right back at it. I ask him to talk about earlier times, about the makeup of the families in the village and to sketch out their histories.

Now, if you're talking about our Liang Village, there's a long history. In this country of ours people have long had reasons to move around: the chaos of war, floods, the migrations never stop. The three main families in Liang Village are the Liangs, the Hans, and the Wangs. The Han family was formed during the Qing Dynasty, in the reign of the Jiaqing Emperor (1796–1820). They came by way of the Guo–Han family area. The Liang family came during the Ming Dynasty migrations, from Shanxi Gongtong County's Dahuaishu. Actually people in many parts of Henan migrated then, too. There was war on the central plains, and many people were dying there, so everyone was a migrant.

The Han family is pretty well educated. They have a high aptitude for learning; many are really capable. Han Lige graduated from Kaifeng University; Han Liting was

Catholic. The land reform campaigns against tyrannical landlords and wealthy peasants hit them very hard.

After Han Lige graduated from college, he was appointed section leader of the Nationalist Party's county militia, and later he was commander of the Pang Bridge Second Division, probably around 1941, 1942. He held this position for about seven or eight years. I'm old enough to remember him coming home to visit. His face was dark as coal, his hair in a crew cut. There was an air of death and war about him, but he was dignified and respectful. About ten *li* from his home, he dismounted and walked the rest of the way, bowing his head slightly and greeting the people he met. After coming back to the village, the Han, Liang and Wang families all went to pay their respects. When the Nationalists were overthrown he fled to Beijing, but in the 1950 "anti-bandit" campaign, the government enacted a broad cleanup. Han Lige was forced to return, but he fought for the opportunity to start a new life. On top of that, his mother was always being struggled against at home. He came back in the autumn of 1950 and started to work at home; at the end of the year they arrested him. At the beginning of 1951, there was a public trial and he was sentenced to death by firing squad. The villagers defended him in tears, saying he was a good man, but he was still shot in the end.

Then there was the "dig out riches" campaign, which forced landlords to turn in their secret stashes of money. Landlords ran all over looking for relatives to lend them money. Han Lige's father was killed as an example to others. When his mother and aunt saw that they didn't bat an eye, they just went and hung themselves, although they dressed neatly and ate *youxuan* pastries beforehand. People felt bad for them at first, but when they saw that they'd eaten *youxuan* pastries first, they started to curse them. His uncle had been in prison. His cousin, the head of the granary, was also killed by a firing squad. He said some things he shouldn't have and had been involved with women. He'd been taking in large measures of grain and only giving out small ones. There was resentment. The executions were all carried out over in the big sports field at the town's Number Two Junior High School. When I go there now I still get an eerie feeling.

Han Lige's younger brother, Han Dianjun, also graduated from Kaifeng University. He hadn't yet gotten a position when the Nationalists were defeated. When he came back five or so years later, he was also struggled against. He fled to Gansu but was caught. Han Lige's wife had her legs broken by debt collectors, and she died soon after. His son Han Xingrong never found a wife. He died a few years ago. That was the end of that family.

Han Liting studied medicine on his own at Fuyin Church. He believed in God and Jesus, same as his mother. Later he became a church leader, a respected elder. Before Chairman Mao, there were many Christians. During the '80s, it became quite popular again for a while; there were many conversions, and they printed pamphlets. Han Dianjun helped, and they sold them. But then he became paralyzed, and there was no one at home to take care of him. Fuyin Church members took turns taking care of him. When his son read the sacrificial rites at his funeral, the villagers all heckled him, giving him what for. When his old man was sick, he didn't lift a finger. What kind of a Christian household is that?

The other large household is Han Jianwen's. They're all Christian, too, and medical doctors. You could call the Han family scholarly. As long as I can remember, they've written all the New Year's couplets for Liang Village.

The Han family has been prolific; each branch has many sons. And yet they're not united. Some of the sons fight among themselves. They argue, compete, take advantage of each other, go to court, and they don't support the elderly. All that is common with them, and they aren't really respected.

At the beginning the Liang family had two brothers, who had a total of seven sons. Each of these sons started a family, and there were seven Liang households. The fifth and seventh family didn't have many children, so they ended early. Today the few dozen Liang families are all descendants of the remaining five.

Compared to the Hans, we Liangs aren't as learned. We've got our share of sad bachelors and village idiots. But the Liangs can fight political battles just as well as they fight among themselves. After land reform, the Liangs became relatively prosperous. We took power, serving under different regimes in positions as exalted as county Party Secretary. The bad qualities of our former branch secretary Liang Xinglong go without mentioning. He was the production brigade branch secretary for some ten years, and the Liangs were bullied all over the place. Once, Liang Qingli chased him around the village waving a knife, intending to chop him up. Liang Xinglong had pushed too hard; even a rat will bite when cornered.

The storekeeper Liang Guangming was also bad news. There were three brothers: Liang Guangfu was a bachelor; Liang Guanghuai starved to death and his wife was beaten to death, so the house and lands all went to Liang Guangming. You know Lingzi, in the Du family? When you two were small you were good friends. After her dad and ma died, an aunt promised her to one of Liang Guangming's sons, but later Lingzi said she didn't want to. Guangming's family took Lingzi's house. They said Lingzi owed the family that much in betrothal money.

The Liang clan's best-known member, Liang Guangji, was the county military head. After retirement his personnel file was lost, and he didn't even have a basic salary. But no one in the Liang family had any sympathy. Why not? Because he didn't support his old, sick father. In the middle of the night his brother brought his father over to his house at the county seat. In the morning he woke up, and looking around he thought someone had delivered grain—turns out it was his father. So now what was he going to do? He went to his relatives, but they all asked him sardonically, so now what are you going to do? Are you going to ask the post office if you can mail him back? That very same day he took his father to the vegetable patch south of the village; he didn't even get out of the car. He told his relatives to tell his brother, "dad's in the southern vegetable patch."

The Wang family isn't worth mentioning. They're all dead wood and never amount to anything. The Liang family holds them no account.

When I mentioned that there are some smaller families in the village, I was thinking of the Qians, the Zhous, the Zhangs, the Yuans, and the Lius. Old Mr. Qian, he never said a word in his life. No one remembers what he looked like. His wife Hua'r was ugly as sin, all sickly and twisted. They had four children but no way to support them. Hua'r got involved with some bachelors from the Zhang and Zhou families to help put food on the table. The whole village knew it.

The various Zhou families are also quite something. Zhou Lihe was an accountant; Zhou Lizhong was a lick-spittle. The father and two sons were nicknamed "Big Activist," "Second Activist," and "Third Activist." Zhou Lihe was a bastard, but he sure worked hard. There wasn't so much as a weed stalk in his fields. Working so hard isn't entirely a good thing, though. When he planted winter wheat, he put on too much fertilizer, and it didn't mature. It grew but it never bore seeds. Later he got stomach cancer. He went to Anyang for an operation, but before he went he still wanted to dry and pack the grain. After the operation, he died at the hospital. In the village they put together a little rhyme:

> When he left he was healthy and active; but he came
>   back to firecrackers;
> When he left he could still eat bread, but he came back
>   boxed and dead.

Zhou Lizhong's daughter Chunrong eloped. In the middle of the night she climbed over the wall and fled. Lame Chang of the Liangs might not know a single character, but he's the best at composing these rhymes. We sang this one around the village:

> On day two of the second month, the dragon lifted
>   its head;
> come to find the Zhou girl had somersaulted out her
>   bed.

Then Zhou Lizhong lifted up his head, to see if someone was still in bed.

All that was left was a coat for a pillow, but he caught them at Lingshantou.

He gave the marriage certificate one long look, hung his head and back he took.

In the '80s, I would go with Lame Chang and a few others to trade in tobacco. When we would take a break on the hills, we would chat and tell stories. Lame Chang said, "Second Brother, I've got it better than you. You owe money, you've got a sick wife, six or seven kids. When are you gonna do better than me? He was giving me a hard time. It was hard to get by. The guys next to me said, "don't talk that way, what takes the dragon a single step, takes the turtle ten years." Now Lame Chang is still Lame Chang. He has a few kids, none of them successful. His eldest went to live with his wife's family and hasn't come back; his second went off to work and hasn't come back either. And then at forty-eight he had two more kids. One drowned; and the other one is on the Internet all day playing games.

I guess it's like the saying, "The Han family is sharp, the Wang family is dumb, and the Liang family shoots itself in the foot."

The sky was gradually growing dark, but Father showed no signs of tiring. Listening to him, each and every feature of the village is alive; the intertwined family stories are all vivid, breathing creatures. It's something you can only feel if you've mixed your sweat and blood into a place, if you've lived there for a very long time. Every village is a piece of history. Every family is a unique form of human life. When Father mentioned Qian Hua'r I suddenly remembered that, when I was small, we had treated the Qians as if they didn't exist, same as we treated the Wangs, even though the Qian family lived across the pond from us. Their daughters were perhaps the same age as us sisters, but we rarely went to their house. They apparently understood the situation: they never brought up their home or invited us to their house to play.

A village is a living being, an organic network. Each household's activities may seem independent, but they are actually bound up in interrelated tensions. The anthropologist Fei Xiaotong suggests that village social structures are a kind of "ranked pattern" with the "self" at the center. In establishing connections with others, no one is a still surface, but rather like ripples on a pond; one ring creates another, extending farther and farther, becoming weaker and weaker. This is why people from larger families can make use of their various family relations to create larger rings of influence. Because they lack these fundamental interpersonal connections, the smaller families, or the families with only a single household, seldom have the opportunity to enter into kinship with the larger families through marriage. They have difficulty creating large ripples and thus being accepted in the village's inner circles. It is also for this reason that their words, actions, and customs are considered "different." Just as Fei Xiaotong says, in this kind of tight-knit village society, they are always seen as the village outsiders. "Anyone of unknown origins is suspicious," he writes. In Liang Village, the Qian family is a textbook example of this phenomenon.

As for the two large families in the village, the Hans and the Liangs, they are clearly the masters. But each also has its set role. For more than two hundred years, the Liangs and the Hans have been fighting overtly and maneuvering covertly. In terms of education, the Liangs have always been at a disadvantage; the Hans have had many Christian households, and because they have been well off, many of them have left to study. In temperament and accomplishment, even in physical appearance, they have seemed exceptional. But this has also made them the frequent subjects of gossip. The Liang family's resistance to the Christian faith must have something to do with this: they felt that following everything the Hans did was a loss of face. In politics, the Liangs have had the upper hand. For more than two hundred years, the Liangs have been clan leaders, branch secretaries, or in charge of village affairs, and it's only in the past ten years that the Hans have usurped this position. Although the Liang family are skilled in political struggle, they haven't been as successful economically. So during the period of opening up and reform, they were naturally eclipsed.

It is already 11 pm. Father has been talking for seven or eight hours, and we didn't even eat dinner. My elder brother and younger sister, as well as my sister-in-law and second and third sisters and their husbands, all of whom came over from the county seat in the afternoon, sit to one side listening quietly. All that can be heard is the click, click of my fingers on the computer.

Everyone is contemplating the things Father has said, and there is a clear sense of something sacred, which I find deeply moving. Their daily lives happen unconsciously; they're only concerned with basic necessities: fuel, food, oil and salt; eat, drink, and be merry. It seems that they have no greater goals. But given a moment's pause, they want very much to think deeply. They are able to understand the inner meanings, and they try to enter that realm.

It's just that life so rarely gives them the opportunity.

Life's Mirror

My brother had arranged with some people in the village to come over tomorrow to talk about fluctuations in the village population and the general economic situation. He said: I thought long and hard but could hardly come up with anyone who could talk about these things.

It was 10 pm by the time we finished dinner, and the few Liangs whom my brother had invited came over. One was the village head. He's in his fifties, the son of the storekeeper Father mentioned earlier. Like his father he has a light complexion and is pretty sharp. He watched me closely as we talked; he wanted to know what I was really up to, what my purpose was. Another was my paternal uncle, a village accountant famous for his prudence. Another, whom I call "Elder Brother" left the village early on to work. At around forty he came back to the village and hasn't left since. He keeps to himself and is rather mysterious. He doesn't drop in on other people, although he doesn't object when others visit his place. One year all his hair suddenly fell out, and since then he's worn a black woolen hat all year round. Finally, there was a middle-aged man who lives outside the village. He's known as somebody who can get things done.

A few hundred years ago, as I mentioned before, the two Liang brothers brought their seven sons here, established homes, and began to increase in number. Currently, there are fifty-four Liang households of substantial size. The number of smaller families is less clear: for example, two brothers left to find jobs after getting married. Their parents stayed behind to help take care of the children. No matter how you divide the family, from an economic perspective they are one small household. Calculated this way, there would be around 150 households of more than 640 people. Young couples in their mid-thirties have at least two children, and a few have three. Two families have left the village altogether. They moved to live in the cities in which they work (selling their houses and land in the village). One family's final whereabouts are unknown, because they haven't been in touch with anyone in the village. Seven families work outside the village, and their children attend school where they live. Their family homes are closed up, and they have not come back for several years, and aren't likely to anytime soon. One family lives in town, but they still have a house and land in the village, and they plan to build a house soon. Three families do business in other places and come back every year or two. They have built nice family homes in the village, so it seems like they're preparing to return in the future. Of the several dozen families who still live in the village, the younger members work outside the village all year round, and it is the elderly, the middle-aged women, and the children who remain at home. In addition there are eight or nine households whose members have never left, but who eke out a living from the land. They are considered the most unworldly members of the village and are the most looked down upon and overlooked.

In the late eighties and early nineties, a large number of people from Liang Village left to find jobs, and in the early years Beijing and Xi'an were the principal destinations. In Beijing, many worked in factories, in construction sites, or as security guards. For a short time, they gathered at the Beijing train station to scalp tickets. In Xi'an, many worked around the train station driving pedicabs. The clan was the nucleus for them all; they exchanged leads and took care of one another. Later some went to Qingdao and Guangzhou to work. A very small number did business, such as working as gas technicians and selling rural food goods in the city.

More than 320 Liangs work outside the village. The oldest, sixty, is a construction worker in Xinjiang. The youngest is fifteen. He followed his uncle to a jewelry factory in Qingdao. More than thirty adolescents study at the middle and high schools in town. For the most part they board at school and come home on the weekends. More than thirty children also study at the primary school in town. Their grandparents take care of them and bring them back and forth every day. The village has more than one hundred people older than fifty. They farm and take care of their grandchildren, and those who still have the energy do odd jobs in town, work on local construction sites or in the village sand-lime brick factory.

There's also a subtle "returnee" phenomenon happening here. The earliest to leave for work left in the mid- to late eighties, and when they were middle aged, between forty and fifty, some of them came back to the village, where they raise crops and do odd jobs in and around town. The others are still working outside of the village, but it's clear they won't be able to keep it up much longer. A few of them don't want to come back, but they're too old to work and are just hanging on. Like a cousin of mine, when he was young he returned from military service, and after his wife had a child he left to find work. He was one of the first to leave. He started as a security guard in Beijing, then he pulled a pedicab in Xi'an. Every year he only came home for Spring Festival. A few years ago I ran into him in the village, and he talked and acted like a city guy who wanted to show what a big shot he was. He looks down on his own wife terribly because she's never left the village. He's gotten used to city life, even though he only pulls a pedicab. Yet it's clear— when it's all said and done, he's going to have to come back.

During the busy season, a few middle-aged women form temporary work units to help villagers with the farming, weeding and harvesting. They can bring in thirty kuai in a day. Younger women, however, live like migratory birds. Both husband and wife go out to find temporary jobs, and then use the money they earn to build houses. The grandparents take care of the kids, who go to school in the village, and the parents come back at Spring Festival or during the busy season. The village head said that over the past two years, the numbers of those coming back for Spring Festival has gradually decreased. During summer and winter vacations, the parents have the kids go to where they're working, and when vacation is over, they send them back to school. Of course this is only for the parents who are working in the same place and live together. There are also a few comparatively successful young people who have earned more money. They've come back home to do business, to sell sand or open wholesale businesses. But these cases are extremely rare. Liang Qingbao is one example. Last year he came back, wanting to open a business selling solar power equipment in the up-and-coming rural areas. He thought the people who were building new houses would buy them, and the market shouldn't be bad. But after a year, he hadn't earned any money and had burned through several years of savings. This year Qingbao plans to leave again to find work.

People gone; buildings empty: this is the fact of daily life in the countryside. The majority of rural people who work in the city have built new homes. Indeed, they have gone to the cities just to earn the money to build houses and pay their children's school expenses. They don't plan to establish roots in the cities, to retire there (perhaps they simply don't see it as possible). Their greatest hope is to work in the cities, earn some money, build a decent house in the village, and afterwards figure out some kind of business to do there.

Husbands are separated from wives; parents are separated from children. This is the most common household situation. Even if a husband and wife go to the same city to work, only very rarely do they eat together or live together. And if they don't work at the same factory or construction site, and eat and sleep in the factory, their ability to simply see one another is limited.

There are a few who don't live too badly, like the younger brother of the village head, whose childhood nickname was "Bad Egg." He used to be known as a troublemaker in the village and was almost sent to prison. He works as a gas technician in Inner Mongolia, where he started ahead of the game and earned a bit of money. He bought a house there and had his children sent to live with him. They haven't been back for four or five years. When the village head mentioned this, his tone was a little strained. It didn't seem like he wanted to talk about him. After they left, I asked my brother about it. He told me why: apparently the village head had sent his two sons to work with their uncle, but it turned out he was so tightfisted he wouldn't pay them. In the end, the head's two sons opened another business in a different part of the city.

The Han and Liang clans have approximately the same number of households and family members; however, many more Hans have gone to college and into business, and their overall standard of living is higher. There aren't more than thirty or forty households of the other minor clans in the village—a little more than a hundred people—and whether they remained in the village or left to work, none of them live better than the Liangs or the Hans.

It's always been the case in Liang Village that "people are plentiful, while land is scarce." In the '50s and '60s there was 1.5 *mu* (about a quarter of an acre) per person; now each person has about four-fifths as much. There are two growing seasons per year: first the wheat season, followed by mung beans, corn, sesame seeds, tobacco, or other commercial products. Because land is scarce, the harvests are rarely large enough to even feed the family. This is why, before the 1980s, nearly every family struggled on the poverty line. By the time spring came, the food would have run out, what we called the "spring panic." After reform and opening up, finding work in the cities created new avenues for earning. No matter what you did, every year you could bring home a little bit of income. It was a way to pay both the larger expenses and the daily expenditures. Because you had to pay tax on farmland and had to come home during the harvest season, many people simply rented their land to other villagers, on the condition that the tenant would pay the taxes and give the owner 200 *jin* (about 220 pounds) of wheat per annum. It was a way for families who stayed in the village to earn money. Even if the early wheat harvest only covered the taxes and the landowner's share, the autumn harvest would be profit. By the 1990s, it was rare to see hungry or poorly dressed people in the village, but the ability to build a new house and live comfortably—that was something only for the village cadre and other successful people, the few families who worked in business or who bought their food, instead of growing it. For the past two years rural taxes have been suspended around the country, and according to the village head several families have wanted to take back land they haven't worked for years to grow wheat or corn. They don't come back themselves, but ask relatives to do the planting and harvesting for them and then pay their wages. There are also those who don't want to bring the land back into production, and this has caused disputes. These disputes have nothing to do with what Fei Xiaotong called the farmers' rootedness in the land. The emotional connection between farmers and the land has weakened; all that is left is a relationship based on benefit.

New houses are more and more common in the village, yet one by one, without exception, their locks have grown rusty. At the same time, the people are fewer and fewer. Only a few feeble old folks totter down the lanes, rest on the edges of fields, or gather beneath the eaves. All across the village weeds and debris rule the land around the houses. They reveal the village's inner desolation, its decay, its exhaustion. Internally the village is no longer an organic, living entity. Or perhaps we should say that its life, if indeed it has a life, has reached old age, and that its very vitality is ebbing away.

2

Where Ruins Flourish

In 1990 Rang County launched an initiative to strengthen rural infrastructure and increase village-level construction so as to accelerate development. It followed the popular adage: "If you want to make loads, first build roads," and invested heavily in manpower and resources for road construction. In 1995, following increased demand by farmers for improved housing, village construction offices circulated 32,000 sets of 12 interchangeable construction blueprints. They built rows of houses and fixed villages' interior roads. While people had formerly lived in earthen and wooden structures, they now moved into brick or cement-block houses. Many rural households built multi-storied structures, while others built retail stores and homes along commercial streets. In 1997, primary and secondary arterial roads and neighborhood roads were opened to the villages. In 2000, in the county's 1,008 villages, 3,094 primary and secondary arterials were opened, for a total of 270,000 meters that allowed vehicle access between villages. By 2006, there were 1493.36 kilometers of paved or cement roads in Rang County, and 578 administrative village units had completed the Inter-village Connection Roads project. Much work has also gone into rural sewer and sanitation infrastructure: as of 2019 work was completed on sewage renovations for 60,000 rural households.

—Rang County Annuals and other government reports

Ruins

Key in hand, Father and I go "treasure hunting" in the old house. This is one of the few times we open up the old house every year. The strange thing is, each time we do, we discover some cherished item: an old photograph, a homework book from elementary school. Once we found a diary of mine from junior high that I had completely forgotten existed. Another time we found an old, damaged comic from when I was in elementary school, which Father had brought back after a trip. Later we kids became a little too obsessed with it, and he hid it in the central room's ceiling.

I walked the road from Liang Village to the school in Wu for a full five years. I followed the road along a man-made pond and from there turned onto the main road. Liang Guangshuan's family had built a small earth hut here, but they never seemed to use it. Instead it served as the most obvious landmark of the village. I would walk through Wu's north side, the Hui District, which was lined with tea shops, mutton shops, and small general stores, then turn onto the small Xujia Street and head into town. On the side of the road, there was a public toilet, and, at another intersection, an amur rose tree, which opened its powdery white flowers every summer, beautiful but almost oppressively fragrant. From there I came to the main road, with the Xinhua Bookstore, the Supply and Marketing Cooperative, a hardware store, and a county government building, next to which was the county central elementary and junior high schools. Altogether the route was more than two kilometers, and I walked there and back six times a day.

Father and I follow the road from Wu, but I can't tell north from south or east from west. Father says, that's the south side of Wu, that's the north side, over there is Xujia Street. I feel lost, floating, as though my feet are suspended above the ground.

The section between the old road and the intersection with the new road counted as part of our village, Father says, because the houses were all built by Liang villagers. There they stand, a row of brand-new houses, small, two-story buildings and single-level homes. They are impressive, with large cement courtyards in front and tall gateways with roller doors. A few old houses are mixed in among them. Father points them out to me one by one. This one is Guangting's house, that one belongs to Liang Guangdong's family, that one is "Bad Egg's" or "Tingzi's." They're all new. The old houses have either been sold on the cheap to other families or abandoned altogether.

The road leading to the old house is choked with weeds. It's hard going, and we trip over roots a few times. As we open the door, dust comes streaming down; standing in the middle of the central room, seeing objects both strange and familiar, I am overcome. Against the back wall is a long composite sideboard with various things on it, among them a portrait of Chairman Mao framed on either side by a pair of couplets, a painting, and some family pictures. Beneath the sideboard is a set of lattice-work shelves holding different objects, and in front a big square table, where we would put out offerings during Spring Festival, though the rest of the year we'd put anything we liked on it. It was also where I would do my homework. You can find these two objects in most northern rural homes. Above the large table, there was a bamboo-and-paper-paste ceiling that Father had put in to prevent dust falling from the house beams. That's where he threw the comic book.

I look carefully over the sideboard and the table and also feel gently around the latticework shelves, but I don't find anything. Can it be this old home holds nothing from my memory? Unwilling to accept this, I pound on the ceiling with a stick. But no comic books are forthcoming, only a stream of dust mixed with ample quantities of mouse poop plopping down onto the floor.

The roofs of the eastern and western rooms are two gaping holes, where water drips all year round into large pits. The bed is still in the corner where the eastern room meets the back wall, but its wood has turned black and it is filled with dirt and dust. Below it you can see the corner of a shabby cotton quilt. This was my mother and father's bed when they were married. At the head of the bed is a wooden chest. It contained my mother's dowry, and in those days it was the only place where the family could lock things up. We would place the family's most valuable possessions in it, including boiled eggs. Indeed, it was from this chest that I once stole an egg. I couldn't stop myself from cracking it open to eat on the sly, but after eating only a part of it, I peeked into the courtyard, where everyone was sitting with Mother in the sun. Many years later, my older sister told me that when I peeked out, they saw egg white stuck to my face, and when I pulled my head back in, everyone knew what I was up to. Apparently I did this a few times, and everyone had to try not to laugh. The western room was where we stored grain, and it also became the girls' room after we got older. After my brother married, we moved back into the eastern room, and he and his wife lived in the western room. When I think now of the moaning that we would hear in the middle of the night, my heart still pounds. There isn't any soundproofing in rural northern homes, and the walls between rooms don't reach the ceiling; they're just partitions hung with all sorts of farming tools.

The real symbol of the old home's demise is not the house itself, however, but the old date tree in the courtyard. It exists as part of our memories, as part of the time, space, and seasons of the countryside; it exists as part of each of us, as part of each family scene. Each year during date season, no matter where I am, I go to buy dates to eat and tell the date-sellers or other buyers that in our courtyard at home we also had an old date tree with fruit like this. Each year during summer vacation, when the date tree was in full bloom and bore its first green fruit, we would sleep beneath it, eat beneath it, play beneath it. We would carry Mother out to lie beneath it. By the end of August, the tree, half-red with dates, attracted an endless stream of naughty children: a tile or clod would land in the courtyard, and a little figure would come dashing in to steal dates, then dash out again. My little sister and I would engage the kids in battles of bravery and wits. At the end of September, in the middle of the afternoon when all the villagers were napping, my older brother and a few friends would climb the tree and whack it with a stick, and sometimes even climb to its highest branches, which they would shake with all their might. The air would be filled with the pattering of dates bouncing across the ground, and the baskets of plump red dates would bring us joy and contentment.

At some point, I don't know when, the old date tree slowly began to decline until it didn't even bear fruit anymore. Now, in the height of summer, most of the trunk is withered, and only a few yellowed leaves remain as a proof of life. After we were gone, who saw the date's lush foliage, its little white flowers, its small green dates? Who ate those dates, mellow, round, and full?

I look out over the rubble and broken walls outside our courtyard: Whose homes are these? Consciously examining the village for the first time, I am shocked to realize that, starting from my own home, it is an expanse of ruins. When I was young, this was the heart of the village. Underneath the big tree in front of Uncle Guangting's was a large platform, and in the summertime, every day at lunch, it would overflow with people, men and women, laughing and gossiping, holding large basins at their sides, eating noodles. In the evening, people would go there to take a break and cool off, and they would sit there until the middle of the night, waving their fans, chatting lazily. Now, everything is covered with weeds and brush, and everywhere you look you see broken walls and rubble. In the corner of one low, fallen wall there is half a collapsed stove, the lid of a pan, and an iron scoop filled with dirt and dust, as if to suggest that once this place was filled with heat and life. Some buildings don't even have roofs; all that's left are the walls or foundations.

Whose homes were these? Trees and weeds cover the ruins, mournful and defeated as a giant graveyard. Facing our house is Lame Chang's house. Lame Chang was always a lazy glutton; Father and the villagers said that when his family was eating noodles, Lame Chang would take his chopsticks, and with a swirl around the pot all the noodles would end up in his own bowl, leaving only the broth for his wife and kids to drink. His house was made of unbaked earthen bricks, and in the rainy season, the muddy yellow water from his house would flow, gurgling, down into our courtyard. Now, all that's left of the house is little heaps of yellow earthen bricks and one side of a wall. Past that is Lame Chang's younger brother's place. His wife left long ago; later, when he was afraid he'd be caught stealing trees and put in prison, he committed suicide. No one knows where their two children are. The house collapsed a long time ago.

Past that, leaning at a 45-degree angle, is a house behind a damaged well. Somehow, a New Year's couplet still clings to the door. The house's kitchen is half collapsed, but the cooking hearth is still there, covered with years of dust and dirt, leaving only two black, eyelike holes where the big front and back pots used to be. Behind the kitchen is a big heap of colorful trash. Whose house is that? I can't remember. Father says that was Guangting's old house. He married and brought home a wife and then had his first child. When he and his wife would fight, we kids would run over and watch. That was a typical rural house, dark and extremely clean.

A little bit farther on, even Father begins to hesitate. He looks around to ascertain our location before he's able to say for sure which house is whose. I count them up: there are fifteen collapsed structures in view. And this isn't even including houses like my own, which are tottering on the verge. That is to say, there are at least fifteen families who have left their old homes, their old gathering places, to start a new life. Father and I make a circle through the village, and as we do I estimate that only about sixty households remain among the ruins.

Are the tall, modern buildings lining the road and these ruins part of the same village? Beneath the hot, bright summer sun, surrounded by the constant chirping of cicadas, I am puzzled. Even though its geographical position is the same, there is an essential disconnect between the village I remember and the village as it is now. China's new era is rising up out of these ruins, creating its new image, its new form.

Without a doubt, the village's internal structure has already collapsed, that is to say it no longer functions as a gathering place of families. These are the ruins of Liang family houses. A long time ago, the village grew in a circle, gradually expanding with the growth of its families. Land was allocated based on distance and the number of family members. The Liang family surname represents a clan, a bloodline, as well as an arena of life and culture. On Chinese New Year's Eve, every family would prepare a braised dish, and each person, according to his or her generational position, would offer a portion of the family's dish to the next family in line. In the end there would be food from the entire clan in each family's pot. Then everyone would wait until breakfast on New Year's Day to eat. When did this custom begin? Why is it done this way? Even the older generation doesn't know. Yet one meaning is certain: it unites the entire family, heart and soul, without differentiation between you and me. If family members weren't on speaking terms but wanted to reconcile, this was the best, the least awkward, time to do so.

Village culture has already changed. While family clans used to be its nexus, economic centers now play that role. The successful live along the commercial roads, so the village is no longer arranged by family. New arenas of livelihood are forming, new communities assembling. These families are clearly the village's *nouveau riche*; they represent wealth, power, and reputation, because not just anyone can buy this land. Those who aren't as successful may still have to live in the old dilapidated houses, which they either fix up as best they can, or else they buy the houses of those who have left. (Most of those houses aren't bad; they used to be the best in the village.) But this also disrupts the clan system. For example, Zhang Daokuan's home is now to the left of my house on land that used to belong to my uncle. There are Zhangs in every village—who knows how they got here. They've had a hard time putting down roots and being accepted and were often allocated relatively poor land, like Zhang Daokuan's family, whose former home was next to the embankment, on a damp, irregular piece of land; the worst in the village, really. But now it's easy enough to buy a better plot from a family that has migrated and to build a new house.

Behind the changes in village structure are changes in China's traditional cultural structures. The structures of agricultural civilization are gradually dying away, replaced by a confused mix.

Agriculture and industry are at war with one another in China's rural areas, and it's easy to see the power disparity. Villages no longer have cultural cohesion. They are like a patch of loose sand, arbitrarily piled together, but quickly scattered again. They have no real cultural function.

I don't mean to indulge in nostalgia, but I do miss that sense of belonging to a village clan, regardless of all the aggravation that comes with human interaction. I don't want to accept this new existence, but the next generation of children is already growing up in these new gathering places. In the future, will these places really be their "hometowns," these places characterized by loneliness, isolation, and contradiction? Lifeless and emotionless.

The first generation that left to find work still intended to build houses in their villages, because those villages were their homes. Demonstrating your wealth in your home village was a clear symbol of self-worth. But the next generation? And the generation after? For them the emotional ties are weak. They've spent very little time in their hometowns, often having left to find work after graduating—or not graduating—from middle school. Their thirst for more is stronger than their connections to their hometowns. And it is for just this reason that their fates, their lives, are so precarious. Where will they put down roots? Leaving the village in their early teens, working in the city without a *hukou*, household registration record, they have no social safety net. The city is not their home, and the village, to them, is a distant object. They have no feelings for it. They have no sense of belonging. The social problems resulting from this double loss are already becoming clear. Repairing this, changing this, will be an enormous social task.

Three *Zhang* Deep in Level Ground

If you've been around northern villages, you may notice that many of them are full of abandoned brick kilns, surrounded by pits of various depths. These are the remnants of the brick factories that were built in the mid to late '70s, one of the rural symbols of "reform and opening up" and China's economic recovery.

Liang Village's brick factory is behind the village, close to the river. In the early 1980s, many villagers earned their living there. They worked from early morning until eight or nine at night, earning enough money to pay household expenses and their children's tuition.

When I was little, kids on their way to wash in the river would pass the big brick kiln in the middle of the factory. Often they would fall into the deep pits hidden between piles of dirt and weeds. The brick factory was a mysterious and frightening place. I once had a nightmare I can still vaguely remember. The brick factory had become a castle. Its doors were tightly closed and there was a suspension bridge. If you wanted to get in, you had to overcome a seemingly endless number of barriers and traps.

How much earth did the village brick factory actually dig up? How deep did it go? You just have to look at the electric pole near the factory to get a sense of the damage. The dirt was dug out around its original base, to a depth of about three *zhang* (about 33 yards). Now it stands there like a lonely flag-pole. If you look beyond it, there's an area of depressed land, also dug three *zhang* deep, with a perfectly flat bottom that extends for more than 100 *mu*. On one side of this large pit is an abandoned electric well with one side dug up. Father says the brickfield used to be two to three hundred *mu* of farmland, filled with our incredibly rich, black soil. In May and June, when the tips of the wheat changed to yellow, it was a beautiful sight. But the land won't grow anything anymore. There aren't any nutrients left.

All around the brick factory are large, uneven pits. They can be found next to the woods, behind the houses, on the river-bank. Some of the trees tilt a little, their coiled roots revealed, because people dug too close. And the high river embankments, which were once like city walls keeping the surging floodwaters at bay, have been pared down almost to ground level.

While we are taking a look at the well, Old Uncle Gui catches sight of us and comes running over.

When he gets closer, he gives us a look and says with a laugh, "I was wondering who had come over to investigate." Old Uncle Gui has a little limp; he's been sick with rheumatism for many years, and the soles of his leather shoes are worn through and muddy. He is wearing a thin jacket, the lining shiny with dirt. Just like father, Old Uncle Gui is known in Liang Village for being a thorn in the side of authorities. He can't stand bad ideas or misguided social movements. He has a fiery temper and will yell at anyone in office. If something wrong or unjust has happened in the village, he'll head right over and let you know. He's one of the older generation, so there's nothing anyone can do about it. He doesn't get along with anybody, so when he was in charge of the brick factory, no one helped him. I ask him to talk about it. Standing next to the well, one foot on the cement foundation and a cigarette in his hand, he tells his story.

It's a typical case: the officials reaped the benefits, while the people suffered the consequences.

It started in the summer of 1975. That's when they built the kiln. It was on village land; they built it within the town limits, taking over 202 *mu* of arable land (about half a square mile). The profits were to go to the village. That's what it said on the contract, that every year each *mu* of land was exempt from 40 RMB and 200 *jin* in grain tax. But that was never honored. I don't know if the village ever got it. In any case the villagers have never seen it. Every year we made some noise about it. In 1985 Zhou Guitian partly took it over. The county government invested in it, and he gave them the profits. He ran it for three years. But the contract was never honored, so we villagers, we put a run on the bank, so to speak, so that he wouldn't succeed. That year our team was short more than 9,000 *jin*. We didn't hand any over. Why? To show that the brick factory contract hadn't been honored all those years. I took it as an opportunity to make things difficult for village head Liang Shuding.

The production brigade department owed payments to your Fifth Uncle. [Old Uncle Gui's father had once been a village cadre.] Even after he left the position, they still hadn't given him a thing. Just after the wheat harvest, I saw Shuding and said, your dad never paid up, now that you're in charge, you really should pay him. Can a debt last over generations?! But he was too good for all that. So I yelled at him, fuck you and your family, you're sucking the people's blood, you just wait, I'm going to report this. So I told the village, and they set up a special investigation team to come and make inquiries about the brick factory. He ran over to the investigation team and said, oh, you shouldn't let Liang Village trouble you, you don't really need to come. But when they heard that, they thought that something really must be going on, so they came and ended up throwing Shuding out. He hated me for that.

39

I ran the factory in 1988, '89, and '90. By 1989, I couldn't do it anymore. I couldn't get along with the production brigade, they kept coming to check on me, wanting me to give them gifts, but I wouldn't do it. I never did. The first year's contract cost 40,000 kuai (about $6,200). Then my own brother started giving me trouble. Everyone was against me, I had no way out. My brother was selling bricks to people in office behind my back. I'd go out for a while, and when I'd come back there would be fewer bricks. I'd ask my fourth brother and he'd say, so-and-so hauled them away. He'll pay later. My fucking foot he'll pay later, we're never seeing that money. One day, I got out the account book and went to find so-and-so. I calculated the bill right in front of him and told him to pay; he was as mad as a snorting hog. I figured no one had ever dared do that before. He's just a little official, but he gave himself airs. What kind of man is that!

Later Wang Xiting did it for three years. He was also unlucky and lost money. Those years it rained a lot, and the bricks just wouldn't dry out. Someone who ran a kiln in the neighboring village couldn't take it anymore and drowned himself in a well. Later, Song Chengxin did it until '95. He made a bunch of money. Things were getting better then, and there was lots of construction. Those were the good days. There were brick trucks going up and down the highway, and in the southern part of the village, people were making coal bricks and hauling those. There were lots of people around. The Qing family in our village even opened a small restaurant and managed a store; they got rich too.

Later, they dug deeper, as you can see, like that [Old Uncle Gui points to the electric well], ground sunk to the level of the bottom of the well. Before, you couldn't see this well at all. Its cover was way below ground level. Do you see that electrical pole? The mound on top of the base marks its original height. They dug out a few *zhang*.

We stopped digging for two years in the middle of all that. The commune gave us more than 30,000 kuai, and told us to go back to farming. I don't know what happened to the money. But how could we farm? We'd dug out all the soil. There were no more nutrients. And where could we get more soil to fill it? Nowadays construction happens so quickly, there's people buying and selling soil everywhere. After that Han Hewa did it for two years. He mostly made money by selling soil. The reason this hole is so big now is because of all the digging he did.

It wasn't until 2002 that the villagers got fed up with Hewa. I always stick with things, I don't stop reporting. I went to the commune secretary. At first he responded quickly, saying, go on back, I'll send some people over to take a look. The second time I went, I said nothing has been resolved. He said he'd make some more inquiries. The third time he told me to fuck off. I said you're party secretary, you're telling an ordinary person to fuck off?! I caused a scene out in the courtyard, I said Secretary X, you come out here, and repeat what you said to me in there! He wouldn't come out. So then I went to the county land bureau, and the bureau chief said he'd come right out to investigate.

He actually did come out, that fucker—he came each time I called. He came lots of times, but each time it was only to eat, drink, look around, ask around, talk a pile of crap, kiss some ass, and walk away. Nothing happened. The brick factory still wasn't closed. I went over to talk to the bureau chief and told him, you don't need to come. When you come you just eat at our expense. You must like our restaurant. He pretended to be confused and said, haven't they closed your brick factory yet? I said Bureau Chief X, if I'm here for no reason, you can lock me up.

When I came to report, I had done my research into the land law beforehand, I knew that digging up arable land wasn't right. So this time when I went, I said, Bureau Chief X, I have the land law right here, do you want me to take it out and read it, so we can see if you're following any of this law?

He said, you don't have to read it. I know it.

It wasn't until 2004 that the brick factory was finally, completely closed. It wasn't due to a rigorous investigation. And it wasn't because Han Hewa decided to do right. It was because there was nothing left to dig. The 100-plus *mu* of land are completely destroyed. And now no one even uses earthen bricks anymore. Everyone uses limestone bricks. They excavate sand from the river, and they take stones and gravel to make concrete blocks. The village land isn't being mined anymore because they've moved on to mining the river. You've seen it, what's become of the river.

As they go over these old grievances, my father and Old Uncle Gui wave their arms, and their eyes shine. In those days the two of them ran back and forth, planning reports; who knows how many people hated them. They were typical village "nonconformists." They were always making trouble; even if their own lives were falling apart, all they did was meddle.

Father sees my distaste, and he shouts at me: "Don't look down on your elders, what we did we did to help our children and grandchildren. You see that 100-*mu* pit! It's a disaster waiting to happen. Liang Village hasn't flooded for the past few years but when it does, that embankment won't hold. Do you remember when you were small and the river flooded? The water filled the village and all the hay piles floated away."

Yes, yes, of course I remember. Amid torrential rain, the village turned into a lake. Everyone dredged the ditches and canals, but the water still overflowed, it just had nowhere to go.

Many families could only put a few sandbags in front of their gates. One summer, the back corner of our kitchen collapsed. There wasn't anything to do but to leave one half wet and cook in the other half. But what could we burn in the stove? All the piles of hay in the wheat fields started to float away. It was hard to get there, even if you risked falling into the pits. Luckily, when we got there, we were able to find some half-dry hay, but the dampness meant that we were all sending up smoke signals.

Father says, "The brick factory was already a disaster back then. If we have another big flood now, the embankment won't hold, they've already been dug away, the water will flow straight into the pit, then straight into the village, and swallow it up. There'll be nowhere else for it to go. Who's going to do something about it? The guy in office now, he said he'd come to the village to investigate. But he's just going through the motions. The villagers are sick of him. Anytime he goes up to anyone they just turn their backs on him."

Old Uncle Gui spits viciously on the ground and says, "One year, the village didn't let Song Chengxin dig a pit. Song Chengxin held a big meeting and said, haven't I, Song Chengxin, brought all of you happiness? In my mind I was thinking, fuck you, you dug out our dirt and you gave a few stupid kids a job, did you bring us happiness? You're fucking with us. They didn't get it. But I got it well enough, and I decided I would bring him down."

Black Sludge

There are ponds scattered around the village. In northern country dialects we call them *kang*, "pits," but the more formal word is *kangtang*, "pond."

Liang Village has six ponds of various sizes, including a large one in front of the elementary school, with a narrow raised pathway twisting through the middle of it. When I was a child, it was the only way for us to get to school. As soon as summer hit, after a rainstorm, the water would rise up and

43

turn the path into a ghost walk, only a few patches visible above the surface. A few of us barefooted friends would hold hands and step from lump to lump until, with a loud "kerplunk," someone would fall into the water. Luckily the pond's edges were gently sloped, and the water wasn't that deep, so it was easy to climb out. If it stayed rainy and gray for a long time, things really got messy. The whole village turned to mud, wet pig manure and chicken droppings floating everywhere. Rocks and broken bricks popped up from who knows where, hurting our bare feet. From my house, it was about 300 meters to the school, and in that short space you would step on manure more times than you could count. Black or yellow, it came squishing up from between your toes, giving off a stink and making your hair stand on end.

Despite all that, the pond in front of the school is still a happy memory. It was filled with lotus roots, and in the summer green lotus leaves spread out across it, sprinkled with tall, pink blossoms, swaying gently in the wind. The blossoms would gradually ripen into lotus-seed pods, round and swollen. We couldn't wait until they were ripe. When the adults weren't looking, my friends and I would link our hands and, making a chain, would wade into the water to pick the closest ones. Then we would savor them, bite by bite, for their sweet fragrance.

There was also the pond with the bluestone bridge that split it into two; the left end of the bridge extended into the village, and that was my family's side of town. On the right it extended toward the main road. Beside it was a relatively wide dirt road, which also led to the main road on the other side of the village. Up above the dirt road was where village families had their private plots of land, where they grew their own vegetables: peppers, eggplants, and turnips. Between the road and the plots was a wild mulberry tree. In late spring and early summer, its purple berries would fill the tree, and we girls would use clumps of earth and sticks to knock the fruit down, where they would smash into the ground and end up too dirty to eat. The boys, however, would zip right up the tree, filling their pockets and then running off in a flash.

The pond on the left was the largest in the village; it almost reached the one in front of the elementary school. The village's main road ran down its center. Perhaps the two ponds were originally linked, and it wasn't until the village was built that they were separated from one another. Two large wheat fields were on either side of the pond, and on the village side there was also a field for drying and threshing the wheat. Weddings were generally held there, as well as funerals, movies and operas, prayers and weeping: it all happened where we milled the wheat. A movie showing, in particular, seemed like a holiday, though the movies were usually only shown because of a funeral. In that moment death and rebirth, tears and laughter were all genuine, even though just before, the threshing yard had been filled with tears and grief and the fear of death.

But once the film was on, that mysterious unknown world dispelled all our fear and sorrow. At one or two in the afternoon, we kids would set up our small stools to hold a spot and then go eat at one another's houses. At nightfall, the white movie screen was stretched out, and the threshing yard was instantly filled with mystery and grandeur. When the movie started, the entire yard went silent, except for the rasping of the spinning film reel and the fantasy world on screen. Everyone was captivated.

As summer began, we would go down to the fields to cut and gather wheat, and at dusk, adults and children, men and women would head down to their designated places in the pond to bathe. We called playing in the pond "duck swimming," but in the river it was called either "washing" or "swimming." The kids would "duck swim," diving around the pond, and in the evening, the adults would wash. The convention was: the east side was for men; the west side was for women. Occasionally some rascal would stage a raid on the women's side, but he was usually promptly beaten until he scurried off holding his head.

Ducks swam to and fro on the water, and fish swam beneath. People washed their clothes, and eels dug into the mud. But the water wasn't dirty at all. In the shallow places, you could even see the color of the stones and the yellow mud at the bottom. I heard the adults say that the pond was fed by a spring, which kept it clean. After the rains, when it became swollen and deep, we felt along the bottom for *luoqiao*, a kind of large freshwater snail. Its meaty interior was delicious when fried.

There was another pond near where the Han part of the village meets the Liang part. It, too, had a path that divided it down the middle. The path wasn't much higher than the water's surface, so after every rain, it just became one large pond. It was three doors down from my house, just past Liang Guang-sheng's, Liang Wanhu's, and Aunt Zhao's houses. There was a level field in front of Aunt Zhao's house, where people would gather. At mealtimes, everyone carried their bowls over, chatting about everything under the sun or flirting with one another. I have vague memories of the conversations between Auntie Han Ling and Ma Qingming: although I didn't understand what they were talking about, the way they covered their smiles, their faces red, was enough for me to understand that they were discussing "those things." Then I'd escape as fast I could—it was a little girl's instinct. Now, many years later, I'm shocked to find that Ma Qingming is a rather wooden, simple sort of person. At home she doesn't say much, and outside of the home she seems even more like a shrinking, timid, rural woman. But when she was joking about the business of husbands and wives, her eyes turned to the sky, her shy, distant expression took on a kind of feminine beauty, an unspeakable appeal. Yet who saw—let alone understood—this appeal? Even though as a girl I sensed this, it took me many years to understand it.

I must admit that sometimes, as time and distance come together to create memory, I may be guilty of sentimentalizing the past. But when I see the village ponds today, I know that this sentiment is born from their demise. They are utterly dead. They cannot be saved.

The pond in front of the elementary school is nothing more than a shallow ditch filled with dead water, covered with black algae and crawling flies. Its former depths, its lotus roots in the dirt (perhaps it was the lotuses that kept it clean), the lotus flowers and pods, they are all gone. They've been replaced by houses and foundations.

Neither the threshing yard nor its pond can be seen. The place where we once somersaulted and watched movies, where we once hid in piles of hay reading novels, ignoring our parents as they shouted themselves hoarse—all that is gone. New houses stand there now, atop who knows how much filled earth. Only a pitiful little triangle of the water remains in the place where we used to swim like ducks.

And the pond next to the tall mulberry tree . . . if you grew up in this village, if you cherished it in your heart, if you came back to look for traces of your childhood, the sight of this pond would bring you to tears. It is black, dead, putrid sludge with nothing growing in it. A tree has fallen across it, its trunk black. The surface is covered in leaves that have been there I don't know how long; they too are black, stuck together into a mass, still as death. People have thrown plastic bottles, tin cans, children's clothes, and all kinds of household garbage on it. You can't get too close. Its stench is so strong you can't open your eyes.

This black sludge, black death, black stench creates a sense of terror. Yet all around it, in front, behind, and to the left, are new houses. My relatives draw their water here. They eat and breathe here. They live their lives here.

That Han family pond, which geese used to fly over, which created the earliest impressions of beauty in a young girl's heart, is now nothing more than a shallow, polluted pit, a swamp, filled with flies and insect larvae. And the pond's legendary well-spring? Did it disappear on its own, or was it stopped up by the houses built on top of it?

This is my village. This is the land where my people live. They earn a little money, build multistoried houses, live happy lives. But can lives built atop this filth be truly happy?

Yet who can I blame? "People from my hometown" who have destroyed the environment, who disregard the ecosystem, who do not value the quality of their own existence? That would almost be an affectation. What they see is the steady improvement of their homes. Even if husbands and wives, fathers and sons, mothers and daughters must live apart all year long, at least they no longer endure days of starvation. During Spring Festival they can come back to the village and sit in their new houses, entertaining family and friends. For these few days, the year's separation, with its hardships and tears, can fall away. This is without a doubt the root of their happiness. They don't know whether or not there is another path. Old Man History has already fixed the course of their lives. They think this is all there is. They endure, and they strive to find a sense of well-being.

So who am I to say? When I look at my family's familiar, good-natured faces, when I listen to their troubles, their joys and sorrows, how can I tell them that this dead, filthy pond should also be a part of their lives?

Chrysanthemum Riverbank

Dawn. I walk through the quiet village, down its small lanes and into the woods. Bird calls of every sort mix together, complex, reverberating, each a tiny quiver of delight. I stand on the riverbank, the morning fog misting the air, the warm red sun slowly rising. It's not a sunrise of dazzling, multicolored rays of light; everything is muted, broad and soft. Gradually, from along the riverbank, in twos and threes, herds of white sheep and cows emerge, heavy and dark. Adults squat on the embankment and children run by, letting out occasional peals of silvery laughter. Fishermen, nearly naked, stand as still as clay figures. The river meanders by, deep and slow. In the fields, dense crops, some low, some tall, all healthy, new and fresh, stretch out in endless green. Beneath the clear sky, in the distance, a faint layer of fog covers the fields. Everything is filled with life, a vast natural beauty that inspires joy.

Who else walks the small, woodland lanes, the river's sandy shores, the grassy riverbank, still and quiet? Who else is listening to this day that has just begun? This day that will pass? This dawn, this midday, this dusk? Human sounds approach, and the birds depart, spirits of nature in retreat. Those little souls, which had welcomed the dawn sun so joyfully, have fallen silent. There is only the occasional call and response, sad, lonely and frightened, as though they are only reassuring one another that they still exist.

In the summertime, when I was a child, everyone in the village ate dinner very early. Adults and kids would walk or ride their bikes, setting off one by one from their homes. At dusk, the riverbanks would be filled with noise. People bathed in the river, then lounged in the shade of the trees by the riverbanks, chatting about everything and nothing, including sweet nothings. They lay on their backs in the pure white river sand, reveling in the starry sky above and the great earth below.

If you came down from the long river dike behind the village, you would find large swaths of deep forest. Within them was a place where people raised deer, and a little swampy lake where pairs of wild ducks lived. When it rained, the entire river dike would turn green and blue.

When I was in my teens, this stretch of river was companion to my first lovelorn sorrow. I skipped school and came here alone to wander along the river, picking purple lilacs; on rainy days, I wouldn't bring an umbrella but would walk barefoot in the grass, trampling the small green plants in the swampy water. The crystal clear water and the soft, fine grasses . . . I was so fond of them all. In the autumn, I would lie on the golden-yellow knotweed, thick and strong. I would roll in it, breathing, silent, watching a fire-red cloud in the western sky, imagining it was a horse coming to carry me to distant places.

The goose-yellow willow trees of springtime; the river water clear as glass; the sweet little deer deep in forest glens; the wild ducks, always in pairs; the fine, white sand—it was all indescribably lovely. My sense of beauty, my love for nature, my thirst for blue sky and white clouds were all formed on that riverbank.

Yet suddenly one day, it disappeared. The dense forest behind the river dike was gone almost overnight. My distracted adolescent eyes hadn't noticed that the trees were being cut down until the green river plain had become an empty wasteland. The small deer in the woods, the swampy pond, the wild ducks, the warblers, at some point they all disappeared. The river water grew lower and lower until all that was left in many places was a dried-up riverbed. The water itself turned black and shiny, like gasoline, like a cloth that's been used all year for cleaning but has never been cleaned itself. Where the river runs wide and the water is deep, the black flow appears calm and imposing, from a distance at least. But in fact it's wastewater from the Summertime Chemical Plant, which has gone through a high temperature evaporation process, and its smell—rancid, fermented, sweet and reeking of blood—makes anyone who comes close feel nauseous and dizzy. White, black, and multicolored foam floats along the water's surface. Where the river eddies, you can use a lighter to ignite the foam, and with a "whoomp" the fire will race along the riverbank, extending out across the foam. It will burn for a hundred meters or more, beautiful really, until you catch a whiff of the smell, which is enough to knock a man over.

Since the 1980s how many rivers in China have escaped pollution? Perhaps if we climb mountains and ford streams to some uninhabited place, we might find a bit of water clear enough to reflect the sky. But the moment it is discovered, its death will not be far off.

The river in our village is only one of countless polluted rivers. It is called the Tuan River, or "Rushing River." It extends for several hundred kilometers, running through most of the towns and villages in Rang County. Li Daoyuan (466?–527) gave a written account of the Tuan in the *Shui Jing Zhu* (*Commentary on the Waterways Classic*):

> The Tuan River travels south, where the Chrysanthemum River enters it. Its origins are the Shijian Mountain Fragrant Chrysanthemum Stream in the northwest. It is also said to feed from Xi Valley. It is also called Gai Stream. Chrysanthemums and wild plants flourish near its source, which is fed by deep pools and springs. Its water is sweet and beautiful and nourishes the valley's land and groundwater all year round. Wangchang, the Minister of Public Works, High Official Yuanwei, and High Officer Huguang drank its water for comfort and nourishment. It sweetened their disgrace. Chrysanthemum River flows southeast into the Tuan, which then flows through this county to the southeast, where it enters northwestern Guanjun County. There the Chu Dam gradually lowers its eight tiers, creating an area of 10 *li*. This reservoir is always filled with sweet water, and its glistening pools never dry up. The Tuan River passes through Guanjun's Eastern Old City, Luyang Village and Wanlintaoju, which was formerly part of Rang County . . . The Tuan River once fed six ponds in Rang County, but during Han Xiaoyuan's time, in the fifth year of Jianzhao, the governor of Nanyang, Shao Xinchen, cut off the river with the Western Rang Stone dam.

In his *Annotated Commentary on the Waterways Classic*, Qing Dynasty scholar Yang Shoujing also includes the following:

> The notes in the Li County *Xu Han Annals* point to the *Jingzhou Records*. The Chrysanthemum River is in Bachen,

in the north of the county; the river has a reputation for its sweet water. Thirty families live there, but they no longer dig wells, instead they rely on the river. They live to be more than 120, and average 100 years or more. They consider 70 or 80 to be an early death. In the Han Dynasty, the Minister of Public Works Wangchang and High Official Yuanwei ordered the county to deliver more than thirty stones of the water monthly to the Nanyang government. It was used for eating and bathing. High Officer Huguang had long been ill, but after he returned south, he always drew this water to drink, and his illness was healed. The chrysanthemums have short stalks and large petals and are sweet to eat, unlike other chrysanthemums.

I imagine the Tuan River of several hundred years ago, passing through our village, with its extravagantly exotic flowers, beautiful and fragrant, gracing the riverbanks, watered by the river. The river so sweet, the soil so fertile, the people so long lived, healthy and refined. What a Peach Blossom Garden . . . like a Garden of Eden.

The River's End

People are gathered by Xiangjiao Dam, near the road that heads to the north side of the county seat. I think perhaps there is some local entertainment going on, but I soon find out otherwise. A teenager has drowned. In the heat of the day, three teens had gone for a swim, and one of them had disappeared. By the time I get there the firemen have been dredging the water for six or seven hours already. People on both sides of the river are crying.

At the riverside, everyone is talking at once. Four or five people have drowned at this spot every year for the past few years. Most are young. Last year two high school students drowned; they had come to visit relatives after taking their college entrance exams. They were seventeen. A few years before, large quantities of sand were dug from this part of the river, leaving deep pits in the riverbed. Now both the sand mining company and all the yellow sand are gone.

As I am chatting with two men in their fifties or sixties, I ask why no one has investigated the sand mining companies' liability. Hasn't anyone inquired with the River Management Bureau? The two men, who look to be retired cadres, think about it, and say, you're not wrong, but none of them are around anymore, and besides, who can say for sure what's going on at the river's bottom? No one has tried to hold the mining companies responsible. Mostly they just say, "What can you do?" "Who could we ask?" "Who would take responsibility?" They might weep. Instead they stand around repeating, "What were those kids thinking? They knew there were whirlpools here, but they jumped in anyway."

The sky is dark when the rain subsides, and the sound of weeping rises suddenly on the riverbank, a woman's voice tearing the sky like a piece of silk. They must have found the body. I run with all the others through the mud over to the river. It is my first time I've stood in the gawking crowd like this.

They found his body. A relative holds him tightly, pinching his nose to stop the stream of white foam while she continues her hoarse weeping. The boy is slim, his eyes tightly closed, his face and body blue. He must have been a handsome young man. Ignoring the people who are trying to stop him, a relative presses on the young man's chest with all his might, attempting CPR. When he realizes it is no use, he begins to cry; then he turns and walks away, as if ducking away from the pain in his heart. The boy's relatives gather on the riverbank and another wail of weeping rises. The more tenderhearted onlookers quietly wipe their eyes, already red.

Even since I was small, I've been called "piss-eyes," and to this day, whenever I hear someone crying, I can't help but cry myself. But this time I have no tears. I am numb, aching with an inexpressible distress, as if a layer of thick fog has covered my way home.

When I return to my brother's house, I tell them about the boy who has drowned by the dam, and my brother and his friends give a good many more examples. Every year a dozen or more people drown in the river in our area. Parents warn their children again and again not to swim there, but if it's a hot summer day and there's a stretch of river, how can you be sure that a group of kids won't be lured in? For instance, one time four young kids, all around eleven or twelve, took advantage of their parents' afternoon naps to go for a secret swim. The result: two of the four are gone. The two who lived didn't dare say anything. Only a day later did they tell their parents what happened. One of the bodies was never even found. Last year a man from the Wang family drowned. He took some children down to the river to bathe, pulled off his clothes, jumped in the water, and with a *zip* he was gone. The children stood crying on the riverbank until someone realized what had happened.

We walk slowly along the river. I want to understand the mining and what happened to the riverbed. No matter what, anywhere a river flows is beautiful, even if it's riddled with ills. On the riverbank, newly planted poplar trees have grown as wide as rice bowls and are filled with budding leaves.

They are part of the "poplar economy," which the new Chinese Communist Party county committee secretary put into place. Whether they will bring in money or not, no one knows, but they have undoubtedly improved the ecology. A pure white road meanders up and down through the wood. Close to the river are thick clusters of reeds, and many of the big, irregularly shaped sandpits left behind by the dredgers. Most have filled with water, and with the gray river stones on either bank contrasting with the sandy shore, the landscape is unexpectedly beautiful. The water and sand are all controlled by different parties; they have been divided by the mining company bosses, and when summer comes and the water level rises, the sandpits turn into large whirlpools, some of which have deep currents that are invisible on the surface. When someone jumps in for a swim, the cold, deep water often stuns them and causes them to drown, or they might get caught in the swirling of the whirlpools.

The dredgers extend across the river, their cranes hanging in the air, dark and solid. From a distance, they aren't necessarily ugly. Beside them are immense piles of sand, and the trucks that haul the sand rumble loudly back and forth. What was once a broad river has been excavated into a tangle of smaller tributaries, which the river water slowly followed as it pleased. Some places are shallow and dry; in others, the current is strong.

By rough count, there are nearly twenty dredgers over about five kilometers of road. That's an average of four per kilometer, though they are concentrated in a few places. My son and his little cousin aren't able to resist, and they start walking into the water, until a chorus of adult voices pulls them to a halt. I run over to the river and drag them out, instructing them to only look from a distance. I was glad I had reacted so fast, but I also felt sad. The peaceful river contains hidden dangers. It could swallow up a human life in a second. The sky may be clear, the birds may be flying, and the current may be slow, but it is no longer possible to bathe in its waters or play on its shores.

What kind of impact does large-scale sand mining have on rivers? To answer this question, I met with the deputy director of the County Water Conservancy Bureau.

Sand mining is important to the local construction industry. At present the country is carrying out construction on a large scale, and there's hardly any construction project, private or public, that doesn't require sand and concrete. Brick-making needs sand as well. It's illegal to dig clay, so we only have fired-lime bricks, which are made from sand and gravel. Where do these come from? Rivers. Sand mining can have an impact on a river's ecology, but the impact need not be great. Sand mining permits must be renewed every year. The scope of the mining, the width, depth and manner are all regulated, so they don't affect the river's course. In addition, mining companies can't mine whenever they wish. For example, there is a provision in the Water Act that says during flood season, sand mining is not permitted. During flood season, dredging vessels must be docked; they cannot mine sand. This prohibition is often broken, however. The government must take decisive measures. Those who don't dock their vessels, or who are carrying workers, must surrender their vessels. If it's done once, fear will do the rest.

Sand mining is an underwater operation, it's hard to be exact. You might only be permitted to dig 1.5–2 meters deep, but on the spot it's only possible to estimate. There's no accuracy. In addition, as the water flows, the riverbed is constantly changing, and it is uneven. You can't take measurements each time before a company starts to dredge.

There is no way to measure.

In addition, objectively speaking, the depth of the water is difficult to determine because of the consequences of the mining itself. It is very difficult to control the operating parameters beneath the water. Any sand mining is bound to have an impact, it's just a question of how much. If you dig too deeply, pools are likely to form. If the riverbed is uneven and someone's walking along in the water, if they come across a pit or a large whirlpool, they're going to disappear.

But on the other hand, even if we didn't mine sand, even if we left the river alone, it's always changing. The flow of the water causes erosion, which can change the condition of the riverbed. As the saying goes, the river flows east thirty years; then the river flows west thirty years. If we jump to conclusions that excessive mining is to blame, that would be unreasonable. Even before large-scale mining, didn't people drown?

The water quality is slightly better now, a lot clearer than before, but the paper mill upstream is going to open again. It is a pillar of that county's economy. When it is closed, the county loses a lot in taxes. So it's always opening and closing. This is typical of local protectionism. There's no way around it. Every county is this way. Equipment to reduce and control pollution is brought in, but it's never used. It's too costly to operate. The higher-ups do an inspection, everything's run for a few days to reach wastewater standards, but then they leave, and it stops. The inspection team is like a mirror: it sees everything, but it doesn't say anything.

Environmental protection efforts have in fact increased over the past few years. Didn't the fertilizer plant in our county close? This was because of wastewater problems. The higher-ups are more and more concerned with environmental protection. The main agents of the Water Pollution Control Act are the Environmental Protection Agency and the Water Conservancy Bureau, working in tandem. Wastewater disposal systems must be arranged with the Water Conservancy Bureau in accordance with the quantity of wastewater output, and must protect our water resources.

With the present reforms, the functions of the large ministries have been integrated. On the whole, it's a good thing. It's a lot more convenient and reduces reduplication and the overlapping of functions.

River pollution does not necessarily imply groundwater pollution. Surface water and groundwater are not always directly connected, and there are no serious groundwater pollution problems in rural areas. But in our region fluoride levels are high, and the groundwater is also high in fluoride. This causes fluorosis and osteoporosis. And in a few places the groundwater contains arsenic, fluoride, and high levels of sodium. In the county census two years ago, 53 million out of 150 million people suffered from fluorosis.

In recent years, the county has implemented safe drinking water programs in rural areas. Last year we gave 35,000 people access to safe water. For example, we dug deeper wells, more than 200 meters below ground level. In the villages we installed waterworks and connected each household with pipes. In the cities, water is chlorinated, but at 200 meters chlorine no longer needs to be added.

I manage the water, but I, too, can only tell the children to stay on the shore. One of my colleagues in the Bureau had a teenager, sixteen years old, who drowned a few years ago. Now parents in rural areas, as well as those who live in cities, won't allow their children to bathe in the river. Before, bathing in the river every night was a pleasure. Where the river runs through the city, the population is denser, and people always go over to the railroad bridge, where the water is deeper. From time to time we put up warning signs, but they're no use. The kids don't pay attention, and every summer they go in.

Throughout the interview, he gives me the sense that I'm making a mountain out of a molehill. These problems can easily be ignored, because they aren't problems for everyone. Or you could say they are problems that are simply an inevitable part of progress. There is no reason to make a fuss about them. The Water Conservancy Bureau cadre says what he thinks over a meal. Perhaps he is much more professional when he is at work. Questions of mining versus the ecology, and the relationship between survival and quality of life, do not factor into their way of thinking. And truly, it can't be helped: it really is impossible to monitor how deep they're digging the sand; you can't stop the mining from happening. It is a legal business, and the demands of industry are great.

Rivers are the lifelines of a country's ecology; the guarantee of a nation's future. Yet, over the past ten years, we have brought them to an early end. We live among riverbeds that are dried up and foul smelling, terrifying and dark. If this doesn't change, catastrophe is nigh. Or perhaps it has already come.

3

Save the Children

The number of crimes and criminal cases involving *liushou*, juveniles who have been left in rural areas while their parents work in urban centers, has more than doubled: In 2007, a total of 53 juvenile crime cases were heard, involving a total of 81 juveniles; of them, 18 juveniles were *liushou*. In 2009, 69 cases involving 133 juveniles were heard; of them, 53 were *liushou*. Great efforts have been made towards education in the law and its application, and strengthening the youth's understanding of rule of law, in a program that has involved 80,000 teachers and students and seen the distribution of 1,200 copies of newly produced legal educational materials, effectively raising the level of young people's legal and self-defense awareness. The joint efforts of many departments have led to visible improvements in young people's developmental circumstances, and rates of youth crime are in decline. In 2016, 33 youth crime cases involving 42 individuals were opened; in 2017, 31 cases involving 40 individuals were opened.

—Data reported by the Rang County
People's Juvenile Court

The Wang Boy

On January 23, 2006, the County Public Security Bureau went to the township high school and pulled the Wang boy out of class. He was being arrested for the rape and murder of 82-year-old Mrs. Liu. She'd been killed almost two years before, but the

Public Security Bureau had not begun its investigation in the village until nine months prior to the arrest. During those nine months, the atmosphere in the village had been tense, especially for the two main suspects: the old bachelors, Qian Huozi and Liang Guangyi. They were interrogated so many times that their mental health was affected. As for the Wang boy, every morning he went to school, and every evening he came home and went to bed. He did nothing out of the ordinary. According to his teacher, he was calm when he was arrested. He said nothing; he did not resist. He arranged his books and materials neatly, as if he had been waiting for this day to come.

When the Liang villagers heard the news, they were shocked. That little bastard?! He was clean-cut, not very talkative. He had a nice look about him. He wasn't a bad kid like the other village boys, who skipped school to play video games on the Internet. His grades had always been good. People had even thought that the Wangs had finally produced a college student.

This was the first time the Wang family had come under scrutiny in the village. On top of that, because of the complicated nature of the case, and the later involvement of some community members, this was one of the biggest events in village history.

On April 2, 2004, Liang Jiankun did as she always did. She woke up at 6 am to prepare breakfast. Then, after she and her two grandchildren had eaten, she put the leftovers on the stove to keep warm and rode them in her three-wheeled cart over to the town elementary school. After that, she stopped to see her daughter, who had married into a family that lives in town.

Aunt Jiankun married into the village from another county. Her mother, Old Mrs. Liu, had only one daughter, and when she was old enough to be eligible for the "five guarantees" (food, clothing, housing, medical care, and burial expenses), her daughter brought her to live in our village. Her mother insisted that she would not live in her daughter's home. She was afraid her grandsons' wives might be unkind to her and that her daughter would be in the middle of it. So she lived alone near the road in a little hut, which Aunt Jiankun had built when she was tending the vegetable garden there.

Aunt Jiankun rode quickly home, thinking of the food that was still on the stove, afraid it might have burned. At the corner, she called out "Ma! Ma! Come eat." When no one answered, she thought maybe her mother had already gone to her place, so she headed toward home. But the house was still locked, so Aunt Jiankun turned back to the little hut, only to find that its door was locked too. Something wasn't right. The chickens were cackling inside. If her mother were up, she would have let them out. So Aunt Jiankun hurried off to find someone to help her break the door down. When they finally got inside, they were met with a paralyzing scene: Old Mrs. Liu's body lay prone on the bed, her feet dangling to the floor. The lower half of her body was naked. There was blood everywhere. On the door, the floor, the bed, and her body. Next to her head was a brick, and when they looked closer, they saw a large gash in her skull. All around, chickens were pecking for food.

After the Public Security Bureau came to investigate, it was determined that she had been raped and murdered. They obtained some semen from the body, and on the other side of the room, they recovered a hoe with some blood on it, as well as some broken fragments of bone. Liang Village was sizzling like a frying pan. Filled with righteous indignation, everyone wanted to capture the rapist who had offended against Heaven and reason.

The Public Security Bureau soon announced that this was an isolated incident, probably perpetrated by a drifter. How were they to know who passed through the village at night, especially by a house so close to the main road? The case was inconclusive, an unsolved mystery. Aunt Jiankun filed complaints with both the town police and the County Public Security Bureau. The Public Security Bureau said they weren't refusing to solve the case; there just wasn't enough evidence. But in 2005, the

Provincial Public Security Bureau decreed that "all homicides must be solved," so Aunt Jiankun went to file another complaint. This time the County Public Security Bureau quickly sent a few people to live in the village head's house to focus their investigation on the village itself.

The men in Liang Village began to panic. Initially, the investigation focused upon two older, single men, Qian Huozi and Liang Guangyi. When they were young, they had engaged in some pretty lewd behavior—harassing women on the road, laughing and even exposing themselves. So they were called in several times, and quickly enough they began to lose it. One ran around the village and town mooning everyone. The other shut himself up in his house. If he saw anyone, he would begin to tremble from head to foot.

Later, the scope of investigation broadened to any and all males aged sixteen years and older. Everyone had blood drawn for a DNA test, to see if it matched the semen found on Old Mrs. Liu's body. It wasn't until some matches were found in the DNA of an old man in the Wang family that the Public Security Bureau finally began to concentrate on the Wangs. Previously, almost no one had thought to suspect them. They were too insignificant.

Soon after the Wang boy was arrested, the details of his confession became known in the village. That night, after he had come home from study hall, he had put on a porno film from his elder brother's collection. His brother, who didn't live at home anymore, had a lot of disks, and the boy knew some of them were pornographic. After he watched it, he went to sleep. In the middle of the night, around 1 am, he used the toilet and then went over to the little hut where Old Mrs. Liu lived. First he used a brick and the hoe to kill her. Then he raped her.

When I returned to the village, the case had already been through a few rounds at court, and the boy was still locked up and under guard. The court had first ruled for the death penalty, but his elder brother and parents had entered an appeal, arguing that because he was under eighteen when he committed the crime, he should not be sentenced to death. They asked people from the Qian family, the Zhou family, and Midwife Zhang to act as witnesses. So the case was reopened and more evidence was collected. This time his death sentence was deferred. But then Aunt Jiankun countered that his elder brother had paid the witnesses, which constituted perjury, so the case was appealed again.

As for the young man himself, no one seemed to think about him, though to my mind he was a great riddle. I was curious: what could cause a young man to commit such a brutal crime? He seemed so quiet and apathetic. What was he really like?

With these thoughts in mind, I sought out one of his aunts. The Wang and Liang family areas of the village are only separated by the road that leads to the fields, and yet the Wangs seem so distant. Even as children, we seldom played with them. I don't know how children make these kinds of distinctions; it seems almost entirely unconscious.

As soon as Aunt Wang heard I wanted to talk about the boy's case, she became very guarded. She obviously didn't want to talk about it. As we sat together, chatting about this and that, I asked about living conditions for the Wang family. I slowly began to realize that after the changes of the past twenty years, more than half of the twenty or so Wang families that had once lived here were no longer in the village. Some had moved, others had no children. Once the Wang boy's crime became public, all the young men who were even close to working age left the village. They would rather go haul bricks than stay. They were afraid people would look down on them.

After I had been there for quite a while, Aunt Wang finally opened up. When he was young, she said, he was never quite right. He never spoke, he was like a closed door. And since he was small, he had lived practically alone. In 1993, when the boy was four or five, his parents went to Xinjiang to farm, and he and his brother went to live with their grandmother. His grandmother died in 1995, and so the boys were entrusted to an aunt. After middle school, his brother dropped out and left home. Some say he got involved with organized crime, and the few times he came back to the village were to evade capture. Later, he opened an Internet cafe somewhere and made some money.

The Wang boy was reserved. He never played with kids his age. But he was good at school and was accepted at the best middle school in Wu town. After middle school, he lived alone and ate in the school cafeteria. In the evenings he stayed at his brother's house. He had come back in 2000 to get married and build a new house, which he fully furnished. When the Wang boy was arrested, he was in his third year of high school. The school was grooming him to be a top student. He had never caused any trouble.

For some reason, as I left Aunt Wang's house, I felt utterly dejected. The way Aunt Wang told it (and consistent with my conversation with the boy's high school teacher), there'd been no sign that he could ever commit such a crime. On the contrary, he seemed an introverted, gracious, and ambitious young man.

Truth be told, when I first heard the story, I had instinctually felt sympathy for him; he was so young, just growing into a young man. Perhaps he was suffering from repressed emotions and urges. And yet he had brutally murdered a woman in her eighties. I wandered around the village. New house after new house, the immense ruins, the filthy ponds, the ducks and the floating trash. It was monstrous, intolerable.

When I found Aunt Jiankun, it was almost dark. She was just heading to the elementary school, but when she saw us, she turned around and asked us into her house, telling me that she knew that at the end of the year she would come and find me in Beijing. She wanted to file a complaint there and believed her case would win.

Swarthy Aunt Jiankun had given birth to three sons and a girl. Ever since I was young, I've felt close to her because, whenever she saw me, she would look at me sadly and say with a sigh that if her little girl had lived, she would have been my age. She and my mother were good friends when they were younger, and a month after I was born she'd had her little girl, who died from dysentery when she was five years old.

Aunt Jiankun was living at her eldest son Wanzhong's house, where she took care of her two grandchildren. Wanzhong's family worked in Shenzhen, and his new house had been built by the milling field. It was imposing from the outside, two stories high with a large iron door to seal it tight. Inside was a different story. Lime was falling from the walls in big patches, leaving marks like giant scars, and the rooms were bare and empty. There was a long bench covered with rags and a dusty standing fan that looked like it had never been used. To the left there was a large bed with some quilts. That was where Aunt Jiankun usually slept. To the right were the stairs. It was strangely cold, sitting in that house. Aunt Jiankun poured the tea and took out some wrinkled tangerines, urging them on me. Then she sat down and began to tell her story.

Until this business is settled, I won't be able to die in peace. I told the head prosecutor, if you handle this sloppily, I'll jump from this building. I'm already sixty-five years old, what do I want with life, I've lived enough. If I die here, there will be no peace for you in the prosecutor's office.

Your great-grandmother's death was brutal. Everyone who saw it wept and cursed whoever could be so heartless. The investigation dragged on for over a year, but nothing came of it. Only after they began to examine the DNA did they get somewhere.

People on the street told me, it was the Wang boy. When I heard that, my heart went cold. How could this boy, who never even spoke, how could he rape and kill? Because he did, didn't he? So cruel, so hateful. The village has been so uneasy. The men so scared they can't keep it together, and this little bastard still going to school every day like nothing ever happened.

At first, his mother went around the village gathering false testimonies. She found his midwife, and some elders from our family, who testified that the bastard wasn't eighteen years old at the time. She also found Zhou Guosheng and had him give false testimony. When he came out of the courtroom, I cornered him: Zhou Guosheng, your bastard grandchild betrayed his conscience, may your grandchildren and daughters-in-law all be run over by cars. And you betrayed your conscience too, may you die a terrible death. What kind of a person are you to give false testimony and betray your conscience? Later I heard that the Wang boy's mother had given him two cartons of cigarettes and a pair of pants.

I ran into Guosheng's wife on the street. I stepped in front of her and cursed her too. If you give false testimony, the next time you're driving your car will flip over and kill your children. I cursed her for more than an hour. The villagers all curse them behind their backs. They said their grandchildren and daughters-in-law deserve to be hit by cars. That's what happens when people's hearts are twisted.

I also fought with Grandmother Wang Shuangtian. They also gave false testimony. If you look at the Wang family children and add things up, you'll see that the bastard was already eighteen when he killed my mother. I said your daughter died in Beijing for no reason, you didn't even find her body, and you're still giving false testimony. You're a Wang, and you say you don't know where the bastard is in the family order, how old he is? If you lie through your teeth, you'll be struck by lightning.

The verdict was decided on November 27, 2007, but by December we still couldn't go pick it up. I went to the prosecutor's office. I called the lead prosecutor. He didn't answer. I called his cell phone. He didn't answer that either.

I waited at the entrance until 11 am, and only then did he finally answer the phone and let me in. He seemed a little angry. He stamped the court verdict and had me add my fingerprint. I can't read, so I had him read it for me.

A judge at the Municipal People's Court called me privately. He said, listen, about this little bastard, my mother is Buddhist, and I've learned a lot from her. When it is possible to forgive, you forgive. It would be a shame to insist on the death penalty. I said, you are tenderhearted, but you're not sitting where I sit. He should live because he's young? My mother was more than eighty and so should die?

I know the Wangs gave these people money. The Wangs' older son had earned a lot of money with his Internet cafe. He was also a thief before he left home. He was sentenced to ten months. As soon as he was let out, he went to find work. He was in and out of the police stations then, too. No one in that family is respectable.

The case was tried five times. When the Wang boy saw me he knelt down. He wanted my sympathy. I didn't even look at him.

I believe that right will prevail. Good always triumphs over evil. If this judgment isn't handed down, I'll jump from the courthouse and show them.

When she said she would jump from the building, Aunt Jiankun's voice, which had been trembling, became firm. Then she went to get the verdict to show me. As I flipped through it, I saw that it included a confession from the Wang boy.

One night that spring, after I was done with study hall at school, I came home to go to bed. Before going to sleep, I watched a porno movie. I don't know how long I slept, but I got up and went over to the hut where Old Mrs. Liu slept. I got the door on the east side open and went in. I found a hoe. I heard the old woman snoring and hit her with the hoe several times. I was afraid she wasn't dead, so I went outside, next to where chickens are kept, and grabbed a brick. I went back inside and saw where her head was and smashed it four or five times. Then I took off the old woman's clothes. I grabbed her neck with my hands. I pulled my pants down to my knees, climbed onto her body and put my penis into her vagina for a minute or two. Then I ejaculated. When I closed the door, I felt around for the lock hanging on the back, and locked it.

So cold. So brutal. I don't know if it's the court's paraphrasing or the boy's original statement, but the description is emotionless. When he was killing her did he feel frightened, weak, panicked? From this statement, it would seem that the killer had no humanity at all. I could think of nothing to say. I was confused—why had I wanted to investigate this case in the first place?

At that time, all you had to do was bring up Old Mrs. Liu's murder, and people would start to lose it, especially over how the Wang family had bought connections to falsify his age. When I asked Grandma Wu about it, she spat in contempt, *pei*! And then added, if I were his ma, I would go straight over to the Public Security Bureau and shoot him myself. What he did was too evil, too brutal. Her words were filled with fury, just like my father's and the former branch secretary's. I hadn't expected that—I thought some might sympathize with him. He was barely eighteen years old, after all. He had been ruthless, but he was just hardly an adult. It was really a shame, I added in a low voice, that he lived at home like that, with no one to take care of him. But as soon as the words were out of my mouth, my father and Grandma Wu cut me off. Think of all the children who live alone. They don't do anything like that. If someone that evil isn't sent to the firing squad, what's society coming to? Only then did I realize that their judgment of the young man was fundamentally moral in nature. Corrupted morals and evil ways cannot be forgiven.

The intensity of the villagers' response to the Wang boy's case reveals their reverence for a kind of primitive morality, woven deep in the village's social fabric. Their reaction was at odds with their fundamental kindness and with the basic way the village worked. So when I tried to say that China's death penalty rate seemed too high and too indiscriminate, and that other countries never had the death penalty while others have abolished it, they were astounded. In their worldview, death was the only fitting punishment for this brutal act.

No one brought up his parents' shortcomings, how a lack of love or a lonely life might have had an impact. To the villagers this kind of reasoning was silly and untenable. Yet how many young people in rural areas were living like this? Who was caring for their mental health?

As she spoke about the case, Aunt Jiankun switched easily to moral terms. It's true that murder is punishable by death, but on a deeper level it seems the case was decided in the court of moral opinion. For example, talking about the people who gave false testimony, Aunt Jiankun brought up other misfortunes that had struck the families, as if to prove their moral dissipation and to paint this as an act of retribution. The examples further confirmed her judgment of their errors. Listening to her, I had a sense of great anxiety, as if some sort of primal justice still lived upon the earth. Daily life concealed it, but it was there, beneath the current "laws." They cannot be separated. People based their judgments upon it. Good is repaid with good; evil is repaid with evil. If a debt has gone unpaid, it is only because the time has not yet come.

I couldn't help but doubt myself: perhaps it was because she had been an old woman, eighty-two years old, with one foot in the grave. Perhaps that's why the crime didn't seem worth a young man's life. Perhaps this was the source of my instinctual sympathy. Perhaps, if he had killed a young adolescent girl, my attitude would have been different. In the end perhaps I, too, was undervaluing life.

After making inquiries through several avenues, I finally got the opportunity to meet the boy. I was nervous, filled with questions. The metal door opened, and a young man, weak, thin, and shackled, came out. He glanced at me quickly with emotionless eyes and then sat down on a stool. He glanced again and then lowered his head. What was the expression in his eyes? Embarrassment? Loneliness? Despair? I couldn't tell. But this was certain: the person before me was a boy, or, if he was already a young man, he still looked like a boy. He didn't even have facial hair. He was still a child, a good, pure, introverted child. He even looked well-mannered.

Sudden tears blurred my eyes, and I couldn't open my mouth. I had been back in the village for so long, and had heard so many sad stories, and never cried. But now, faced with a murderer, I suddenly fell apart. Looking at him, the causes ceased to be causes; all of the factors, which were not causes, joined together to form tragedy. I couldn't imagine him brandishing a hoe or a brick; I couldn't connect the young man before me with that act of violence.

What could I ask? All my questions paled in comparison to this scene before me. Who could understand how, on a lonely night, the pent-up frustrations of his teenage heart spilled over into darkness? Who could understand how loveless day stacked upon loveless day led to this cry of anguish? Who had attended to his burgeoning sex drive? What attitude should I adopt before him? What frame of mind? I didn't know. I was at sea. Sympathy? Anger? Grief? These words all seemed too simple.

The final judgment was passed down in April 2009. The Wang boy was sentenced to death for premeditated murder.

Aunt Zhi

A few days ago my father arranged to get together with his younger brother, the village accountant, at his house for a meal. My uncle intrigues me. Last time we ate together, I had the sense that he was a deep one. Whenever he touches on a crucial subject, especially regarding the village's current economic situation, he promptly changes the subject without expressing any sort of opinion. Even when father presses him, he only prevaricates.

When we get to Uncle's house, my cousin Qingdao is already there. Another man is there, but I don't recognize him and Uncle doesn't introduce him. A first course of cold dishes is already on the table, and, to one side, a card table is set up. It looks like we won't get a chance to talk. Sure enough, as soon as Father comes in Qingdao shouts out, "What took you so long, Second Uncle, it's only a few steps away, and we still had to call you more than once, come to the table, let's get to it." In town, people will deliver hot dishes to your door by car (for a fee, of course). Uncle explains to me that he doesn't generally eat out and only occasionally gets delivery like this. Neither Father nor Qingdao seem happy about it. Qingdao doesn't want anything to drink. Last night he had a few too many—he drank himself into the ditch.

Uncle and Father tell him that's why he should keep it up. They press him until Qingdao's face has taken on a drunken flush. The issue of the Inter-Village Connection Road Project came up. According to my father, the project's main road had already been sold to the sand mining companies on the river (it's the only main road that goes there). It was sold for 170,000 yuan (more than $26,000), but nearly all the money was siphoned off by the new branch secretary. The accountant ought to know the details better than anyone, but Uncle talks in circles and doesn't say a thing, except, "It's always this way. There's really nothing to do about it. There are always too many places

73

to spend money. Even they don't know how much they took." In other words, his lips are sealed.

After the meal, the cards come out. I go into the courtyard to chat with Uncle's wife, whom we call Aunt Zhi. Her little grandson is a couple of years older than my son, and the two, already friends, are playing in a pile of sand by the entrance. The village accountant's house is much nicer than the former branch secretary's; it can't be more than two years old. Like the branch secretary's, it was built on a reclaimed pond. From the road, it looks like a one-story house, made imposing by its high foundation, but from the back, where the main entrance is located, it is exceptionally pretty. What from the front looks like a high foundation is actually only the top level of a two-story structure; the elevated road hides the lower floor. The courtyard, covered in cement, is neat and clean.

Uncle's house has many urban amenities. Three rooms were even designed by an interior decorator from town. "Interior decoration" is a word that wasn't heard here until a few years ago; it only came into vogue over the past two years. There is a chandelier, a TV console, and bookcases. Everything is the same color, with a sort of European feel, but on closer inspection, you can see that the materials are low quality and the workmanship is poor. More to the point, the modern-looking place is filled with small stools, broken bamboo chairs and an old nineteen-inch TV, and the rooms are filled with old farmers wearing their clothes from the '70s and '80s. They seem so out of place in the overdesigned rooms that the effect is comical.

The bathroom is at the bottom of the stairs. It has a squat toilet and running water, but it's filthy. The white ceramic tile and toilet bowl have turned black. In the corner is a basket for toilet paper that has long since overflowed, and the sink is covered in black filth. There's a towel above the mirror and a bar of soap, but it's hard to tell what color the towel is. The bathroom is urban in form, but it is being used according to rural ways. In northern villages, folks don't give a thought to bathrooms, those most important of facilities.

Aunt Zhi says it cost more than 100,000 kuai ($15,000) to build the house, but the money all came from her son's work on the oil fields. She and her husband had nothing to do with it. When I ask about the design and style, she gives a little snort, "it was all designed according to my daughter-in-law's vision. I don't see what's so good about it, squandering money like this, none of it practical. The three rooms on the second floor are all connected. In the future my daughter-in-law wants to come back and see if she can open a shop. You can't live your whole life away from home, you know." Of everything said in the village, I hear this sentence most often.

Aunt Zhi has a glowing complexion with white skin that we don't often see in the village—she looks like she has money. Like Uncle, she's cautious with words. Leaning on the entrance, she watches her grandson closely, scolding him from time to time while she chats with me. I've been a frequent visitor and Aunt Zhi's wariness has gradually abated; she has become more willing to speak with me. When I ask when her grandson came to live with her and where her son works, I am surprised by her response:

When did my grandson come to stay here at home? When he was less than ten months old. My son was hired at an oil field in Xinjiang, and he told my daughter-in-law to go with him. His grandpa and I have been taking care of our grandson ever since. They come back once a year at Spring Festival and stay for a couple of weeks. One summer they had us go live there. I tell you, what a place, there's nowhere to escape the heat, and it's small, just one big room, really it's no way to live. The child couldn't stand it either, so we didn't even last a month. This year they had a little girl. My daughter-in-law had it all planned out. She wanted to take the eldest back and leave the little one with me. I said I wouldn't do it. The older one is more than four, after all; he has feelings. Now's not the right time to take him. Besides, I'm old. The past couple years I've had lower back pain, and when it acts up I can't stand up straight. I had to go for massages in the village. There's no way I could take care of a ten-month-old. After Spring Festival, my daughter-in-law left in a huff. I don't care. Afterward, this little guy missed his mother. I said we'd send him to Xinjiang, but he won't go for love or money.

He was upset. He said, Gramma, if you say that again I'll go jump in a pit. His dad was on the phone listening, heartbroken. He said, bring the child here, but I didn't want to, if we went, what would we do? There's nowhere to live, it's hot enough to kill you, and I'd have to take care of the entire family. It would be too much. His grandfather says I spoil him. He says I take him everywhere I go. I know the harm in pampering, but I can't help it. The boy doesn't bring up his mom and dad anymore. When his dad calls, I shout for him, but he won't come. I know the child is hurting. But tell me, is there a house in the village that isn't like this?

Nearly every household in the village is the same, with *liushou* (left-behind or rear-guard) children and elderly— the so-called "rear-guard." Folks in their fifties, sixties, and seventies are raising their grandchildren. Old men and old women take in the grandkids and take care of their food, drink, shit, and piss—some mothers don't even send money, so the grandparents still have to work in the fields. Some take care of five or six grandchildren, their sons' and daughters' kids. How can you live that way? Three children leave six grandchildren, and it's like they're competing to leave their kids behind, like they're afraid they'll lose out. In some households, the son says, don't worry about farming these seven or eight *mu*, I'll give you some money, raising five or six kids is enough work. It's easy enough for us to earn money elsewhere, don't mess with the fields. But the money's never as much as they promise. And with the parents away, it's not just a burden on grandpa and grandma, it also has an impact on the kids' schooling.

One morning I had just gotten out of bed, when an old lady came over. She was dressed up neat and tidy, and said her tire was low on air, and she wanted to borrow a bike pump. I asked where she was going so early, and she said she was going to visit her daughter, to help her with the harvest. Her children had all left the village to work, leaving behind five grandchildren. I said, so many small children, and at your age, you're still farming? She sighed, What can I do? The children never send any money. I said, in that case why do you even care what they do. Give the children back and take care of yourself. But it's easier said than done; if you don't take your own family's children, who's going to take care of you in the future, when you get old?

And there were two old folks who took care of four grandchildren—both their sons' and daughters' kids. On a hot day they went down to bathe in the river, and all four drowned. In the end the old couple committed suicide by taking poison. You tell me, what has this society come to?

The kids now are all naughty, too—they've gotten sneaky. In one family the kid was always playing games online. Saturday and Sunday he went into town to rent anime or drama series, and he would spend the whole day watching them at home. He didn't even eat. His grandma scolded him, but he didn't care, so they told his parents, and they reprimanded the boy on the phone. You know how bad that kid was? A few days later his parents called again, and he told them that his grandma wasn't taking care of him, just playing cards, not giving him anything to eat, not giving him any money. He got his own grandma in trouble, you see. She was so mad she swore up and down the village, saying she'd never take care of that little snake again. But it's not that she wouldn't, it's that she couldn't. You tell me, a couple of sixty- or seventy-year-olds becoming parents again, becoming teachers and principals, are they going to do a good job? At the elementary and junior high schools, not a single student is doing well. They don't do well at school, and no one is taking care of them at home; then during vacation they go stay wherever their parents are working. They don't study anything there either. They only watch TV. Their parents just spoil them.

Everyone's leaving town to work and get rich, but the children's education has become a problem. The village schools are low quality. The young parents have left home and don't care for their own children, and the grand-parents can only keep them fed and clothed. They can't educate them. Those math problems, who can do them? Even the best societies have their problems. This is our problem.

I am astonished to hear Aunt Zhi say that her five-year-old grandson wanted to "jump in a pit." A five-year-old child would rather kill himself than open the wounds in his soul? How much pain must he be carrying inside? That conflict must be ripping him apart, hindering his development. How could he be healthy or happy?

Aunt Zhi spoke of "rear-guard children," a phrase that has become very popular in the countryside, so common that ordinary old folks use it. I finally understand; they've tacitly accepted their historical circumstance. As she speaks, Aunt Zhi's face remains calm, so much so that it seemed almost mocking. When I ask her if she didn't feel sad about it all, she says yes, how could you not feel sad about it, but it was the same for everyone.

Again and again I explain the emotional damage done to children who live apart from their parents when families are separated. (This was perhaps a little cruel.) Aunt Zhi keeps repeating the same thing: What's to be done? It's the same for everyone.

The consequences obviously haven't sunk in: the situation is too common, too ordinary. It seems natural. How could an everyday state of affairs be tragic? The tragedy and suffering is a feeling only we "tourists" or "visitors" have. Faced with separation as an everyday occurrence, what can they do? Spend each day crying bitterly, being unhappy? You can't live like that.

But seeing the tender affection in Aunt Zhi's eyes as she watches her grandson, you can tell that she is completely aware of all this. She has only taken the pain and suffering and hidden them away. She can't cry over the child all day; nor can she offer too much comfort for his tears. In rural life, women must be hard in the face of hardship.

Grandma Wu

One of the characteristics of all villages is that they follow the highways. Perhaps it's because that's where the business opportunities are, although no one is doing anything at the moment. A few villagers sit in their doorways cooling off. As we walk by, they greet my father warmly, but when they see me, they become more guarded. It's the typical rural reserve. As far as they are concerned, I belong to another world.

Uncle Guangwu's son Yiheng, older than me by ten years or so, is squatting by the side of the road. He looks much the same, although his body and demeanor have shriveled into those of a farmer. He and some other relatives are playing cards in the doorway, and they stand up to say hello. They haven't changed much, and yet somehow seem very different. The passing years have marked their souls and their faces. Zhou's wife, pale and round, peeks out to see who it is, but when she sees us, she hurries back in. Her husband was in prison for a few years and died of illness not long after his release. Everyone thought she would remarry, but she has remained a widow. Father said she found a husband for her daughter last year but didn't move out of her house near the road. No one in the village says anything, because she's kept her widowhood for so long.

We can hear Grandmother's Wu bright, forthright laugh from the road. She's a fat and kind old earth mother, whom I haven't seen for many years. She used to live in a thatched hut by the river. Once I went to look for her, but there are many lonely huts there, and many lonely elderly folks, and Grandma Wu wasn't among them. Father said she'd moved back and was living with her youngest son, Guangliang.

It was his son who drowned in the river. His parents were working in the cities. Grandma Wu was taking care of him.

Uncle Guangliang's new house is next to the road, and we can hear Grandma Wu laughing as we approach. She is so surprised to see me. Is this Qing, she asks, using my childhood nickname? She looks so different! I too am surprised when I see Grandma Wu. I had expected her to be old and gray, debilitated by sorrow, but she is still full of energy with the same cheerful, optimistic look, just as I remember. But she seems a lot shorter.

The courtyard is square. In front are three new, single-story buildings. The middle one also serves as the main gate, which leads through the courtyard to the back main building. The inner courtyard is made of lime and cement bricks; to the right is the kitchen and to the left are the pigpen and chicken coop. The old house is behind the main building. Grandma Wu says they had planned to build a new house in the back, but Uncle Guangliang ran out of money. They spent nearly 80,000 yuan just building the front three houses and had to borrow another 30 or 40,000. Grandma Wu brings out two big mugs of hot water from the kitchen and asks if we'd like to add some tea. I say no thank you, but Father says he would, so she gets a small box and adds some bits and pieces to his water. It's a habit left over from some twenty years before, when villagers bought tea leaf scraps at the store because it was cheaper.

Grandmother Wu is sixty-seven years old. She has pure white hair combed smooth and arranged neatly on the top of her head. Her face is darkened from the sun, but it is bright and smooth, and, in contrast with her hair, looks very young. She has a loud voice and loves to joke; her humor leans toward self-mockery. She's known in the village as a capable, reasonable elder. As we talk, her seven- or eight-year-old granddaughter sits by her side, fidgeting and talking to herself. She tries to interject several times—she seems to really want our attention—and it is aggravating to see Grandmother Wu try and stop her and then finally give up and let her talk.

Most of your eldest uncle's family works in Beijing. He and Heiwa, his eldest, are at one construction site, and your aunt is there, too, although she doesn't work. His daughter works in Guangzhou. They're just doing what they can to put food on the table. Your aunt says she has high blood pressure, so she can't work. Only forty and not working, she's got the good life, eh? Who wouldn't have high blood pressure, sitting around all day? Do some work and it'll come down.

The house they built is really nice. Outside to the left— that two-story building is the one your uncle built. But he doesn't even make it back every year. He says he can't earn anything because of the Olympics. He wants to come back, but what can he do, it would cost almost 1,000 yuan for the three of them to come back, it would take him ages to earn that.

Your second uncle, Uncle Guangting, never left. He has a brick kiln on the east side of the river. He has people working for him, and it seems like he's making some money. His wife doesn't work either. She plays cards. What a life, not to work. Their son is twenty. He just came back from Qingdao a couple days ago.

Your uncle Guangliang works at a jewelry factory in Qingdao run by some Koreans; it's mostly fake stuff, gold- or silver-plated. After they finish plating it, they send it back to Korea to sell, or sell some of it in China at double the price. It's a scam. His boss is strict, and whenever he asks for leave to go home or take a vacation, they deduct it from his wages. He asked for two months last year to come home and build a house. He didn't get a penny of his yearly bonus. Is the work dangerous? What's dangerous about it? They're all working there, and nothing's ever happened. Maybe there's dust, toxic metals, but who can prove it? Xiaozhu never said what caused his illness—even before he died. Your uncle Guangliang got him the job. He worked in the factory for eight years. When he first got there, the money wasn't good, but he kept at it, and eventually he was earning 1–2,000 kuai a month.

Your uncle Guangliang's eldest son is the one who died. Your Aunt Li tried to get pregnant for two years after that, but nothing happened so they adopted this girl. [Grandma Wu points to the girl near her.] She's a lot of trouble. They waited a few years, and then three years ago your Aunt Li finally had a set of twins. It's good and all, but how can they take care of them? They both work and can't take care of small children. Your Aunt Li, she takes care of the boy twin now. She isn't working; she's just taking care of the little bastard. Her aunt is taking care of the girl twin, but she's not planning to for much longer, because she'll have grandchildren of her own soon. This little girl's *hukou* is registered with her second uncle's family. When they got *hukou* for the twins, they also had to spend 2,000 kuai for the birth permits.

They've asked for this little girl in Qingdao. [The little girl swears: "Asked, my ass." It's a sin. The little bit she's been raised has been my doing. Aiya, it'll be the death of me. Don't mention the piss and the shit, schooling is the real trouble. Our village hasn't had an elementary school for a long time, so she goes to school in town, and I have to take her there and back. At first, your aunt Guiping's house was near the road, so the girl would eat her midday meal there. But now your aunt has left to work and all that's left are her parents-in-law, and they only eat two meals a day. How can I possibly ask them to feed her? So this September when school started, I had to start taking her home at noon, then back again. It's not safe on the road anymore, not like before when you would go yourself. I take her morning, noon, and night. There and back six times, each way is two kilometers. It's going to be the death of me. I can't handle it. When I get back I still have to cook. After I've cooked and eaten I go back and get her. There's no time to rest. Off I go again.

Now we're looking at a tuition-free school, but it's still a hassle. They call it tuition-free, but the school still comes up with ways to get its money.

What about child support you say? What child support? Nobody says anything. I have three sons, and they give a little when they can. Last year, your uncle Guangting built this house and borrowed 30 or 40,000. This year he hasn't given me a cent. I'm raising this child for him. Who am I going to complain to? It's your other uncles who have given a little bit. At the New Year, your aunt gave a little bit. Your second uncle gave the most. He only has one child and so isn't too burdened.

Who says you don't need to spend money in a year? Never mind social occasions—we got sick in the spring and had to spend more than 200 kuai. Most of the time I'm healthy, but who can say when you're going to get sick? This leg is always going numb. It's cold. I'm sixty-seven years old, I'm done. [The little girl starts running around, which seems to annoy Grandma Wu, who snaps at her.]

Your grandpa Wu died eight years ago this October. He was sixty when he died. He drank his stomach rotten.

When they did a gastroscopy, it was all mush. He was determined to drink, no matter what anyone said. He had started a vegetable garden, and when he went to sell the produce, he'd drink. And after he sold them he would drink some more. Or he'd sell them all at once, at a bulk discount, and go drink. I'll tell you how he died so fast. He'd sell all the vegetables before noon, then he'd go to the teashop and make a strong cup, half filled with leaves. Then he'd drink all the way home. They sell booze by the side of the road, that goddamn awful stuff they pour out. You don't know where it comes from, and it clearly rotted his guts. It wasn't a sudden death, exactly, but he was gone two or three months after they discovered it.

That was around the time when your uncle Guangliang's boy died. He was eleven. If he'd lived, he'd be twenty now. Aiya, he was a handful, monkey-brained, uncontrollable. After he died, your aunt Li came back, but she wasn't looking for trouble. People had told her; she knew he was a handful. We used to hit him with a v-belt, if you just brushed him he'd cry his eyes out, but the minute you stopped he'd be laughing again. That day after school let out, everyone came back except him. Where was he? On the way home from school he had tried to catch a frog in the mud over at the Zhang family pond, so he was playing over there.

Before dinner, he went with Qingli's kids down to the river. I was at home cooking. Not long after, there was a kid in front of me saying he had disappeared in the river. Your second aunt ran over in a panic saying, there were people dredging sand nearby, they saw him. Your second uncle, all the Liangs are already there. I ran past the brick factory, crying as I went, how was I going to explain this to your aunt? I took a shortcut, steep and filled with holes, my legs catching in the weeds, but I felt nothing, except that I had no strength, my knees went weak, I fell and went tumbling over I don't know how many times. As I ran to the river's edge, I could see a group of people feeling around in the water. Finally Guangxiu got hold of him from his foot and yanked him up. There wasn't a bit of water in the boy's belly. On his face, just a little yellow mud. He had been killed by a powerful whirlpool. I can still remember his face when he was pulled from the water. Pale as death. Bluish, eyes closed, peaceful. It didn't look like he struggled. He must have been killed in an instant. I sat down on the sand. I couldn't get up. The little bastard. He had drowned. I held the child's body and I cried. What could be done? Old Father in Heaven, take my life for the child's. I don't need it.

After that, I went to live in the grass hut by the river. I was so tired. My heart was heavy and empty; I had no strength.

All day long I would think, if only I had made dinner a little earlier, when he got out of school he would have come home to eat and wouldn't have gone down to the river. It was my fault, I had insisted on working in the fields a little longer, so dinner had been late. He did make me mad sometimes, the little bastard was a handful. How many times did I hit him or yell at him in a day? He never listened, he never really did. It's not good to dwell on it. And I was also afraid that your aunt Li would lay into me when she came back. I just had no good explanation. They give you your grandchild to take care of, and what do you do? Your uncle Guangliang might not have spared the rod, but he sure loved the boy.

They say it's because of the sand mining, and it's true. They're all digging sand, digging deep, making eddies and whirlpools. Many people have died in those whirlpools over the past few years. That's what everyone says, but who's listening? You can talk but no one does anything, and who can prove that the child drowned in a whirlpool caused by sand mining?

Your uncle Guangliang wanted to adopt the little girl and bring her back for me to raise. I said no, I couldn't care for her. She was only two years old. I had Guangguan's older girl, and I was already tired enough; my body ached from head to toe. No way.

There's some trouble with everyone in the family. A couple of days ago Heiwa suddenly came back to see the doctor. They may work over there, but they have to come back here to see a doctor, no one can afford it in Beijing. At night he was breaking into sweats, and he had a hard time urinating. The county doctor said it was really serious, a case of gonorrhea, they had to operate. That scared him. We didn't know what he'd been getting up to over there. Then he went to your brother's clinic. They took a look and said it was no big deal; a few IV drips and he was fine. It's your own people who are going to treat you right.

People are coming and going at Grandma Wu's, and she keeps being interrupted, but when she begins to talk about her grandson's death, her expression changes, and her voice grows low and thick. She breaks off, as if recalling the scene.

I imagine Grandma Wu running toward the river like someone possessed, her legs weak, her body coated in sweat, her limbs covered with scratches. But she would never get there in time. Even if she ran forever, she would never get there. Who can know her dread, her fear? She'd taken care of her grandson for years. She'd cared for him more than her own children. And how would her sharp-tongued daughter-in-law react? And how heartbroken would her son be, her youngest and most-beloved son? Even though it had happened many years ago, the scar hasn't healed. This is one thing she can't distance herself from with a little self-mockery.

Just then a woman from next door comes over. She says Aunt Li's aunt called and said she is bringing Guangliang's daughter over, that her own daughter-in-law is about to give birth, and she is afraid the daughter-in-law will be unhappy if the girl is still there. When Grandma Wu hears this she sighs and says, you can't get away from it. I said I wouldn't raise her for him, but I can't just turn my back on them while I'm still able to do something to help.

I take the road past the brick factory, walking slowly toward the river. It is the way Grandma Wu took that day, rushing toward the river. She will never reach the end of this road. She will never finish preparing her grandson's meal. And that eleven-year-old troublemaker won't stir up trouble anymore. Suddenly I think of a children's song I used to sing as I walked home from school:

> The stool wobbles,
> I harvest the grain.
> Cool wind,
> Gentle rain.
> I run home,
> Grandmother, grandmother open the door,
> Your good little child is back from outdoors.

Liang Village Elementary

From our old house we once again take the road that leads to Liang Village Elementary School. A wall encloses its square courtyard with a playing field in the front and a flagpole in the middle. When I was in elementary school, I would stand in the courtyard every morning while they raised the flag. At the back of the courtyard is a row of two-story, red-brick classroom buildings, with five rooms per floor. Most of my childhood was spent here. At 6 am the morning bell would ring through the village sky. Kids would yell to one another, walking in the dim dawn light to start school. I think most villagers used that bell to tell time, to schedule their days.

Liang Village Elementary has been closed for nearly a decade now. The playing field has been plowed into a lush vegetable garden and all that's left of the flagpole is its cement base. But the buildings are still there.

Xing, who watches the main gate, comes out—maybe he heard us talking. He's happy to see us. He takes the keys from inside, mumbling to himself. The door won't open; animals trying to get in to eat the vegetables have dug up the ground.

We head back to the classroom buildings, which are all more or less ruined. The doors have nearly rotted away, practically collapsing into dust with a push. Through the broken glass, the classrooms were an even more harrowing sight. Some rooms on the bottom floor are filled with old furniture, beds, sofas, wooden tables, stools, pots and pans, and homework books from who knows when. They must have been the teachers' rooms. Perhaps they thought that they would come back, and so nothing was put away. In some rooms there are broken desks and chairs, tipped over onto the ground. One room, with a bed and a coal stove, looks as if someone lived there recently. Xing said one of the Liang family aunts lived there for six months. She'd gotten into a fight with her daughter-in-law and had nowhere else to go.

Following the stairs, which have lost their railings, we go up to the second floor. In each room there are rabbits, chickens and other animals, and the ground is covered with chewed up pumpkins, dirty water basins, hay and other odds and ends. These must be Xing's animals.

As I stand next to the second-floor railing and look out, I realize that the school building is located at the highest point in the village. Standing there, you can see the ruined houses, cooking smoke rising into the dusk, and I think, when they chose this site for the school, maybe they meant to give it pride of place? What growth has this school witnessed? What flourishing? And why had it been cast aside? I decide I should talk with a former teacher, Liang Wanming. He helped found the school and knows its entire history.

88

Liang Wanming is a slight man, past fifty, in an old man's cap. His gray-blue clothes, in the style of the 1980s, seem like they haven't been washed for quite some time.

The sky is already dark, and Wanming's wife turns on a light. Its pale white glow, flickering and ghostly, makes the large living room feel gloomy and cold. A grandson, around two years old, runs in and out of the room. His cheeks are red and swollen, perhaps from the rural winter cold, but his daughter's clothes are relatively fashionable; you can tell that she's worked outside the village for a long time. Gentle and quiet, and a little bit shy, she comes and goes from the kitchen, watching me timidly. Liang Wanming, who was a teacher for many years, enunciates clearly and chooses his words carefully. He has his own opinions, and he often surprises me with what he has to say.

We had a hard time getting our village school going. We started in 1967 with a combined class, in a borrowed room in someone's house. The Bureau of Culture and Education sent us a teacher, which meant it was a real school. The next year, the production team collective built a two-roomed earth-brick building. Afterward, when Zhou Zutai came to teach, they added a room, and also someone to cook— Zutai's mother. Then they added three more rooms on the western side. That was the earliest version of the village school—a row of buildings. During the Cultural Revolution it was just that row of buildings. I remember it so clearly. When the production brigade held a struggle session against your dad, it was in front of those buildings. That's where the masses would gather to hear the criticisms or the daily instructions from above.

I am fifty-five years old this year. I graduated from junior high school in '78 and went to the agricultural college for two years. Then I came to teach at the school. When I got there, there were already three rows of buildings. The school was largest in the late '80s. It went from first to seventh grade and had six or seven state-appointed teachers and 200 students. Your sister-in-law started in 1981. At that time, the government was subsidizing rural education and school construction, and the main building that's there now was built during that time. The government gave a little bit; the village raised a little bit; and the villagers provided the manpower. Our school was the first in the township. The Educational Department presented us with a stone tablet that said, "The Party and People of Liang Village Commemorate the School's Foundation and the Promotion of Learning." I remember it all so clearly. Everyone was really of one mind about building the school. No one tried to steal or be sneaky or evade work. There was no ambivalence when it came to acquiring an elementary education. We started building in the spring, and every family came out to work. The weather was still bitter cold, but everyone worked enthusiastically, talking and laughing, willing and happy. When you went to school, Liang Village was thriving—100 percent of school-age children attended school. Wu's central primary school came in first on the exams, and Liang Village came in second. Several teachers, Guangdao, Han Pingzhan, Han Lige, were well known. They made their mark in the village. It was a strong academic environment. In the mid-eighties, it didn't matter if the kid was a moron; if he could walk, he was going to school. If a child in the village didn't go to school, the teachers would go to the house. Our county even scored first on the college entrance exams, the first in the country! It was tremendous. And now look at us.

I stopped teaching in 1992; I was discharged. Back then they were trying to deal with the private teacher issue: there was an annual quota for how many could become proper teachers, and the others were let go. They said that I was on the list, that it was part of the plan. What I didn't know was that the education office director was making decisions based on who gave him gifts, and I'd lost out. In 1992, the country incorporated all private teachers. No more could be added. There was no opportunity for me, so I had to stop.

There haven't been any students in the village school for ten years now. The school had to shut down. Some parents took their children out, so there weren't enough students to form classes. At first they were just going to have first, second, and third grades, and the rest would go to town for school. Later, the Township Educational Office didn't send any more teachers, and that was the end of the school. A few years ago, the headmaster took the flagpole down and sold it. It was stainless steel, and he figured he could get 100 RMB or more. Then he stopped going there, and now it's just Xing looking after the place.

They say this sort of thing is the result of population movements and family planning policies, but frankly speaking, it was the village head and branch secretary who brought it down. The higher-ups sent four teachers, and when they came, there should have been subsidies. Teachers' salaries were low, so the village was supposed to give subsidies and find someone to prepare meals. No matter how poor Liang Village had been in the past, we'd always given the subsidies. Now they said the expense wasn't authorized, the village secretary wouldn't provide it. Teachers came for a year, or half a year, and then left. If the village had been proactive, gone into town to negotiate or to report, or to the Department of Education to say we want teachers, I think it would have been fine. Teachers will teach anywhere, and our Liang Village isn't the most remote place in the county. Besides, how are you going to talk parents into bringing their kids to the school? They all think it's too far. And the village head just couldn't be bothered. Of course, he was better off *not* saying anything.

Every year there are educational program fees. Even with no school, there are still the program fees. The money just goes into their pockets.

If you look at the number of school-aged children in our village, we could have first, second, and third grades, no problem. But no one takes the time to organize it. Last year, some villagers wanted to take over the school buildings for raising pigs. They let them out in the yard during the day, and in the evenings put them in the classrooms. Someone changed the sign on the schoolyard door to read "The Liang Village Pigpen, Imparting Knowledge and Educating the People." Some kids did it. Later, the Bureau of Education said it was unbecoming, and they made them shut it down.

Everyone's so negative now, only worrying about themselves. The young people have all left for work, and no one takes care of things here. When the school was thriving, we sent an increasing number of students to college. We were strong back then, we produced so many college students. In the '80s, all the parents wanted their children to go to college, and more than a few were getting advanced degrees.

Expectations aren't that high anymore. Over the past ten years, students have clearly lost their confidence in schooling. This was the result of a change in the country's college educational system. They don't consider applicants; they only collect fees. So when the students are done, they have nowhere to go. Before, if a child didn't go to school, their parents would take a rod and beat him like crazy. They don't do that anymore. Now college costs 40 to 50,000 yuan at least; they might as well go get a job. Even if they test into the schools, and even if they graduate, who has the 100,000 kuai it takes to get a good job?

But when you get down to it, parents still have the same idea: if their children want to go to school, they'll help them get there, even if they have to sell their houses or their blood. They still feel that it's good for their children to have an education, to have knowledge. A parent's first wish is for knowledge. But just think: the dropout rates are much higher now than they were in the '80s. We may be "modernized," but educational levels have fallen. Post-junior-high dropout rates are extremely high. Students are 100 percent against going to school, they don't go. The biggest barrier to progress in education is online games. The parents work somewhere else, and grandma and grandpa are in charge of the kids, but they can't control them.

Ai . . . How do I feel when I pass the school? I feel bad, like you feel seeing a bachelor with no kids. But you couldn't fix it up if you wanted to. The chairs and tables have all been taken. The school doesn't look like a school; no parent would want to send their kids there. Now the adults take their children to town every day for school. Everyone is sick to death of it. Farmers don't punch the clock; they're in the middle of hoeing a field, and they have to drop the hoe and go pick them up. I figure there are a few dozen families in Liang Village. At 6 am, they all get up to make breakfast. At 7 am, they take the kids to school on bikes or carts. They do it again at lunch. They do it again in the afternoon. They don't have time to get anything done. Families with money send their kids to "boarding schools." But what are they? I've asked about it, and the educational level is terrible. The grades are all faked, and during exams, the teachers write the questions on the board and explain them. Students aren't able to do them on their own.

The problems with the rear-guard kids being raised by an older generation is that they are spoiled, and as people start earning a little more money, their parents send them spending money, which teaches them bad habits. For example, Yiheng came back a few days ago, just because of his son. He's in high school, but he skips school every day and either gets on the Internet and plays games or else watches VCDs at home. His grandparents get so mad their bodies shake, but he just swears at them. Every house has hundreds of VCDs. If the adults aren't at home, the kids watch them all day.

He may be just an elementary teacher who left his job long ago, but you can tell that he is not most worried about the closure of the school itself, but rather about the fact that the village's pro-education, progressive spirit has faded away. Perhaps the village's real decline can be seen in the ruins of the school, its future dissolution.

Closing a school is very easy and very common. There are many practical reasons to do so: the population has decreased, expenses have increased, friction with parents, and so on. But from the perspective of the nation's cultural cohesion and continuity, it's not just a question of the school, it's that the school's closing has created a sense of loss and absence in the village, which then slowly permeates the villagers' lives. Most of the time this loss is intangible, but in the end it displays its terrible destructive power in tangible ways.

As Wanming tells it, when Liang Village Elementary was thriving, the villagers were spirited and lively. They worked in the field with gusto, and the ringing of the school bell gave them a sense of self-respect and pride. But now they all just live their own little lives, and money is the most important thing.

They might still get angry or worried about their children's education, but in the end they're not truly concerned about it. That atmosphere of culture and education grows fainter and fainter; people no longer feel like this is an "educated village" as they once did. Of course parents still hope their children will go to school, and when they're working to build a house, their first priority is still a better education for their children. But the impact of economic perspectives and money-consciousness has been this: when the parents are absent, the children simply don't want to go to school. They leave school as soon as they can to find work. They don't seem to think much about what work they'll do or even what work they can do. And, to make matters worse, going to college no longer guarantees a better life.

Uncle Guangsheng's son Xiuqing tested into the local university, a third-tier, four-year school, majoring in administrative management. The yearly school fees were 10,000 RMB plus the cost of living. Uncle Guangsheng, his wife, and even Xiuqing's little sister worked to pay for his schooling. But after he graduated, he wasn't able to find a job. He took the civil service exam several times, but nothing ever came of it.

Xiuqing, bookish and slight, has been living in a rented room in the city for several years and doesn't want to come back to the village. Finally, this year, he went with the other young villagers to find a manual job. When you bring it up, everyone just shakes their heads and sighs. Uncle Guangsheng lives in the worst house in the village, and his daughter is already twenty-five and has no plans for marriage. There were other children who went to vocational schools, but only one of them found work in his field. All the others are low-level factory workers. What is their status? It doesn't seem right to call them farmers or migrant workers. But are they urban salaried employees? White-collar workers? Absolutely not. They exist in a sort of limbo; they don't want to return to the rural areas, but the cities haven't truly accepted them. They never earn enough to let them forget where they came from. They can only struggle on the margins.

Very few middle-school students from Liang Village have gone to attend school where their parents live. Instead the parents pay for boarding schools. A few live in teacher-organized "study camps," which are common in the provincial capital and towns. The parents pay more than 1,000 RMB each semester, plus the students' room and board, and the students live either with the teacher or in a rented room. The teachers are in charge of both the students' schoolwork and their daily lives. But the results aren't good. My sister's son attended this kind of school, and when we asked him questions from his textbooks, he answered "I don't know" to everything. If you ask which family's kids are doing well, the old folks all sigh and say girls might do a little better while the boys all skip school to play video games or get on the Internet. They never bring their grades home to show their parents. Usually they do two or three years of junior high and in the summers go live with their parents. Eventually they stop coming back.

Around thirty village students go to the elementary school in town. There's no lodging and no cafeteria. The noon hour break is two hours long, so the parents, grandparents, or other guardians have to pick them up and bring them back. If you happen to be in Liang Village before 6 am, or at noon, or from 4 to 5 pm, you'll see a strange sight: a crowd of old women and men, riding their three-wheeled carts hurriedly, yet still very cautiously, either to or from the town school.

Most troubling is how the idea that "education is useless" is gaining more and more traction. When I was young, poverty kept children from school, not parents who didn't want their children to go. But today, education doesn't seem to offer the same kind of opportunities, and so after some fretting, parents often let their children off the hook. This means teachers no longer have the same kind of authority. For example, my cousin's wife is a middle-school teacher at a highly regarded school. Parents used to do everything they could to get their children into her class. Now they spend all day playing mah-jongg. She says very few of the children want to be in school, and cutting classes is as common as eating lunch. Teachers have also lost their desire to teach. Many parents treat school as if it has temporary custody of their children: As long as the children stay in school, and stay out of trouble, that's all that matters. When they're a little older, they can go work. It's not simply rural utilitarianism, or the children's ignorance, or even a decline in teaching ethics. A sense of disappointment in and impatience with education permeates village society.

I never knew this stone plaque stood in Liang Village. Nor did I know what an event the school's construction was. I went back to the school and asked Xing about the plaque. He said that a large rectangular stone was under the pig trough. That was it. After we moved the trough aside and gave it a good brushing, the characters emerged in a vertical row: "The Party and People of Liang Village Commemorate the School's Foundation and the Promotion of Learning." Below that was written, "Liang Village Citizens Educational Unit, Autumn 1981." Imagine the entire village building the school together. As they piled these bricks, these stones, what were they talking about? How did they feel? Were they proud? What were their hopes? What expectations did they have for their children? This collective force, this unity of purpose, does it still exist today?

People from a neighboring village had had the idea to rent the Liang Village School and set up a pig farm. To our surprise, the local Party secretary approved. The way he saw it, the school wasn't being used for anything else. Why not make a little money? So they turned the classrooms on the first and second levels into pigpens and built a few rows of pigpens in the schoolyard. All day they drove the pigs back and forth. The former school was filled with the sounds of people shouting and pigs grunting—or screaming as they were slaughtered. For a while, Liang Village Elementary was lively again. Some kid erased "Elementary School" from the sign on the school gate and changed it to "pigpen," so the sign now reads: "The Liang Village Pigpen Imparts Knowledge and Educates the People."

At dusk, the village is quiet. I turn back to look at the school in the twilight. Staring at those ten large crimson words my mind starts to wander. When did "elementary school" become "pigpen"? When did education cede way to pig-raising? If the school's disappearance was inevitable, what can be done to revive the villagers' vanished spirit? How can respect for culture and thirst for knowledge once again fill their hearts?

4

The Youth Who've Left

In September 1991, Rang County established the Export Labor Development Company. In 1993, the Urban Development Company created offices in twenty-nine townships and municipalities with job market listings. In December 1996, the municipal Export Labor Development Company changed its name to the Second Employment Agency. By 2000, a total of 18,000 people had received pre-job training or retraining in a new field. This created an export labor force of 2.196 million young and surplus laborers with economic returns of 1.144 billion RMB. As of October, 2020, a total of 583,480 individuals were considered re-employed (301,256 participated in official labor export programs, 282,224 engaged in unofficial labor export, 109,614 attended facilitative training programs, and 33,863 attended vocational training programs). Their combined monthly income was 1.1 billion yuan; for a combined total income of 14 billion yuan.

—Rang County Records Major Events

Yizhi

Yizhi is my elder brother. He's on the chubby side, and swarthy. Around his neck he wears a small Buddha. I heard that once, after he had fought with his wife, he went to a temple in the mountains to pray for the return of their love. He's a high school graduate and once was a bookish young man. He and his close friends were all romantics, pure-hearted lovers of literature with beautiful and complicated romantic entanglements. When summer vacation came, they would meet at one another's houses and then head off together in search of their girlfriends. Yizhi always kept a journal and he liked to write love letters. When he left to go work, he and the woman who was to become my sister-in-law sent dozens of letters back and forth. She only had a fifth-grade education, but he seemed to have found an outlet for his emotion.

When I get to their house, my sister-in-law is cleaning up a large pile of wastepaper. She says Yizhi bought it to practice calligraphy on—he'd spent 100 kuai on it, but a year later he hadn't written a single character. So she is stuffing it into two large bags to resell. As she tells me this she starts laughing. Your brother is making a study for himself upstairs, but he doesn't want me to tell you. He's afraid you'll laugh. We go up together and find that sure enough he has a spacious study, with a desk, chairs, and a customized bookcase.

Yizhi picks up a large bag filled with his diary and letters from the corner. As we talk he flips through them and laughs, saying he'd been full of poetry and art back then. I ask him to tell me about his work—and his romantic history.

You mentioned Juanzi. I had noticed her by fifth grade. I thought she was beautiful. I'll tell you true: in elementary school I was often the number one student in the county. And I wasn't bad in middle school either. Why didn't I do well in high school? Because all day long I was thinking how, how. When I was in fifth grade, her family subscribed to *Liberation Army Literature and Art* magazine. Her dad was a high school teacher. I went over to her house—she wasn't there, but I read the magazine. I remember it so well, it was a little chilly, but I kept on reading until my eyes went blurry. After a while Juanzi finally came back and called, "Yizhi!" I lifted my head and thought: there's a fairy before me. So I answered "Juanzi." It was such a beautiful feeling. My junior year was all unrequited love. Once, just to see her, I rolled off a second-story roof. I would also slap myself in the face. Later I became friends with her younger brother, although my motives weren't entirely pure. It was so that I could be closer to his sister. When junior year was almost over, I wrote her a long love letter, I'm guessing it was twenty pages or so, and I gave it to her in secret. Juanzi wrote two words on it: "Too Late!" I was devastated. The next day I got my head shaved to signify a fresh start, but I never really focused on my studies. Later, Juanzi's family all followed her father to the city. I knew it was over, so I stopped thinking about it.

The next year, because of problems at home, I still wasn't studying well. That's when I started thinking about leaving school. One day in the fall I sold some corn, 100 kuai's worth. I wanted to go to the city, but Elder Sister didn't let me, so I just ran away. I rode the bus to Xi'an and then headed out to Xinjiang to look for our uncle. I wanted to get far, far away, then just start another family and never go back. I regretted it as soon as I left. The winter was too harsh. I stayed for all of twenty days; Uncle didn't welcome me, he gave me the cold shoulder. After that, I had Elder Sister send me 200 kuai and came back. She was really mad—blaming iron for not being steel, you know. I hadn't met her expectations.

I came back on October 15, 1989. I was still thinking of going back to school, but when I told the head teacher, he said, Don't bother. You're not much of a student, you'd be better off getting a job. Well, fuck that guy. I have my pride: if I've got to get a job, I'll get a job. So I did. First I worked in the city with our cousin's construction team. I earned five kuai for ten hours of work. I would make dinner at Elder Sister's and at night I would go see movies or write in my journal. I did construction work for four or five months. I helped the bricklayers, tossing bricks up to them. The first day of work I was tossing down buckets of ash, and I put a hole in my boss's head. I ate a lot then. You could buy six steamed buns for a kuai, but I would eat them all in a single sitting, so I never saved any money. There was this girl who I'd been friends with when we were students, she'd gotten in to college. She wrote me a love letter, but I didn't answer. I didn't think it was appropriate. I was just a farmer; I couldn't do that to her. Besides, I didn't like her all that much.

Third Sister said, you should learn a trade. That was during the off-season and there was nothing to do in the fields, so we went to Gansu and Shaanxi to learn how to cover sofas and make chairs. So, with leather and sofa springs on my back, I went with Third Sister's husband to Yichuan County in Yan'an. I think we went to Gelou Township first. People only eat two meals a day there, unless they're doing heavy labor, then they eat three. We ate three. First we stayed in a hostel, but we wanted to find work because then you could live and eat at the owner's house. I wasn't writing in my journal anymore, and later I couldn't remember where I'd left it. We started at a house in East Gelou. They were a prominent family in the area, and the guy's mom was nice. They welcomed us. After we started, news got around, and relatives and neighbors gave us work. Business wasn't bad. We were pretty happy. I was still a romantic, and there was a mountain—not a big one, you could run up to the top in no time—but when I'd finished work, if there wasn't anything else to do, I'd go to the top of the mountain and wax lyrical over the scenery. I worked for more than a month until Third Sister's Husband said, Yizhi, Yizhi, you've been working for more than a month and you can't even saw a piece of wood straight. You're a high school graduate but you can't do anything! That really hurt my feelings. Wasn't I doing a good job? Later, I got in a wrestling match and broke my arm and fingers. I had to rest in the hostel for three weeks or so with no way to earn any money. My hand filled with pus, so we found a razor blade, but there wasn't any anesthetic, and two people had to hold me down while they cut it open. It hurt beyond belief. And when we had to dress the wound, it hurt like crazy too. The doctor was a young woman—not bad looking either. Our brother-in-law joked and said, when you go get your wound dressed, you should chat her up. If you do it right, you could bring her back.

But how could I do that? The local police said we were unauthorized workers and did everything they could to get rid of us. We had to leave in the middle of the night. It was cold, and we built a fire on the side of a hill to warm up. I was thinking about going back, and it looked like it was time. I hadn't paid the hostel, and I had borrowed money for food in town. I owed more than 200 kuai in total. There was no way I could get married. When I think about it now, I still feel bad.

After that, Dad and I sold vegetables and cold noodles in the city. Dad said I should hurry up and get married, it would calm me down. Elder Sister also thought I should hurry up and get married. There was a girl called Xiuyu who liked me. I didn't have any feelings for her, but she wasn't bad looking. Ten days after our first meeting, they were pressuring me to get married. Later she and I were going into the city, and cracking jokes along the way. Xiuyu said, a guy like you, what kind of girl do you think you can get? That pissed me off, so I rode off and left her. If you don't respect me, I can't be bothered.

It was after that I met Chunzi. You know all about that. I went over to our sister's to help them build their house. Chunzi was so innocent. She also loved to read, and she worked hard and was eager to get ahead. Oh, and she was pretty. We fell in love.

Later I went to work in Beijing. Why? Our families told us to get married, but we didn't want to, we were so poor. So I said, I'll go to Beijing first, and if I do okay, then you come and join me. I left for the first time in 1991, and I worked on Hepingli Street, in Chaoyang District, at the Cherry Blossom Garden Spa. Later they made me a manager, and at one point I was managing nine people. At that point I was still only making 260 kuai a month, though later it increased. I cooked my own food, but the cooking gas was free. I told Chunzi to come to Beijing, and she worked in Haidian district. To get from her place to mine took more than two hours one way. At first we were crazy about each other, but later, she met this guy where she worked, and the two of them ended up together, they were hot and heavy. I said to her, Chunzi, I need to take you back home. I still was under the delusion that people at home could talk to her, and we'd be fine. The day I took her home, I drank too much and made a scene. Chunzi's mother said, Where do you get off acting like this, when you're not even married! What will you be like after you're married?

So I went back to Beijing and drank for a month straight. I cut my wrists, hurt myself. When I was with Chunzi, I had become friends with one of her friends, a really good guy. I said to him, after I leave, frighten her a bit, do whatever you think will work. He said, You guys were together three or four years, and she still was like that. What will she be like in the future? That guy was good-looking, tall and brawny, actually he was the kind of guy Chunzi liked. Now that I think about it, Chunzi had never been out in the world before, and then all of the sudden she was alone in the big city. She got a little bit lost. But she really hurt me. I never thought she could change so fast. We'd been together three or four years. When I see her now, I'm still a little mad.

In 1994 I left Beijing on the second day of the New Year and arrived home on the third. I was in bad shape. I hadn't earned enough money to live on, and in all that time, I'd only sent home 2,000 kuai. When I got back they started talking about marriage again, and our uncles and other relatives introduced me to people. Elder Sister took me to see them. She'd yell at me the whole time. I spoke to a few, but nothing worked out. On the morning of the twelfth, I went over to Uncle's for a visit. Right after I got there, Father came running over and said that Dongwa's wife's family had a daughter who seemed pretty good. I should come check her out.

So I went over to Dongwa's. The girl was pretty—delicate—the only one of all I'd seen who seemed pretty good. I poured her a cup of tea and asked her if she liked tea, but she said she didn't drink it. I liked the way she talked. We saw each other on the twelfth of the New Year. [My sister-in-law, laughing on the side, adds, When I saw him I thought, this guy isn't good looking at all. A black helmet of hair, small eyes, only when he talked did he seem okay, sort of refined.] Well, it was love at first sight. Your sister-in-law is the last of my love stories.

I went back to Beijing in the third month of 1994. But I had nothing to do there. A lot of us from the village were scalping tickets at the Beijing Railway Station. So I went and scalped too. Usually it was a matter of cutting in line. Bang, bang, make a scene, a bit of slapping, a bit of cursing, and then you try to look threatening enough that they'll let you get in front of them. Then you charge the buyer thirty to fifty extra. Once, I cut in front of a police officer from Chengdu. But I wasn't scared: how was a police officer from Chengdu going to enforce the law here? I even beat people. After I broke up with Chunzi, I was so angry I was self-destructive. Later, you know what some of us did? If there were ten or so people buying tickets, you'd say I can help you buy them, but after they gave you the money you'd take off. The Beijing Railway Station is always crowded. Lines snaking everywhere. Once you'd pushed through a few groups, they keep track of you. You'd just take the money and go. But I wasn't the one doing that, once I'd made a deal I would wait in line. Later I was stopped by a plainclothes policeman. When he saw my ID was for Rang County, he said I must be no good, so he took me in. They knew about people from our county; we were notorious. First they took me to the local police station. When we went in, I saw a kid locked to the stairs with finger-cuffs, his toes barely touching the ground. It looked so damn painful. Back then they beat people brutally at the train terminal police station. I saw it with my own eyes. They'd tell you to squat there, and then they'd go arrest someone else. If someone needed to go to the bathroom, the police would take a hard rubber stick and wham! That's how it was when I went in. First they worked me over with the stick. I said I hadn't scalped any tickets, they only brought me in because they knew I was from Rang County. Later they didn't beat me too badly. They put me in a small room, about ten meters square. There were forty or fifty people in it. You couldn't sit down. We were all so crammed we were forced to stand. When they put me in, someone said, stomp him, and I was going to get ugly, but there was a boss in the room, who came over to beat me up. They made fun of me, but I said fuck your sister, do you want to die? In the afternoon they took me over to the Changping Detention Center. After I got there a little hoodlum who'd been in there for ages beat me up.

I was shut up in the Changping Detention Center for two days and two nights. On the third day they took me to Anyang Detention Center. When they were bored, the policemen would pick one of us to amuse themselves with.

They'd say, You, come over here, and then they'd slap you
around a few times. I swore under my breath, Fuck your
sister, there's no justice here. But they heard me, and the
police asked, Who said that, and of course I had to be
the hero and say it was me. The policemen said come over
here. They hit my head seven or eight times with a leather
belt while they kicked me brutally. They told me to stand
military style. I stood up straight with my chest out and
they hit me; I raised my head and they hit me again, and I
raised my head again. I stood there for two hours. They
beat my face to a pulp.

I also had to fight when I got to Anyang. The prisoners
there were also beating each other up. Those of us from
home had talked it over on the way. When we got in, we
had to strike first, otherwise we'd end up sleeping next to
the toilet. The police in Beijing had taken our money. After
we got to the Anyang Detention Center, the four of us
fought as soon as we got in. We cleaned them out, took
their stuff. We made them sleep next to the toilets, while
we slept next to the door.

The second day at the Anyang Detention Center they
told us, if there was money to get you out, you could go. If
there was no money, you'd be working at the tile and brick
factory. So I was forced to go work at the Anyang Municipal Eastern Tile and Brick Factory. What really happened
is that the Anyang Detention Center sold us to the factory
for 100 kuai. Then they were done with us. I took one
look, and fuck, if you stayed there long, it'd kill you. The
dust was bad; the sky above the factory was gray. A few
people holding sticks were watching the workers closely.
Whoever went slow got hit. We lived in some shacks made
out of corrugated asbestos sheeting. If you didn't starve,
you'd freeze. A few of us started thinking about escaping.
We'd eaten in the early morning and we started working in
the afternoon. We were scooping out dirt from a deep pit.

One side was high, and on the other people were watching. They had us take a break for tea, and I pretended to be gung-ho and offered to get the tea. We'd agreed to all escape at the same time, but two had run off first, and the guards beat us two who were left with shovels and sticks. And then they kept an even closer eye on us. You know how we slept? They would take our clothes. You were just in your underwear. The watchman would hold the clothes while he slept on the other side. In the middle of the night I tried to pull open the bars on the window but couldn't move them. We got up the next morning just as the sky was beginning to turn light; the guy threw our clothes on the ground and told us to get dressed. In the night, I'd stolen some clothes, I don't know whose. I wore them lying in bed, wrapped in the quilt. He opened the door and then went around to open the other door. I just ran straight out the door. Someone yelled from the kitchen, someone's getting away. I picked up the fire pincers, thinking if anyone tried to grab me I would beat him to death.

They called to people on the road to stop me, but I bowed my head and begged, I said, Elder Brothers, I've been here half a year already, I can't endure it any longer, if I don't run away I'll die. They knew how brutal they were at the brick factory and said, Hurry, go, run! When the people following me saw that they wouldn't catch me, they gave up. I ran until my shoes fell apart. My heart filled with terror; it would have been a disaster to get recaptured. I ran into a village where there was a local bus, but I didn't have a cent on me. They said it was one kuai to the train station. I said I don't have any money, I just escaped from the brick factory, I don't have a thing. When they heard I'd come from the brick factory, they were very sympathetic and let me ride for free. Later there were problems at the factory, they beat someone to death. After that was exposed, the Anyang Detention Center was nearly shut down. Those people were bad through and through, not a bit of conscience.

When I got to the train station, I got myself a ticket—I knew how to do it. When I got off in Beijing, I ran into some of the guys, and we went to Aunt Guo's place near Jiuxian Bridge. We had a great meal, and I was asleep as soon as my head hit the pillow. But I had eaten too much, and the next day I had diarrhea. Later, I thought it was a good story, but at that time I was terrified. If they recaptured you, they could beat you to death, because no one would ever know.

I met your sister-in-law in early 1994, and I worked in Beijing until October. Then I came back. I'd worked enough and in any case I wanted to get married. I was already twenty-four. But even after all that work I'd never earned any money, and I had to borrow 200 kuai to pay for the trip.

When I got back I made arrangements for the marriage. Then I started studying at the medical school. I didn't leave after that. And I didn't write in my journal anymore.

Take this journal and see if there's anything you can use. It's the life of a rural, literary youth. But don't laugh at my style.

Here are some excerpts from Yizhi's journal:

1994.3.10 (**Lunar Calendar** 1.29)
Overcast
The years flow by.
The red in my cheeks is gradually fading. Wrinkles, that symbol of old age, appear one by one, climbing across my forehead. I pass my twenty-fourth year in silence. The wheel of life has already turned twice.

1994 **The year of my birth sign**
Empty eyes, a weary heart, a man who has achieved nothing.

The poet Li Bai once said: Life is like a dream, from unconsciousness to consciousness, from elementary school to middle school, and from middle school to high school, then on into the world, everything seems like yesterday. Yet yesterday's concerns are nothing but clouds and mist.

What is fate?

Fate is helplessness; fate is chance; fate is fortune; fate is the excuse of the clever in moments of uncertainty; fate is not taking yourself too seriously.

Fate is nothing.

1994.3.15
Cold and clear.
The question of marriage.
Inscription: 1994 CE Lunar Calendar 1.12. Sunny and breezy. Yizhi and Qingdong went to Zhuang Village in a neighboring county. Saw Doudou. Chose Lunar Calendar 1.24 to marry. Yizhi's happiness knows no bounds. He wrote this in commemoration.

The floating life is nothing but a dream.

On the first day of the New Year, in the evening, I bought a train ticket; on the afternoon of the second, I left; at 4 pm on the third, I arrived home, my body travel weary, my face haggard.

A traveler returns home.

It was not only physical and mental fatigue. He suddenly felt his age; he felt misery; he felt helplessness, the ruthlessness of time; he felt his twenty-four years.

His youth, his vitality, seemed to have vanished overnight.

On the morning of the 6th day of the New Year, Father rose early to go to the city. I talked with Elder Sister about my life. On the 8th, 9th, 10th until the 12th, I had blind date after blind date until my face lost its color and all my confidence was gone. I grew pale and wan.

On the morning of the 12th, before I had risen, as I was considering my departure, my father scolded me. I was utterly demoralized.

Who would have thought that on the 12th, that very day, the weather would turn out to be so extraordinarily beautiful, everything would go so extraordinarily well, and the Bai girl I met would be so extraordinarily beautiful.

I spent several sleepless nights in loneliness and worry. On the 17th, I went to Zhang Village again and set everything up. On the 20th, Mr. Bai paid a call. On the 24th, Doudou and her maternal aunt paid a call. And we were engaged.

Nothing is certain in life. All is chance.

1994.4.11
Overcast
Will Beijing welcome you?

The sound of New Year bells linger in my ears, the warm comfort of New Year's Eve is not yet spent. Young people, near and far, have shouldered their backpacks and gathered friends and companions. Some go north. Some go south. Every major train station swells with the tide, the trains overburdened and behind schedule. Delayed at the train station, the number of people waiting at the stations never seemed to decrease. Like rings of sand, they are endless.

I, radiant with happiness, my face glowing like a spring breeze, step onto a northbound train, filled with beautiful dreams. On either side of the street, I see large signs that read "Beijing welcomes you." Filled with thoughts of love, our ancient city feels so warm, so hospitable. It welcomes you!

I got to Beijing on 2.13. On the 14th I had some drinks with Hongdang at a restaurant and got a little buzzed. Who knew that the following morning, when I let my guard down for an instant, I would be taken in by a plain-clothes policeman, and then, by the afternoon, sent over to the Changping Detention Center.

It was about four or five *li* [1.25 to 1.5 miles] between Beijing and the Changping Detention Center, which is more than 10,000 meters square and surrounded by high walls topped with electric fencing. This gave the milky white buildings a sort of imposing disharmony. In the detention center, between the male and female sides, was a high observation tower, evidence of the "dictatorship" of the proletariat. A kind of involuntary force swelled deep inside your heart, so even when you got angry, a small amount of unfeigned caution remained.

I was under police escort the entire trip, but I maintained my dignity. Then, as soon as I entered an interior door in the detention center, a little hoodlum kicked me right in the chest and liver. There was no warning. I grit my teeth in pain, but I couldn't hold back my anger and shouted, "Fuck your mother! You want to die?" He made as if to hit me again, but seeing my face twisted like an angry fiend, he swore too. Then he searched my body, and when he was done, threw me on the ground like a male prostitute.

The detention center had two levels. On the upper level, they kept people who had submitted complaints or were there for violent crimes; on the lower level, they kept rural migrant workers and ticket scalpers. Rural migrants were the majority. Some were old and disabled; they had desig-nated cells on the east and west sides. When it was time to eat, the sick got special treatment. At mealtime you could eat white *mantou* or diluted noodles, and most of the workers lined up to eat. Some carried sticks to keep order. After one group had finished, the bastards in charge of the tin trays would pass them to the next group without even rinsing them. The next group would knock the leftovers off the trays and then go get their food. It went on like that until the three or four hundred people had finished eating. The mute in charge of handing out the corn pone and other food would push his wobbly food cart out, and that was the end of the meal.

We'd eat a little past 10 am. That was breakfast. Then there was the afternoon meal at a little past 4. When that was done, the day was over.

The sky began to dim. A few bastard officers took up sticks and drove the prisoners into the cells, where they lay down side by side, close together on the ice-cold cement floor. There were no blankets, not even any rice straw on the ground. The room overflowed with migrant workers, each with their own moods. Not long after they started snoring, one by one, despite the cold earth and frigid ground. Despite the fact that other people's feet were in their mouths.

1994.4.14 Thursday, clear

I slept for two days before I shook off the dread of the escape and begin to think straight.

At noon I went over to Xiao Zhang's. He'd said they were making a movie behind Tucheng Park, and we went to look. All I could see on the west side of the park was a group of men and women rushing around. Then a movie camera lifted into the air. When we got closer, we were surprised to see the Beijing comedian Liang Tian. He's a small guy with a small nose and small eyes and a small square-jawed face. He spoke slowly, in a low voice. Standing in the crowd, he looked like an ordinary guy. But when it was time to start filming, his face changed into something extraordinary.

I was riveted by his every movement. Then I had an idea. I would take this notebook and have Liang Tian sign it. A fine moment for a film buff! But then I looked at how I was dressed, and I lost my nerve. I stowed that idea deep.

1994.4.15 Friday
Clear
Yesterday I saw Ouyang Shan's *Three Family Alley*. Today
I saw Zhang Xianliang's *Half of Man Is Woman*. Ouyang's
film was clearly influenced by *How the Steel Was Tempered*,
especially in the portrayal of Zhou Bing and Chen Went-
ing, and in Zhou Bing's characterization, though in Zhou
Bing's portrayal there was a clear tendency toward aesthet-
icism. I happened upon Hao Ran's book *Golden Road*. It's
so optimistic, but . . . what about now? Where's the golden
road? The roads have only narrowed. Stay at home: starvation and poverty. Leave home: scorn. We rural youth
have no exit.

Now Zhang Xianliang's *Half of Man Is Woman* seems
like something written by someone with a sick mind to
describe a sick society. This book once was criticized because
of its description of sex. It pales in comparison with Jia
Pingwa's *Ruined City*.

1994.4.17 Sunday
Clear
I am at a loss, uneasy. It's as if I live in a vacuum, cut off
from the rest of society. On the streets people come and go.
All complete strangers to themselves. In this city I am nothing more than an ant. To go unnoticed, to be stepped on,
to be loathed. No one knows you exist. No one knows that
you have family, that you have a love, that you too experience life's sorrows and joys.

This is my experience. The experience of a migrant
worker who left his home and village.

Of course I have relatives, friends, a spouse. Of course it
only takes me a day and a night to reach them, although
it feels like 1,000 *li*. It's not only the distance. I spent this
year working in Beijing. But, come hell or high water, I'll
never come back to this shithole. This inhuman life.

Juxiu

Juxiu lives in Xiangfan, but she calls as soon as she hears I'm back from Beijing. That same day she and her son come back to the village. Juxiu is one of my two best childhood friends. The other is Xiazi. Xiazi and I tested into the teachers college, and now she lives in town and teaches at the elementary school. Three adults and three kids all holed up at Xiazi's house, making a large bed on the floor. Juxiu's family left Liang Village in the late '80s. After her elder brother finished middle school, he went to Xiangfan, Hubei, and eked out a living in a shantytown south of the river. He eventually put down roots and then brought Juxiu's parents and brothers and sisters over. Only Juxiu refused to go. We were in middle school, and Juxiu didn't want to do business or work. She wanted to go to school. She wanted to live out her dreams. So she lived alone at home. So Juxiu's home became our meeting place. We would go there to do our homework, chat, write in our journals, argue, talk nonsense. On summer evenings, we'd sit in the courtyard, looking at the moon, writing little compositions and then reading them to one another. We'd bathe in the river, take walks. We looked on the sand, the river, the meadows with our tender, girlish hearts. In our third year of middle school, in the winter, the three of us went once again to ask the headmaster if he would turn an abandoned warehouse into a place for us to board at school. And this time we actually succeeded—Juxiu made her persistence clear; she wouldn't leave until the headmaster said yes. The three of us squeezed into a single bed. She and Xiazi both wanted to be next to me, because I slept hot like a furnace. They spoiled me—they both loved me best.

After Xiazi and I tested into teachers' school, Juxiu repeated the ninth grade, but she never got into that school. At that point, her parents pressured her into coming to Xiangfan because they needed help with the business, and it didn't seem like she was ever going to get in.

I've wanted a life like yours, but I was never able to get it. I've also been reflecting on how my lack of success has to do with my personality. If I weren't so stupid and naive, maybe I wouldn't be in the situation I'm in today.

When you both tested into college, and I did two more years of high school and still didn't get in, those years were really tough. Ma and my sisters set up a small vendor's stall to support me. I wasn't going to give up, I wanted to go to college, but it didn't work out. You know how much they blamed me. After I left school, I went where my parents were living, and I started to get a stall together. But I wasn't suited for it. I always had my ideals and dreams. There wasn't anything else to learn, so I started studying tailoring, thinking in the future I could be a designer and open a big clothing store. It seemed like a classy profession.

I discussed it with my Ma. I would study tailoring for one year, and if it didn't work out, I would come right back and run a stall. The shop where I apprenticed was really far. Every day I had to go ten *li*, there and back. The master gave us endless amounts of work, but we only did pants. Every day we had to do twenty pairs. The other apprentice and I would compare our work. The earliest I would get home was 12 midnight and half of the time it was 1 am. I rode my bike alone. Going up this big hill every day was the hardest. I couldn't ride the bike up, I'd pedal and pedal and start falling asleep. This happened over and over, and then I'd get a shock: why wasn't I home yet? You can imagine how sleepy I was. Every day, even when it was raining, even if it was windy, it was the same. One day, going up the slope, I just couldn't ride, I had to walk, and a hoodlum came over and put his hand over my mouth. I kicked at him as hard as I could, and I think I got him between the legs, anyway he let go and ran off. After that, I thought that if there were a boy who would go with me every day, I would marry him. That was my sincerest wish at the time.

After I'd studied for a year, I found the teacher was still keeping some things from me, so I thought I'd study on the sly. The other girl had studied for a year and a half and still couldn't do it, so I secretly took a look. When I went home I cut out two pairs of pants. They weren't bad. They even seemed better than the teacher's, and I decided I wanted to open my own shop. I had to scrape together one or two hundred kuai, so I asked my ma and brother again for help. My ma couldn't help me, but my brothers had actually started a slaughterhouse, which was already earning money, and they wanted me to work with them. I said I wouldn't. That was degrading work, it didn't fit with my dreams.

In the end my brother gave me 600 kuai. But my heart was heavy when I took the money. I bought a sewing machine and the other tools I would need, and I started doing piecework and repairs. I started by making things for my family. I made some mistakes and some people got angry, but I was very patient then, and was able to calm them down. I did my apprenticeship in 1990 and then started on my own in 1992. 1992 and 1993 were the hardest years. My family saw I wasn't earning any money, and so they wouldn't lend me any more. So I went to get a loan. I knew a woman who said she would lend me some, but in the end she changed her mind. I was so upset. I drank half a *jin* of liquor by myself. I was sick about it, wondering when I would be able to make it. That was the one time in my life I got drunk. I felt it was all utterly hopeless. Some people introduced me to a guy, but I wasn't interested in him at all. All I wanted was 5,000 kuai, so I could start fresh, but there just wasn't any money.

After that I met Lao San, my husband. That was one mistake on top of another. I'm the romantic type, and back then Lao San was young, with beautiful pale skin. He liked to play the flute, read books, and all that. He seemed so sophisticated and urbane, and I fell for him hard, so we started dating. I was still making clothes then. I would work every day until late in the night, but I was really happy. Every morning I would get up early to exercise. I would go to the top of the dam and sing with all my might. My ma always yelled at me for that. My tailoring shop wasn't growing, and no matter how hard I worked, I wasn't earning any money.

Tangerines are abundant in Xiangfan, so afterwards some villagers and I started to buy them up and then use our local connections to transport them all over the country, although mostly to Kaifeng, Hebei, those areas. It was really hard. When you bought them, it was easy for the locals to throw in bad ones without you noticing, but when you went to sell them, you could only get rid of the good ones. We could never raise the prices, and it was hard work. It was also hard to be on the road. Sometimes I ate only one meal a day, which ended up damaging my stomach. And I still wasn't earning any money. Sometimes we'd even lose twenty or thirty thousand on a load. I transported tangerines for two or three years and hardly earned anything.

That was when I started being dissatisfied with Lao San. He has no business sense and he can't handle it when things get tough. He'll never come help when you call him. My brothers set up a job for him, but he didn't work hard. We always fought. My brother told me, this guy you chose, he can play music; he can sing; he can play the fool and make everyone laugh, but he can't earn a living. Actually, in my heart I knew that Lao San couldn't do business. He can't get tough with people, he can't compete. I'm the same way. That's why I don't make any money. But you still have to earn a living.

I went to Hebei with my brother in around 2000 to help a brick factory recruit workers. I would get people at the train station to come with me—you really have to understand human psychology to persuade people in just a few minutes. It was really hard. We rented a little apartment in Shijiazhuang. We had to go out every day, even in the brutal wind. Then we would go into the station waiting room or wait at the exit.

I wanted to help these people. I only recommended them to places I'd heard were good and paid salaries regularly. I couldn't help it if some of them turned out to be bad. Being in the middle was so hard. Every day we had to get up at 5 am to go and find workers to persuade. Most of them were from Yunnan, Guizhou or Sichuan. My wages came entirely from my broker's fee. And then the Public Security Bureau would also arrest us, so we had to dodge them, and we had to fight with other brokers for the workers. We would fight until blood flowed. I really didn't know how my life had come to this. Sometimes, I would sit alone at the train station, and as I sat there I'd want to cry. I had done all I could for a good life, how did it come to this?

I did that for three or four years, but I always felt I couldn't keep it up. I met a woman and opened a clothing shop again, but it was in 2005, which was bad luck. Right when I started, the clothing industry went into a slump. I'd put in all the money I made in Shijiazhuang, but there weren't enough customers, and the business didn't do very well. I gave it up.

I went back to Xiangfan. My brother's business was doing well, and he needed people, so he had Lao San do transport for him. See? In the end, we still had to depend on my brother.

Now things are like this: We still have one tangerine orchard, worth 40 or 50,000, and we're owed about 30 or

40,000, that's all we've got. I opened a teashop, really a place to play mah-jongg. Of course I have to prepare the tea, but if there aren't enough people, I also have to join in the game and even put down money. Now I'm so used to it that if I don't play for a day, I get the itch, but it's hard to earn money that way. Everyone is a friend or relative. They might not pay in advance, but they'll pay once they earn some money. Some won't ever pay.

Now I think the worst thing in the word is dreaming. If I hadn't held onto my little dreams, would I have fallen so short? Would I have married Lao San, that good for nothing? It would have been better if I had married someone like my brother. Now I admire him most of all. Originally, I thought my brother was too rough, too uncouth. Now I see he's somebody who can get things done. He doesn't shy away from dirt or hard work. He tries everything. Lao San isn't tough, and he doesn't have the least bit of talent. But when it's all said and done, he's not a bad guy. He's just ordinary and a bit conservative. He should have an office job, something where you don't take risks. Our conflicts come from the fact that we don't think the same. When we first started dating, we would talk about our feelings, our dreams. Now we don't talk, if we say more than three sentences, we start to fight. He doesn't try to bridge the gap, and I feel like talking to him is casting pearls before swine.

When I opened my tailor shop, I still had dreams. No matter how hard it was, no matter how much work, I thought I could keep it going. My life was full and I was happy. Now we make a better living, but I'm not happy. I even feel bad about myself. I can see that you all are fulfilled. Me? I have nothing, and my days are unhappy.

When I dream at night, I still dream about when we were in school. If I can't answer a test question I get so nervous I want to die, but in my heart I'm so happy because I've gone back to school. I'm studying again. After I wake up is the worst. Sometimes I see that old country lane and the three of us sitting in the sunset, on the riverbank, going for a walk, staring into space. I've dreamt this so many times. I don't know if it's nostalgia or what. Spending these two days with you, I feel as though we've returned to our youth, and I am so, so happy, so trouble-free, so deeply moved. I really want to go back to our school. I have such an emotional connection to it. If I had been able to go to college, at the very least my spirit would have been richer.

What I'm thinking about now is making my son a successful student. Partly so I can realize my own dreams. But I think my son is pretty worthless. He's like his father, he represses everything, and his father hits him. On top of that, our environment at home isn't good. Our house is a teashop, a mah-jongg parlor, and that has its influences.

I'm planning to buy a house. We have to. Children need to have a place. After we get a house, you'll have to come over.

Ai . . . sometimes I think the future is grim. I don't have any goals, but I should. My dream life would be to weave the material and the spiritual together, like your lives do. It's a more fulfilling kind of life.

While she was talking about working as a broker for the brick factory, Juxiu's face blushed dark red, and she was on the verge of tears. She's ashamed of this part of her life. That's partly why she stopped doing it.

On another level, it's true that her dreaming, her "idealism," harmed her. If she were like her brother and had quit after elementary school, if she hadn't harbored those ridiculous dreams, if she had been able to give all that up, to get off her high horse and work like her brothers and sisters, to find a boyfriend who knew how to earn money, well, it's unlikely that her life would be as hard as it is now. But, can you really say that sticking to your ideals is wrong? Why does Juxiu's life seem as if it were turned upside down? Her mother's contempt and her brother's ridicule—there's a reason for them. She's not pragmatic, especially because she's always dreaming about something else. She made unrealistic choices based on these illusions.

But it is because life never gave her the opportunity to achieve her ideals that her idealism and romanticism became weaknesses, keeping her from a better life. You can see her feelings of inferiority in her irritability, in her defensiveness, in her glance, in her way of speaking and her mannerisms. I can sense the humiliation she has suffered. But I am powerless. Compared with Juxiu, my life has been so smooth that it seems almost pale and uneventful. I studied and then I got a job. Smooth and steady. I made my dreams a reality. I write, reflect—my life has depth. And this is what Juxiu yearns for. She set her ideals when she was young. But when life threw her into a different sphere, she didn't have a chance.

I know Juxiu is concealing other darker, more complicated experiences, even though, of the three of us, her character is still the simplest. She doesn't seem to completely understand the ways of the world or how things work. There's a naiveté in what she says. As we listened, Xiazi and I would glance at each other from time to time, looks of understanding and sympathy. We had the sense that she was still an eighteen-year-old girl, filled with childish idealism. A young girl who inevitably makes a mess of things.

We decide to stay at Xiazi's for three days. Every evening it rains, but during the day it is clear, and the early morning air is damp and fresh. We take the kids down to the river, and it's like we have returned to our childhood. We follow the river on crisscrossing little roads, always ending up at the back of the village, near the graveyard. Seeing my mother's grave, I wave and say "Bye, Ma, I'm leaving!" Strangely enough, this warms my heart. Tenderness rises from the pit of my stomach and floods my body. It is as if my mother were still alive and I am just heading out, shouting goodbye as usual. How good it would have been to do that every day. If only I had had a moment like that.

We walk again across the fields on the small lanes once filled with silent sunset hopes. Returning to the village, we search for traces of the past, Juxiu again innocent and unaffected, her spirits high. Until she speaks to her twelve-year-old son. Then she trembles with irritation. It is clear she has set her hopes on him and that he didn't care about school. We run into some people from the Han family, and Xiazi introduces us. It's like déjà vu. We all walk together along the old road we once took to school, but I am left cold. In the end, all we want is to find a place to eat with air conditioning. After we sit down, we start to talk and laugh, and the road is forgotten once again. This is its fate.

As it is Juxiu's.

Chunmei

Summer 2008 seems especially hot. At noon I chat with my brother and then go upstairs to organize the tapes from the past few days. They took a lot of time and work, but the results aren't good. Sometimes there are a lot of people around, and their loud voices drown out my primary interviewee. And more than once we end up talking about something other than what we'd planned. But the diversions are also interesting, with new, unexpected things unearthed.

All of a sudden, my sister-in-law runs in saying "Hurry, come and see, Chunmei drank poison!" And then like a whirlwind she is gone.

I take off my headphones and can hear all sorts of noises and the sound of weeping in the front courtyard. People are shouting, Chunmei, Chunmei, wake up, wake up! I hurry downstairs and see my brother taking something out to the woman lying in a wheelbarrow and pouring it into her mouth. It must be something to empty her stomach.

Chunmei is unconscious, but she looks as if she's in pain. Amid the sounds of her rescue, her eyes flicker from time to time, and it seems she might be responding. The attempts to revive her are successful; she seems to be regaining awareness. She opens her eyes and looks around, and then suddenly grips her mother-in-law's hand tightly. In a hoarse voice she says, I don't want to die, I want to live, I don't want to die, save me, I'll be good. She says it again and again and then loses consciousness, her hand still gripping her mother-in-law, as if it were the lifeline that might save her.

In the short time she was awake, she also managed to spit out: If I live, I'll make you a new pair of shoes.

An hour later Chunmei's feet twitch a few times and then all movement stops. My brother checks her pulse and shakes his head. She is dead.

I silently withdraw. Over the next few days, Liang Village, which is usually so quiet, bursts with noise, and for the first time, Chunmei's house, on the east side of the village, becomes the center of town. People gather around the door or stand beside the pond, discussing what happened. A few Liang family elders gather in my cousin's home and talk for a long time. They first decide to send a few senior members to inform Chunmei's family. After that they begin to discuss the burial. Her husband doesn't work in the village, and it will take him three or four days to make the trip; the weather is so hot, it will be hard to preserve the body. Then Chunmei's father, mother, brothers, and other family members, about twenty or so, arrive crying and cursing, armed with sticks and hoes. They break all the pots and pans in Chunmei's mother-in-law's house, and then they go after my uncle and his wife. They won't allow the funeral. They insist on waiting for her husband so that he can give an explanation. So we send someone to get him.

Her husband, my cousin, is nicknamed Ge'r: "Rooty." He graduated from middle school and is one of the few from the village who works in a coal mine. He doesn't have a phone, and he never left the number of the mining company, but he comes back every year for harvest and Spring Festival. Only now does everyone realize that there is no way to contact him. They bundle a young man from his family onto a train to go find him. "Escorted" by Chunmei's older brother, my uncle goes to buy the best coffin and a large quantity of ice to put around it, to keep down the intensifying smell.

Chunmei was tall and one of the prettier young married women in the village. Her round face and her large eyes were always alert and curious. But she wasn't popular; she was both strong willed and relatively incapable. She didn't get along with other women, and when they passed on the road, they'd give each other dirty looks. Yet when Chunmei died, the women were deeply shaken. They gathered in groups, talking about it. The curious thing is, they immediately stop talking when I join them and just look at me guardedly before changing the subject. Perhaps there is something I don't know. It's true I don't really know these young women; I left before they got here. Later, my brother tells me that Chunmei is closest to the wife of one of our cousins. She was Chunmei's only friend in the village. My brother introduces us; she is a high school graduate who has her own views and relatively modern ideas. I ask her for an interview and learn the reason for Chunmei's suicide.

I am telling this only to you, you must never tell anyone else. I've been so unhappy these past few days, so troubled. I blame myself for Chunmei's death. I had a part in it.

Before Chunmei and Ge'r had been married a month, he left to go work. Normally Chunmei would have gone with him, but she gets carsick—when she rode to the county seat, she nearly died from vomiting—so she said she wouldn't go for anything, she didn't dare take the train. Later she had a little girl, so then she really didn't want to leave. Although Chunmei was short-tempered and often fought with her mother-in-law and with others in the village, she had a really good relationship with Ge'r. I never saw them fight. When Ge'r came back, he would ride his bike around with their daughter on the front and Chunmei on the back. They would go to market in town or to visit Chunmei's parents or to see relatives. Sometimes they left their daughter with his mother, and the two of them would go into town for a date. They rode the bike, one carrying the other. They were really close.

People might say that Chunmei didn't know much and that she was a little dumb, but they also knew she was hardworking and tidy. She worked all day long, and their two little rooms were always neat and clean. There wasn't a speck of dust on the beds or tables. When she went to work in the fields she gave it her all, and at home she raised chickens, ducks, pigs, and for a while also rabbits. She worked too hard, really. Her greatest wish was to build a large house like Huan's and not to live crammed in with her mother-in-law.

This year things changed for Chunmei. Ge'r didn't come back for Spring Festival. He called the former village secretary to say that the mine needed someone to guard it, and the pay was doubled, so he planned to stay. Chunmei hadn't been able to get to the phone, and she was feeling resentful. You don't know, but the last time Ge'r came home was last year at Spring Festival. He didn't come back for the midyear harvest, and now he wasn't coming again. If he came for the summer harvest, it would be a year and a half that he hadn't been back. Chunmei was heartbroken, and she hit her daughter, swore at the animals, and glared at people. Sometimes she would close the door and not go out for the better part of the day. Who shuts their doors in broad daylight in the village? Her mother-in-law wasn't happy about it and said she couldn't live without a man. Chunmei made it worse, saying who says you don't need a man, you're out and about every night. Her mother-in-law was so mad she couldn't speak. Actually, her mother-in-law is a Christian, and she's always away from home. At New Year's, when others are all together, the young couples visiting their relatives, Chunmei is left all on her own. It wasn't easy for her.

After the New Year, Chunmei came over to chat, and we started talking about this. At first she was embarrassed, but finally opened up, and she cursed Ge'r up and down. I could tell she actually just missed him. So I gave Chunmei an idea. What if she wrote him a letter, saying she was sick and asking him if he would hurry home. At first Chunmei was too embarrassed and said she couldn't write him a letter; they'd never written letters before. Ge'r had gone through senior year of high school, and he can write and read the newspaper. But Chunmei was mostly illiterate. How could she write? I said if you can't write, I'll write for you. I'm a high school graduate, for better or for worse, and I'm pretty romantic. When your cousin was working as a sailor down south, we would often write letters and send each other pictures. It was great. Every time a letter came, it made me so happy, no matter how tired I was. Chunmei knew we wrote letters, she envied us for that. Eventually, she agreed. So I wrote a letter to Ge'r for Chunmei, making it just a bit more expressive. After I was finished, I read it to Chunmei. When she heard what I wrote she yelled: Who says I miss him? But she didn't tell me to change it. So I finished it and sealed it and addressed it, and Chunmei took it over to the town post office and mailed it.

After this, things started to get bad. The next day, she started waiting for a response. She sat at the village entrance every day, or sometimes even over at the post office. As soon as she saw the postal carrier, she would follow him around, afraid other people would know what was happening. She also wanted to drag me along. I told her, it takes more than twenty days for a letter to get there and back.

But she wouldn't listen, and after more than a month there was still no response. I started to think, maybe the letter had the wrong address. It didn't seem likely. We had copied the return address Ge'r used when he sent money. Whenever she had a free moment Chunmei would come over to ask: What's going on? What's going on? I said, Why don't we write another letter. Maybe the last one went to the wrong place. So I wrote another letter, and I had Chunmei take a picture to put in for Ge'r to see and write back. In retrospect, I was probably trying too hard, I should have just tried to comfort her. I added fuel to the fire and led Chunmei into a dead end.

This time she waited more than twenty days but Ge'r didn't even write, much less show up. Chunmei stopped coming to me, and when I went to see her, she barely acknowledged me. She sat at home with the door closed all day long. She didn't pick the peppers. She didn't clean the floor. When her mother-in-law criticized her, she didn't bite back like before. I was really worried, so I secretly wrote Ge'r a letter, and I even went over to the former secretary's house and asked him if he could look up the number Ge'r had called from, but his phone didn't display incoming phone numbers. I looked online, too, but I couldn't find the mine where Ge'r worked. You tell me, what else could I have done?

Before, when Chunmei and I would go to market, she was always arguing with the people who sold clothes or the ones who sold shoes or apples. She always did. She was as noisy as hell. But now she didn't say a word. Her eyes were empty, and she just bought whatever was in front of her. She was so meek. Her face was red and her hands damp and hot. Then for a while she became crazed. She fought with everyone she saw. Her husband's grandfather, her mother-in-law, her daughter, she nearly burnt all those bridges. And no one knew why.

Her mother-in-law said she was "love sick," that she missed her man so much she'd gone crazy. The two of them fought, and her mother accused her of this in front of other villagers. She had no face left after that, so she just locked herself in her room and didn't come out. But it seemed like her mother-in-law was right: for the past two months she hardly had been able to work. She was always confused, and more than once when she went down to work in the fields she set her daughter down and then came back without her. She also stopped cooking, and when she saw a man in the village she ran as if he wanted to catch her. You could see things weren't right. People started to stare at her and talk about her behind her back. It pissed me off, too, and when they asked me about it, I told them to back off. But what could I do? Ge'r didn't contact us. This didn't necessarily mean something was wrong; it's normal not to be in touch. Who's in touch unless something's wrong? When it's time, they came back on their own.

I thought we'd better wait it out until next harvest. Ge'r would surely come back then. But that stubborn bastard still didn't come back. Now, last year Ge'r didn't come back at the harvest either. Everything is mechanized now— the machines just bag everything up and deliver it, and you don't need a lot of laborers. But here things were different. Chunmei wasn't going to last much longer. She would die from it. She had repressed it until it made her ill.

Still, all that wasn't too bad. To put it coarsely, in the spring the cats all yowl. People are the same. You just push through it. But a few months ago, something happened in Wangying, a neighboring village, and Chunmei started to dwell on that. A young married woman hung herself. Why? Her husband came back, and the two of them got along beautifully. They were always together, for a dozen days or so. For a month after he'd left again, this woman's nether regions were always itching. But she just put up with it—she was too embarrassed to go see someone. But then she started to have a fever, and she had to go to the doctor. They took a look and said it was a sexually transmitted disease. They also asked her who her husband had had contact with, and they drew blood to see if she was HIV-positive. All the villagers knew about it, and the woman was so ashamed and angry that she hung herself.

Now what does this have to do with Chunmei? As soon as Chunmei heard, she came over ranting like someone possessed. She pressured me, asking if Ge'r had done something bad. Is that why he doesn't come back? I said how was I supposed to know. And I said at the mines, it's all men. There aren't any women there. Chunmei said, no, she saw it on TV, the mines are surrounded by women, they do that professionally, and they were sure to have diseases. She wouldn't listen to my explanations, so I said, take your daughter and go find Ge'r. Don't all the large mines have places for families now? Or rent a house and live there. As soon as I said that, Chunmei collapsed. She'd never left home, she'd be confused and lost, scared to death, and besides, if she spent months and years searching for Ge'r, everyone else would laugh at her. And she didn't want to leave her land, she'd been working hard growing hot peppers and mung beans, and she was going to spread some fertilizer for turnips and cabbage. Ge'r didn't earn enough to build a house, how could she give up the land?

Chunmei didn't bring up the idea of going to find Ge'r again. But from time to time she'd go over to Wangying and wander around, asking about where the man worked, what the woman was like, how they'd caught the disease. She would come back and ask me again, if he's with another woman will a man get sick for sure? She was jittery and unstable, and it made me feel bad. You see, your cousin works elsewhere, too. As a sailor, he's been to every port, and what port doesn't have that kind of place? I'd never thought about it before. It's not easy to earn money, and who has the spare time and money for that? But lots of people can't help it.

Three days ago she had a big fight with her mother-in-law. I'm not sure about what. After the fight, Chunmei went to the fields to spread fertilizer. But when she got back she suddenly realized she'd spread it on the wrong fields. She'd spread two whole bags of fertilizer on someone else's fields. She ran back and walked in circles around the edge. She didn't look right to me, and I followed her. But on the way back she suddenly disappeared and went and drank insecticide. I said, are you stupid or what, so many men work outside the village, if we were all like you, would there be anyone left?

Ge'r comes back three days later with the man who had been sent to find him, and Chunmei's family comes again with their anger. In the heat of the moment, Chunmei's elder brother even slaps Ge'r a few times, but Ge'r just stands there, back straight. He doesn't hit back and he doesn't wipe away tears. He seems to have no tears. Perhaps he is numb or in a state of shock. He doesn't seem to understand why his wife killed herself when their lives were getting better and better. I don't approach him, even though I really want to ask if he received Chunmei's letters. If he had, why hadn't he written back? And communication is so easy now, why didn't he have a cell phone? Didn't he miss Chunmei? Didn't he miss her body, still smooth and full?

But then again, what's the point? To the villagers, it isn't that big a deal. It isn't the New Year or spring planting season, or fall harvest, so of course he couldn't come home, that would be inconceivable. It would just be a waste of money. And to express feelings and emotions, that's even harder. They've developed the ability to "repress" themselves. Issues of sex and the body are things that can be ignored. Yet how many hundreds of millions of people are part of this migrant army?

Would it be too difficult to consider this "small" question?

With reform and opening up, "export labor" began to influence the local economy's major targets, because only people who leave to work can earn money, and only this money can drive the local economy. But how many partings and reunions, how much emotional turmoil comes as a result? How many lives are ground down to nothing? This never seems to be factored in. Men leave the village. They come back once a year or at most twice. Never more than one month per year total. They are all young or in their prime, when their physical needs are most intense, and yet they repress those needs for long periods of time. Even if husbands and wives work in the same city, only very rarely are they able to live together, simply because construction sites and factories are not required to provide married housing. And because it is very difficult to rent a place on their salaries, they often live at their respective workplaces. So even on the weekends, where can they meet? Where can they be intimate? It's a hidden question that is hard to discuss; if they're living in the same city, they are already considered fortunate.

This sexual repression has created many different problems in rural areas, and rural morality is on the verge of collapse. Migrant workers masturbate or visit prostitutes to relieve their needs. Some even form temporary new relations at their work sites. This causes an increase in sexually transmitted diseases, remarriage, illegitimate children, and other kinds of serious social problems. Women who remain in the villages must also repress their sexual urges; some turn to affairs, incest, and sexual relations with other women. This, in turn, allows the seedy side of the village to flourish. Some men use it as a pretext to sexually harass women, often successfully. Cadres are said to have "three wives and four concubines," and many criminal cases arise from women's jealousy and rivalries.

The general disregard for the sexuality of peasants also reveals a kind of deep discrimination. Our government, media, and intellectuals, in their inquiries into migrant workers' problems, usually discuss wages and only rarely sex. This suggests that if the workers were allowed to earn more money, then all their problems would be solved. Or that if their wages were much improved, issues of sexuality and intimacy could be intentionally ignored. But why? Don't these migrant workers have the right to both earn money and to live together as husband and wife?

They finally hold Chunmei's funeral, and she is buried in the field where she hadn't spread her fertilizer, her own body given to enrich this soil. On the seventh day, Ge'r goes to Chunmei's grave and lights firecrackers for her. Then he leaves to return to work.

Yi

Yi's last name is Yuan—he's the only one in Liang Village with that surname. At seventeen, after he dropped out of school, he and his family left the village, going to the ports in the south to eke out a living. They fought with the locals for territory, and by dint of endless hard work and a lack of fear, he finally found his footing. He started a wholesale seafood company, and for a while everything went smoothly. He even became an influential figure in the area.

Perhaps he heard from my brother that I was at home and working on this project. In any case, he wanted to come back and tell me his story. So one day, a large Volkswagen comes to a screaming halt in front of my brother's house, a long trail of dust behind it. Soon after Yi, his mother, and his son climb out. Yi's face is oily and shiny. He is wearing a thick gold necklace and a white singlet, muscles bulging beneath it. And although he is short and a little fat, he radiates aggression. He speaks directly, but when he talks about past events he immediately becomes emotional; he even tears up a few times. Yi's mother looks younger than she did when she was living in the village twenty years ago. Her skin is white and rosy, and it's obvious that she is an elderly person who lives well. His son seems to be only eight or nine. Yi said he brought him along to teach him something. He said, these kids don't know what hardship is; they don't know what their dads had to suffer, what they had to endure, to get to where they are today. Yi has come over from another county, where he is discussing the possibility of developing an aluminum mine. He talks for about three hours, and then he gathers up his son and mother and hurries back. Friends are waiting to talk with him. He is confident in his ability to earn money and especially in a future career working with government-owned businesses.

This life of mine has been really hard. It would take me days to tell the whole story; you'd have to write a book.

When we lived in the village, we didn't have enough to eat. After we built my mother and father's house, we owed a shit-load of debt. We'd been told that herding sheep or selling shoe soles was a way to earn money. We wanted to do the latter, but the team leader wouldn't let us. My mother got down on her knees, but it didn't help. So then I raised sheep until a thief put a hole in the wall and stole them. Was that bad luck or what?

This will show you how poor we were: When mother and father left to sell shoe soles, they gave us kids twenty-seven packets of noodles. Not the kind you get at the supermarket—one *jin* per pack—it's the kind they make in the rural areas, the short kind. At most half a *jin*. There was no corn or anything like that. We—my sisters and I—lived on those for one month and twenty days. After school my four sisters divided up the work: fetching firewood, tending the fire. And then every day it was watery noodles with some wild vegetables or sweet potato leaves, stuff like that, until in the end it was all gone. Then I tried to borrow food. I went all over the village. Everyone was poor then, who would give anything to these parentless children? We almost starved to death waiting for them to come back.

Since we were the only ones in the village with the surname "Yuan," we didn't have much status, and as the main family, you Liangs often pushed us around. People got into arguments with us about the land for our house, and Wanming and his family would hassle us. Once I took a kitchen knife in one hand and an iron pick in the other like a crazy person. I fought them all to the ground. I was in my early teens at the time. Liang Wanming was my teacher. He said Yi, son, why are you fighting me? I said you've gone too far, you've cheated my family one too many times, you feudal tyrant!

Later my parents came back from Hunan, and soon after the house accidentally burned down. The corn was burned up, and the bedding and everything else was lost. My father walked around the house while we sat on the ground weeping. We wept because there was no way out. Later we rented a cheap room from the production team.

When I was seventeen we left for Yang County. My ma borrowed 100 kuai from her family, and we bought a machine to grind soybeans into tofu. My parents made it at home, and I sold it in areas where we had family. One winter, there was a huge snowstorm. It doesn't snow very often in the south, but I still had to go out to sell the tofu. It was too slippery, and as I went uphill, my bicycle fell over, and the tofu spilled everywhere. I sat down and wept. I wanted to die.

Later I thought about expanding our business. Yang County is apple country, you could earn more money dealing in apples. I made contact with a customer. He would make several thousand kuai for a boatload of apples, of which he'd give me several hundred. I was ecstatic. That was the first pot of gold I'd ever earned. But then other people got me drunk and stole the money. I wept like a baby. It was all a set up—they'd cheated me.

Later I traded in fish. People bullied me. They hit me. They'd try and make me kneel down, but I wouldn't. They could beat me to death, but I wouldn't kneel. After that, I hardened up too. If you wanted to get by, you couldn't be soft. If you were soft, the locals would make short work of you. I started to get to know all the bosses on Yang County's main roads. They thought I had nerve and respected me. They said kids from Henan were all such and such. Actually we had no choice but to stand up and take a piece of the sky. That was when I started to get to know people, to communicate with them, to find people like me, and loyal ones, to make an alliance.

Later I sold fresh fish and seafood products wholesale at the port. That's a money-making business. If you aren't aggressive, you won't make it. I put my life in danger many times. For example, there was a guy named Zheng. We had bad blood. There was a guy who delivered fish to Zheng, but I stole his customer. The man heard that I would pay a little more. The Zheng family wasn't happy about it and went to get the guy armed with knives. I got my knife too. We both saw blood that day. While they were trying to hold me, I hit them from behind, while my sister's husband came straight on with a wooden club. He gave a guy a concussion. Later they put out word that whoever saw me or my brother-in-law should split us in two. At that time he was only eighteen or nineteen, like me when I got to Yang County six or seven years before. In the end, I got my knife to fight it out, and as a result we all paid the same price. I had to pay off some officials, then the whole thing was more or less over. No one knew anything about the law back then, the local police tried to talk me out of it, and I said they'd pushed me too far. Only later did I realize that what I'd done was considered excessive self-defense.

There was a guy from Yang County in the same business, the same village, same territory. He was the town boss, really a big deal. What he says goes, that kind of guy. He was in with the Zheng family, and he wanted my family to get out. So he went to my friend Li Lao'er, who I call Little Yaba, to negotiate; he was pretty well-known. I wanted the two sides to meet on the level, but they wouldn't listen, and my friend lost face. Then we really had our backs to the wall. We either had to wrap it up and take our asses back to Henan, or we had to make a firm stand in Yang County. We set up a command center at Li Lao'er's place. The three of us were the commanders. My brother-in-law was the lead commander, and there were around twenty or thirty men. My brother once chased Old Zheng and some of his men from the third story down to the first with a knife. He stabbed eight of them altogether and did time for that.

After that fight, I had to go pay to patch things up a bit. We had no understanding of the law. My brother-in-law paid a heavy price; he was sentenced to eight months in prison. I spent tens of thousands to avoid a lawsuit and was in for two months. My brother was in for eight years. It was big news in Yang County at the time. It also established my status. I live in Yang County now, but no matter what's going on here, they listen when I talk.

I'm still in the wholesale fish business. When business was booming, I earned more that 200,000 a year, but my take home was about 70 or 80,000. The rest I gave to friends. When there is meat, everyone eats. You have to reward loyalty for people to do their best for you. These past few years, circumstances have changed. With limited buyers and wholesale, our yearly business is now only 60 or 70,000, far below my costs. I had no choice but to go start a factory. These past three years were a failure. I didn't earn any money. I came back to Yang County to refine oil but was cheated by a friend who took the money and ran.

So there were seven or eight years that were a total failure. In the '90s I had 1,000,000 or more in my hands, but then I lost almost all of it.

So I opened a teahouse in Yang County and did a bit on the side. We set up a gambling joint like an underground casino. Three of us opened the teahouse together and we earned a few million kuai. In the process, I started working with this aluminum mine factory. Seven of us were in it together, and each of us put up a few hundred thousand. We found a professional factory director, but he wasn't good at daily operations, so we lost a little. Later, conflicts arose between the seven of us, and we argued over the factory. The guns almost came out. I took out cash and divided it among them, and now I am the legal representative. I've already invested 12,000,000. We might need more than 20,000,000 in the end. But we've already been given the national seal of approval for the quality of the goods, and factory owners are buying the goods I've put out. We'll be profitable soon.

I have a lot of specialized knowledge now. You wouldn't understand all the vocabulary.

People have to have imagination. I finally understood that officials and businessmen are part of the same family. Now I can sit together with the county commissioner and the public security bureau chief. Before I was the kind that got locked up. Now I'm an entrepreneur not just in name, but in reality.

Afterlife

Among the row of houses on the corner of Liang Village Road is one with an especially big courtyard. It doesn't have a surrounding wall, and its cement base runs all the way to the road. It's somehow both open and imposing. It was built in 2007 and belongs to Liang Guanghe. Behind his back some villagers say that the house was paid for with the blood of his son and daughter.

It's true, in a sense. Guanghe and his wife are honest people, and his dream was always to build a grand house. For twenty years they slowly saved, bit by bit, but they never had enough, and they didn't want to borrow money. So they gave it their all: Guanghe, his wife, and his children all left to go work. For several years they didn't come back even once. But before the accident, their dreams were still a distant reality. The house was built two years after they received the compensation. Since then, Guanghe hasn't left the village; in fact, he very rarely leaves his house and is only seldom seen in the village. I've been back all this time and haven't seen him once.

After dinner, traces of light cross the sky, and the village is wrapped in an unusual stillness. There's nothing new or fashionable about that stillness; it's the simplicity, the serenity of the ruins, with their ineffable sense of time everlasting.

Father and I go for a walk and find ourselves in front of Guanghe's door. It's ajar and dark inside. Father calls out a few times, but no one answers. Then, just as we are about to leave, Guanghe comes out, his pale face suddenly emerging from the darkness, phantom-like. He is so emaciated, you can see the veins on his skull, and his nose seems strangely pointed, his skin slack, like a terrifying, bloodless ghost. He moves slowly, stooped and crooked, like a man of seventy or eighty. I start in fright. In my memory, Guanghe is a rather handsome young man, someone with deeply etched features, which now make him look even sicklier. He greets us, and moving a few stools, has us sit down near the doorway. Then he calls to a little boy, telling him to go and get his father, a former village secretary, Liang Xinglong. Guanghe does all of this slowly, his voice weak, and his body as thin as paper, as if a gust of wind could blow him over.

After a while Guanghe's father comes out, as does his wife, whom we call Aunt Hua. She is still full of fire and vigor, with thick eyebrows and big eyes, a strong body and a voice that rings high and clear. Her appearance doesn't betray the family's tragedy. Rural women are always tough, much stronger than the men.

I want to talk about what happened, but I can't bring myself to say anything. Father can't seem to talk about it either. A few times I almost bring it up, but then I stop. Guanghe's eyes are downcast, even though his father, the former secretary, is still hale and hearty. He cares about politics and has insights into the current political situation. I look closely at his neck, his hands, and his bare chest. All are scarred, especially his chest, which has a long slanting scar across it. Qingli gave that to him many years ago.

By the time we leave Guanghe's, the sky is completely black. As we walk along the main road, we listen closely to the sound of the crops, of all shapes and sizes, breathing. The entire earth seems to undulate with breath and life. Late at night is especially beautiful. The sky is peaceful, the crops mysterious and full of breath. They almost seem to be walking beside us.

A beam of white light flashes here and there, gradually growing closer. As we draw near, the light pauses, reflecting onto our faces. Someone says, Er'ye, what are you doing here so late? Oh, just taking a leisurely spin, Father replies. What are you doing? I'm catching cicadas. As he says it he shows us the bottle in his hand. It's about half-full of dirty water, which he pours out, showing us the cicada inside. I ask him, what did you catch that for? He answers, there's a place in town that buys them one kuai a piece or at the very least 6 jiao. After he goes on, Father says that's Shangwen, the eldest son of the Zhous. When he and his wife left to work, his father Old Zhou took care of his son, but he didn't take good care of him, and the boy fell in a well and drowned. When Shangwen came back he drove his parents out of the village. He wanted to kill them. He scared them so much they went into hiding for two weeks.

When we get home, Father tells me the details of Guanghe's tragedy.

It happened on October 18, 2005. It was around 6 pm, sunset, when the students were just leaving school.

Liang Liang and his elder sister Liang Ying are Guanghe's two oldest children. Liang Liang had picked Liang Ying up on a motorbike and was going to bring her back to the village. She was pregnant, around four or five months. She was a good kid; she took care of her parents and her husband's parents. She and her husband had opened a furniture store in town. Business was good. Her husband's elder sister was blind, and she often took care of her, too, so their relationship was a good one. Liang Liang had just gotten back that day from where he was working in Guangzhou, and he was going into town to bring his sister back to eat with the family. Taking the turn at the intersection by the high school, they were hit by a small sedan. The driver's surname was Pang. He was a director at a Grain Control Office. Pang's brother was in the Public Security Bureau, criminal investigation vice-captain or something like that. Pang was drunk and going too fast. He hit Liang Liang's motorbike while he was passing a farm vehicle. Liang Ying was knocked into the vehicle and taken all the way into another county, about seventy or eighty li from here. Only when the guy started to unload the vehicle did he discover there was a corpse in it. By then it was already 10 pm, and it scared the owner half to death. He didn't know what happened, but he quickly reported it to the police. At the site of the accident, when he saw someone had been killed, Pang made a call and soon someone came to get him out of there. But bystanders reported it to the police. Liang Liang was taken to the hospital, but he died not long after. The villagers and Liang Ying's husband's family looked all over for Liang Ying. She had been with Liang Liang, there was no doubt, so how could she just disappear? It wasn't until the next morning that the Public Security Bureau's investigators got to our police station and figured out that Liang Ying had been knocked into the vehicle and carried into another county.

Guanghe and his wife were working in Xinjiang and weren't able to get home for a few days. His younger brother Guangtian was taking care of things at home. Liang Ying was taken to a crematorium, and Liang Liang was placed in the hospital morgue. Pang sent the village Public Security Director over and offered to settle things for 70 or 80,000 kuai. Guangtian didn't think that was enough for two adults and the child Liang Ying was carrying, that was three lives altogether. So then Pang sent a few influential people from town over to mediate, saying 95,000 was the final offer. Guanghe and his wife came back three days later, and their grief . . . well it's no use saying. They cried and cried over their son, and then they cried and cried over their daughter. They cried until they lost their voices. The villagers tried to console them, saying don't cry, it won't bring them back to life, you should hurry and think about being compensated. At first, Guanghe said he didn't want money, he wanted a life in exchange, for Pang to be sentenced to jail. They said, they're dead, and if you don't get any money out of it that would be a loss of both life and property. And your son and daughter are watching from below, they wouldn't want that either. So Guanghe stopped talking like that. For a while there was a bunch of people around Guanghe's house offering ideas—both out of sympathy but also doing the math, thinking in case he gets a lot, then maybe they could borrow some.

Finally they found a connection in the local Public Security Bureau office. They took him some gifts and asked him to speak on their behalf. They said the lowest possible compensation would be 200,000 kuai, but Pang wouldn't agree. The local bureau folks said not to worry about it, hold out for a while, just don't sign a settlement. It counted as a major traffic incident, and other than paying for damages, he could be sentenced to prison. Later, Pang sent lots of people over to mediate with Guanghe, but things stayed deadlocked. Finally Pang played the trump card, he sent word that he wouldn't budge on the money, he'd go to prison if he had to. This put a lot of pressure on Liang Guanghe. He was worried the other party was too powerful, that even if he went to prison he'd be out again soon, and maybe not pay anything at all. Guanghe asked all over for people's opinions, but there wasn't any other way.

Pang had also asked around, he knew that even though the family had people on the outside, Liang Guanghe's family, especially his father, the former branch secretary Liang Xinglong, had had conflicts in the past, and it was highly unlikely that they'd be able to count on outside help. So he didn't care about what Liang Guanghe did; he just silently put on the brakes.

The whole business lingered at a stalemate for a while. Liang Liang and Liang Ying still hadn't been buried; they were in a freezer unit at the crematorium, which was costing a lot of money every day. Guanghe and his wife cried until they had no more tears to shed. They couldn't bury their son and daughter. The other guy didn't care, and they had no one to help them file a lawsuit. After keeping it up for a month, Guanghe was so thin he looked completely different. In the end he couldn't hold on any longer and found someone to mediate. They set the compensation price at 157,000 and it was more or less settled. Liang Ying's husband's family also got a portion.

Later, someone in the Liang family who harbored animosity toward Liang Xinglong ran into someone else in town and told them the whole story. He said it was karmic retribution for Liang Xinglong. You don't know what unconscionable stuff that son of a bitch got up to when he was secretary. He's evil through and through. Old Father

Heaven took revenge not on him, but on his grandson and granddaughter. The other guy was thinking, don't I know it, that asshole sure gave me a hard time. The fucker is finally getting his just desserts.

Most people in the village were devastated about the two kids, but on the other hand, they also thought Liang Xinglong was getting what he deserved, for what he'd done when he was secretary.

Rural people are pragmatic. When someone dies, the most important question is money. But that way your pain and grief and love for the deceased turns into a price you haggle over; everything becomes cold, emotionless, cruel. When people try to understand how things happen in rural areas, they often condemn and look down on this behavior. It seems like money has become more important than life. But who can see into these people's hearts?

Just as I am about to leave the village, Guanghe goes to the county seat to see a doctor. His tongue has suddenly become paralyzed, and he throws up everything he eats. He hasn't been able to keep anything down for ten days. I don't know the results of the medical tests, but my older sister says it is maybe mental illness, something is off. I have my doubts; could this be caused by depression? I think of Guanghe emerging from the darkness, his weary, haggard face. Death seemed close behind him. How can we know how his son and daughter's deaths affected him? When the grey-haired deliver the black-haired into the earth, is that not the deepest of sorrows? Without son and daughter, what aspirations can he have? And this new house, what stress does it add? What guilt? How does he react, in his heart, to this phrase, "Paid for with the blood of your son and daughter"? A sudden windfall like that can provoke even slightly jealous folks to say things they wouldn't normally, never mind the truly greedy ones. I think quite a few people borrowed money from Guanghe. Everyone knew how much money he had; there was no reason for him not to lend it. So when he put all that money into building the house, it was tantamount to the villagers losing a hefty sum; it was a thoughtless, inconsiderate thing to do. It made the villagers resentful. And it might have added to Guanghe's guilt.

5

Runtu Grows Up

For Spring Festival, the municipal government has adopted measures for both temporary emergency relief and special assistance to be given to the rural elderly, ill, and disabled, including those affected by work-related disabilities who have no other means of support. For destitute families, the municipal government has adopted temporary emergency relief measures in addition to special assistance to aid families by resolving challenges to their livelihood. In 1998, the city government drafted "Provisional Strategies to Protect Citizens of Rang County Cities and Towns with the Lowest Household Incomes." Those whose average household monthly income was less than 80 yuan were designated for assistance. In June 2004, the Rang County Assistance Policy for Destitute Households in Rural Areas was officially launched. In July 2006, an additional 9,388 households, totaling 22,500 people, were included under the purview of rural subsidized assistance.

The minimum poverty line for rural residents was raised from 174 yuan per person in 2019, to 253 yuan in 2020, while households registered as below the poverty line qualified for A-level support of 335 yuan per month. In all, 53,373 rural residents received support: a total of 16 million yuan was disbursed to them between January and September of 2020. Support for rural residents deemed to be in extreme poverty was increased from 5,044 yuan in 2019, to 6,000 yuan in 2020. 9,936 rural residents qualified for this standard, receiving a total disbursement of 60,589,000 yuan in extreme poverty support.

—The Rang County Annals Civil Administration

Qingli

It rained heavily all night. At dawn everyone came out to inspect their houses, afraid that the standing water might seep into the foundations. Sewers have always been a problem in the village. There isn't a village-wide sewer system—each house handles its own waste—so when it rains, streams crisscross the village, and neighbors often fight about issues of drainage.

Elder Brother and I go over to check on the old house. There are two large puddles on the east and west sides, but the water hadn't flooded the foundation yet, and the house isn't in danger of falling over. As we head home for breakfast, we see Qingli on the other side of Qingshi Bridge, a basket over his shoulder. His jacket is wide open, showing his beach-ball belly, and his pants are held up by a piece of straw rope. In one hand he holds a meat cleaver about eleven or twelve inches long. When he sees my brother in the distance, he breaks into a large grin and calls out a greeting.

"Uncle is back. When did Auntie arrive?" His voice is low and hoarse. Under my breath I say to my brother, "He looks pretty normal, why does everyone say he's still crazy?" "Let him talk for a second and you'll see," my brother whispers back dryly. Then he calls out, "Qingli, you're out and about early, what are you up to?" Qingli says, "Since the water's high, I got up a little after five to go catch some fish. I got a big catfish." He walks over and holds the basket out so we can see. Inside is a large fish, about four or five *jin*, its whiskers still quivering. Brother and I both exclaim in admiration. When Qingli hears this, he insists Brother take it. He sets the basket on the bridge and starts to look for something to string it up with.

148

I tell him I want to take his picture, but he doesn't seem to believe me. "Really?" "Really, you stand here and pose. Put the knife down, it doesn't look good." But Qingli won't put the knife down, so I say, "Put the knife in the basket, then after we've taken the picture, you can get it back out. Ok?" As I say this, I go over to take the knife. Suddenly Qingli's face turns ugly, a savage light in his eyes, and his grip tightens. My brother sees the change and hurries over saying, "Just take the picture. Just take the picture."

Qingli suddenly seems to understand. He pulls up his shirt, sticks the knife in his pants, and then pulls the shirt over it, so you can only see its faint outline. I ask, "Are we ready?" Qingli jumps up and says, "Hold on, I haven't posed." He goes over to a tree and leans against it, crossing his legs. He seems pleased—he must think this looks good. After the photo, he tells me several times that I have to give him a copy. I promise I will.

I want to chat more, to better understand his mental state. Nine years before, Qingli suffered a sudden mental breakdown. He got a knife and went over to the former branch secretary Liang Xinglong's home with violent intent. Liang Xinglong, terrified, ran around the village with Qingli at his heels. He hacked at his head, his hands, his legs. He cut his chest so deeply that you could see his ribs. He also slashed Liang Xinglong's wife's waist and hands. For a 2 mile radius, it was the news of the year. Somebody even made up a little song:

In Liang Village there's something new,
Qingli cut Xinglong through;
he cut his arm 'til it hung by a thread, he cut his guts all
  to shreds,
so much so, he was almost dead.

I ask Qingli how he's been, but he replies with his own question: You're back from Beijing, what were the Olympics like? But before I have time to answer, he's talking about how incredible the Olympics are. I'm surprised—he doesn't seem stupid at all. But then I start to have trouble following him. He keeps his hands wrapped around his chest and his eyes pointed at the sky, mumbling unintelligibly, almost meditatively. He rambles: food policies; security management; what people die of where, and although his thinking is mostly related to important national events, it's incoherent and incomplete.

As we leave, Qingli insists we take the fish. He finds some thread on the ground and strings it up. My brother says it's too much to handle, but Qingli won't hear it. My brother has no choice but to carry the large fish home. On the road, my brother says, "What were you thinking trying to take Qingli's knife? Don't you know how dangerous that was? Since the attack, that knife has never left his side, sometimes while he's walking he pulls it out and waves it around. No one touches it. Think about it; since he attacked those people, no one's gone near him."

So why did he want to give my brother a fish? Because during the lawsuit my brother helped him find a lawyer and a mental health institution to do an evaluation. Qingli hasn't forgotten.

After breakfast, my brother fills in the details of Qingli's attack.

Qingli is maybe around forty-four years old. He used to have a small business as a bricklayer. He knew what he was doing and worked hard. But the rest of Liang Village bullied his family. His father was the stubborn type who didn't put much stock in personal loyalty and couldn't win people over. He wanted to curry favor with village cadres, but it didn't work. Everyone looked down on him. During the Cultural Revolution he was on top for a couple of days, but he was really only a hired thug. When Father was criticized, he followed the others and kicked and hit him. He didn't have a single friend in the village, and people only rarely dropped by his house or drank with him. Qingli could get things done, although when he interacted with people he was a little like his father: antisocial. He didn't have many friends. But he made more of an effort than his father at greeting people and saying hello.

Qingli didn't earn a lot of money, but he married a woman with expectations, who was always calling him a good-for-nothing. Actually, no one here had any money then, and after Qingli moved into his own house he did fine, relatively speaking. But his wife was stubborn, and the two of them bickered and fought a lot. Qingli couldn't outargue or outfight her, and he seemed a little depressed. Everyone thought he seemed a little off, but nothing actually happened.

The tension between Qingli and Liang Xinglong began with a conflict about their houses. Qingli built his house next to the pond, pretty far from Xinglong's house, but it blocked Xinglong's sewer. Actually it wasn't really that big a deal, we all dig our own sewers, and if we're worried they won't drain we just make some minor adjustments, and it's usually OK. But Xinglong had been branch secretary for a few years then, and was in the habit of using his power to take advantage of people, so he went over and yelled at Qingli. Qingli wouldn't have it and said a few words of his own. He even pushed Xinglong onto the ground. After that Xinglong's sons said they had to punish Qingli. Who did he think he was harassing the most powerful elder in the area? They had to pay him back, otherwise who knew what the nutjob would end up doing. So Xinglong's three sons went over to Qingli's place, held him down, and beat him up pretty badly. Later they went to the production brigade to work things out, but the director of the village Public Security Bureau was related to one of Xinglong's sons. You tell me, what chance did Qingli have? They said Qingli was in the wrong, and because he had hit Xinglong, he had to pay 500 kuai for medical expenses. After that, Qingli really went off the deep end.

One night, when Liang Xinglong's son was on his way home after watching TV at the Zhou house, someone slapped him on the shoulder just as he was about to open the door. When he turned around, someone stuck him with a knife. They thought it must have been Qingli, so they went over to confront him. Qingli said he didn't do it, but no one believed him. So they beat him up again. This time, it was even worse for Qingli. His wife took his son and left. He couldn't find them. Maybe they went to go work somewhere. Anyway, they didn't even leave a note.

It was maybe a few months later, during the summer of 1999, I forget exactly which day, Qingli appeared with a cleaver in his hand—we didn't know why—and walked over to Xinglong's house. First he hit his wife. He knocked a hole in her head and chopped off her finger. Xinglong ran terrified through the village and Qingli ran after him, hitting his neck, his shoulder, even his legs a few times. People tried to pull Qingli away, but he went after everyone who got near him. We all thought that was the end of Xinglong.

Xinglong and his wife were both sent to the hospital, and Qingli was locked up in the local police station. The couple was badly wounded, and Xinglong's family had to pay 16 or 17,000 kuai; his brothers fought like bastards over who would put up the money. When the medical assessment was done, they found that by law Qingli could be sentenced to prison for a minimum of fifteen years.

I don't know who first had the idea to get Qingli a lawyer and have a mental health evaluation done. His father came to talk to me about it, but at first I decided I shouldn't get involved. There is bad blood between Xinglong's family and ours, but I didn't want anyone thinking I was using a public offense to right a private wrong. Later I thought about it some more and it seemed like a simple matter of upholding justice. If Qingli were mentally ill, then he shouldn't be treated unjustly. So I agreed to help him find a lawyer and a hospital for an evaluation. They established Qingli had a manic-depressive disorder.

During the trial, the judge asked Qingli, "Liang Qingli, why did you try to kill Liang Xinglong?" Qingli said, "Fuck his sister, I wanted him dead, that's all. I wish I'd cut him worse." The judge asked a few more times, but he just said the same thing. The judge couldn't make a ruling like that, so soon he declared the court adjourned and had Qingli sent to a mental hospital for evaluation. Later, on the local level, they did an evaluation and said he did have a mental illness. A few months after that, Qingli was found not guilty and released.

I don't know if it's because he's afraid, or if he wants to scare people, but after he came back, he's got that knife on him whenever he leaves the house.

They're depressing, these old village stories that repeat over and over again. Even with the changes of the past decades, the inner logic of village life remains the same. As far as Qingli is concerned, fair laws saved him from punishment, but what about his mental health? Who is responsible for its deterioration?

My brother says I should visit Qingli's house; perhaps it will help me gain some insights. So after lunch, we go over. He lives by the pond near the village entrance, but I never really noticed his house before. It's the kind they built in the '80s, with bricks and earth and a clay tile roof. The walls are half brick, half earth, but for some reason he bricked up the windows on the east and west sides.

When Qingli sees us coming, he looks really pleased and asks us in. The house is dim and smells like a garbage pit. In the main room there's enough light to make out the furniture, which seems randomly scattered around the room. There is a small, beat-up table, covered in dust, and a couple of stools. There's also a long, brick bench at the back of the room, piled with all

sorts of stuff covered in spider webs. Nothing appears to have
been used in a long time. The western room, with only a bed, a
broken mat, and some clothes, is almost completely black.
There's no pillow. There is just the knife, glimmering menac-
ingly in the dim light.

The smell in the room is unbearable, so we don't stay long.
Originally I had wanted to take some pictures, but I'm afraid
Qingli won't like it, so I don't bring it up. Elder Brother suggests
we go see the pigpen. It's also pitch black, but there aren't any
pigs. Instead it's filled with wormwood grass. As we leave, Elder
Brother says that Qingli goes to the river every day to cut the
grass. After he fills the pigpen up, he throws it all away. I ask
why, and my brother says to keep his knife sharp. Qingli adds,
"Fuck, if I don't use the knife, and it gets dull, then what will I
do? What if I need it?"

Kunsheng

It was probably ten years ago, in the summer, that I first saw the
family living in the graveyard. After a spell of heavy rain, my
brother, elder sister, and I went over to clean our mother's
grave, and my brother mentioned that a family was living there,
on the other side. They were from another village, and he didn't
know why they had chosen to come live in our cemetery. I was
curious so went over to take a look. The land on the far end of
the cemetery had been carefully altered to include a threshing
area, rolled flat, with piles of grain and stalks that had not yet
been ground; below them a layer of wheat kernels had sprouted.
There was also a well and a homemade millstone. Two men
were building a house in a central open space. The walls had
just been built with homemade bricks, and it looked like they
were about to set up the roof beams. Nearby was a small
thatched hut.

The two men turned and watched us closely, but they didn't
say anything. Only after my brother gave each of them a

cigarette did they relax a bit. I bent down and peered into the hut. When my eyes adjusted to dim light, I was shocked by what I saw.

The hut was unfinished. In the front there was something like an entryway, behind which was a wall made of dried corn stalks pasted together. The rain had penetrated this fragile screen and the narrow space was filled with water. In the "kitchen," rain and mud had spilled onto the stove, and there was no apparent place to eat. The only dry spot was in front of the cooking stove—a space about the width of three chairs, in which three people huddled together. One, staring dully straight ahead, seemed to be the mother. There were also two small children. One was lying on her stomach on a straw mat, her hair tangled across her face. She didn't move at all. The other, who was a bit bigger, about ten years or so, was crying. It didn't look like there was anything to eat. My brother went over to the girl on the ground and could feel she had a high fever. He spoke to the woman, but she made no response, so he went outside to the two men. They said she'd gotten wet in the rain the night before and started to run a fever.

My brother and I returned to town and got some medicine, noodles, crackers, salt, and firewood. Then we went over to the hardware store and bought some thick plastic fabric ten yards wide. When we returned, the scene in the little room was the same. I gave the crackers to the older sister, but she didn't eat them. She turned and called gently to her sister, "Little Sister, Little Sister, crackers." But the little girl didn't move. My brother had the two men help the woman out of the hut. Then he asked the older sister to turn the little one over and hold her in her arms. The little girl's face was bright red, her eyes tightly shut. She hardly seemed to be breathing. My brother gave her a shot to lower the fever.

I couldn't figure it out. This space, three chairs wide, was the only dry place in the hut. At night there were five people: the sick child, the older girl, the two men, and the disabled woman.

How did they get through the night, and the buckets of freezing rain? Even now, when I think about it, I get a pain in the pit of my stomach. This has remained a riddle to me.

Now, as the small hut at the end of the graveyard comes into view, I can see two people, one old, one young, working that same bit of land. The older one is swinging a hoe, while the younger one is crouched on the ground gathering something. When they see us, they stop, stand up, and stare at us. The older one is head of the household. I haven't seen him in ten years, but he is already an old man. His hair, which looks like it hasn't been washed in a long time, hangs down past his shoulders, gray and matted. And his dirty and tangled beard covers most of his mouth. It also looks like he has cataracts; the whites of his eyes are large, and he doesn't appear to see well. The young girl beside him watches us with a large smile. She looks livelier.

We ask the man to come over to the side of the field, but he doesn't seem to have heard us and instead just watches inquisitively. The girl comes over instead, shyly and cautiously. My older sister takes out fifty kuai and hands it to her, but she won't take it and looks over at the old man in the field, as if for help. At that point, he comes over. We can't tell if he's mumbling something to himself or if he's trying to communicate with us. My sister stuffs the money in his hand, and after pushing it away several times he accepts it, although we still can't make out what he's saying. We keep asking and finally get the gist of it, something to the effect of: It's hard to spend this shiny white silver. We don't really know what he means. Like Qingli, this man has been alone for so long he has lost the basic ability to communicate.

I am especially curious about the little girl. She is small but has healthy, rosy cheeks. Her eyes are curved and smiling, sweet and innocent. I wonder: Is she the older sister or the younger one? So I ask her, who else lives with you? She says her older sister is married, and her mother died in the spring.

So she must be the little sister I saw ten years ago who was so sick. How wonderful that she's grown so tall! She tells me that her sister married someone in Guizhou. I ask why she married someone so far away, and she says she doesn't know. As for herself, she never went to school and can't read. She went to Guangzhou to work but came back before long. Because she can't read, there was too much she didn't understand, and she was afraid. After the farming season is done, she plans to help out at a cafeteria in town. They've agreed to pay her 500 RMB a month, plus room and board. The cafeteria has already asked her a few times; they're waiting for her. When I hear that I'm happy. The girl is earning her own keep; at the very least she can provide for herself. I ask where she and her father are living now, and she says with the work team—they have a house with a *kang* (a traditional bed-stove). The village cadre found it for them; the house they built here was always falling down. I look around and can see what she means. The land is too low, and it would easily take on water in the summer rains.

I suggest I take a picture of them, which pleases the old man. He smooths his hair with his hand, but it won't stay flat. He spits a few times into his hand and is finally able to sweep it back into a kind of pompadour. The girl stands next to her father looking at me, her feet together, her hands tugging at her jacket, her mouth in a shy smile.

My heart trembles, with either excitement or happiness. She's survived the hardest years, and now is healthy and cheerful, innocent and wholesome. Her future will probably be better. I don't tell her what I'd seen ten years before. She would have only been five or six. Does she remember? I hope not.

It's noon by the time we head back. We pass Qingdao's house, where he's invited a high-ranking crowd—people from the local government—to play cards. Qingdao sees us passing by and calls us over, introducing us to everyone. He seems to be showing us off a bit.

I bring up the family in the cemetery and only then learn the man's name is Kunsheng. To be honest, it hadn't occurred to me that he had a name.

People call him "Beardy." When he was young, he enlisted as a military driver, but he didn't come back after he was discharged. He found work in Yunnan and Guizhou. People say he was good with his hands; he could weave bamboo mats, even adding multicolored characters and flowers. He built the well and storage cellar and house in the cemetery with his own hands.

Qingdao says something must be wrong with that guy's head. He has land in his own village, and he even has some brothers, but for some reason he lives in a place like that. Back when he built that house, he came to ask me for bricks and he didn't seem dumb. I said, what am I going to do, tear down my house and give the bricks to you? Qingdao's tone is filled with contempt.

I ask Qingdao if the government has any specific policies for people like this, subsidies or the like. Qingdao says of course there is, and folks at the village level have always watched out for him. Before, when he was living in the cemetery, they kept saying that he should come live in the village, but he didn't want to. Later, when the house collapsed after heavy summer rains and winter snows, he grudgingly agreed. They arranged a space for him on an old *kang* in a team member's house. His wife died in the spring, and the village paid for the burial. He enjoys the "five guarantees," including seven or eight hundred kuai every year, along with three or four hundred in subsidies. People usually give him flour and blankets and clothing, so he doesn't really live too badly. He is better off than honest folks in the village who work themselves to death. Qingdao's voice is scornful. Everyone else seems in agreement.

A young man playing cards interrupts. Qingdao explains that he's the town's civil administration cadre, in charge of this area, so he knows the situation best. The young man said, "This Kunsheng, he may look pitiful, but he's actually no good. One time he got drunk and went to the county government to lodge a complaint, he said no one was taking care of him. The guy in charge didn't want to hear it, so he came out and yelled at him. He said, We serve you like a living god, what more do you want? If the government wasn't taking care of you, you'd have starved to death. I said, Get him out of here. We can't let him make a scene, but Kunsheng wouldn't listen. Later I said, If you don't listen to me, I won't help you anymore, and the civil administration won't help you. And if you cross the line, I'll have you taken over to the local police station. After that he stopped.

"He's not poor at all anymore. He's too smart. We gave him two *mu* of land in the village, which he farms, and the land in the cemetery is in good shape now, too. It can hold water, so he uses it to grow lotus roots. He has money in the bank. I reckon he's got 10,000. Last year he sold his eldest daughter. They gave him 5,000. The two girls were adopted, and he doesn't really care about them. And his clothes, he's got lots, he just doesn't wash them."

All this makes Kunsheng sound completely amoral. He drinks and causes trouble; he extorts money from the government; he sold his daughter; he dresses as if he were poor on purpose. I think to myself, if this really is Kunsheng's other side, I shouldn't be so sympathetic. If he's amoral, if he's lazy, if he doesn't understand the difference between right and wrong, he's not worth it. Yet it's very clear that the person they're describing and the Kunsheng I've seen are not the same man.

Or perhaps he's being considered through two different lenses. They see him differently. Did he really sell his daughter? Maybe the girl's in-laws gave some money. But Kunsheng shouldn't have that kind of money, he ought to be in utter poverty, he ought to have nothing, only then would he deserve sympathy. And as for the drinking, someone who enjoys government subsidies shouldn't be drinking, that's degenerate.

People like Kunsheng have already been excluded from the village moral code. They are not a symbol of the village's inhumanity: on the contrary, because they are cut off from the world, because they are unintelligent or different, they have become a moral stain on the village, the mocked and rejected "other." For this reason, they do not deserve care or assistance. In our culture, "life" and "people" have no value. Only if you are part of the system are you given the respect, recognition, and value that correspond to your position. This is why, when you are driven from a community, you find yourself more and more alone. You become "a discarded object" unworthy of respect or aid. Deep in their bones, the general population and the politicians don't think these people deserve assistance; they only take action because of the new rules.

Lumpy Ginger

By the time we're ready to eat, it's well past 1 pm. But, as they say, "In the country, there's neither food nor tea, 'til almost three," so this is actually early. Just as the food is served, a wizened old man comes in, his hands and legs black as lacquer from coal dust. He yells out, in exaggerated tones, "What? It's not even noon, but you're all at the table!" My brother makes a minimal response. Father, acting very unlike himself, doesn't welcome him at all. I look at him closely; could this be Lumpy Ginger? In the few years since I last saw him, he's aged tremendously. His eyes are cloudy and his back hunched. But the lumps on the back of his head still stick out. My brother asks him to sit down but doesn't offer him anything to eat. Lumpy sits for a minute, muttering, as he scans the room. He doesn't seem to recognize me. I don't know why, but I don't say anything to him either. After a minute, Lumpy suddenly says to my brother, "Yizhi, son, I didn't finish the bottle last night, get it and give me a drink." My brother pulls out a bottle as if he had it ready in advance, and sure enough there's just a little left at the bottom. Elder Brother murmurs something polite about there being so little, but Lumpy Ginger replies in earnest, "No need to open a new bottle. A little bit is fine." There seems to be about two glasses, and after Lumpy Ginger downs them both, he wipes his mouth and asks my brother what time it is. It's 2 pm, and Lumpy Ginger, suddenly flustered, says, "Aiya, fuck, it's late, your Ninth Gramma must be waiting on me." Then he climbs on his beat-up bicycle and, swaying from side to side, rides off.

I start telling my brother off for not being very civil, and he and Father both burst out laughing. They don't dare be civil; rude as they are, he still comes over almost every day to ask for a drink. If they were at all nice to him, he would start coming at lunch and dinner, and in the middle of the day when he's supposed to be at work. They don't want him to come over more, so they just keep some liquor at the bottom of a bottle for him. He hadn't been over for a while, because Ninth Grandmother got angry with him and was threatening to go back to her parents' home. He had to stay at home to keep her from leaving.

Lumpy Ginger's last name isn't "Ginger." He's a Liang like us. We have the same lineage, and since he's over sixty, if we were following the generational order, I would call him Fourth Grandfather. But no one knows his real name. When I ask Father and some of the village elders, no one can remember it. As for why he has this strange name, everyone just smiles. If you look at the back of his head in profile it's really bumpy, just like a piece of ginger. In fact, even from the front you can see mountain peaks sticking out.

As I remember him, Lumpy Ginger was always that skinny, but his back wasn't hunched, and he didn't seem so worn out. He was always humming a tune and sometimes burst out into a Shaanxi folk song. I've never heard anything about his parents, and his home is just an old broken-down house that leans to one side. He used to drift around most of the year, only showing up from time to time. He doesn't cook, so he would eat here and there, always appearing right at dinnertime at whichever household seemed to be doing well. But his eyes sparkled with life, so no one begrudged him a little bit of food. In our family, every time we steamed some buns, Lumpy Ginger would come over, humming a tune. He wouldn't let anyone else knead the dough or cut it into sections. He could knead two buns at a time, one in each hand. We would watch his hands as they rolled around and around, sometimes tossing the dough in the air, sometimes moving quickly on the chopping board. It seemed like magic, how quickly two perfectly round mounds would appear. His buns always smelled especially delicious, and when he took the lid off the pot, the sweet smell would have us falling over with hunger. Of course he would eat lunch with us, downing three or four buns in one sitting, driving us to distraction. We were so poor then, and flour was rationed. In one meal he could eat three day's worth of our flour.

When Lumpy Ginger finally came back to stay, it was news for a year. Even years later, people still like to talk about it. This is how the story goes: A light rain was falling. The village bachelors were gathered as usual by the main road, making eyes and shouting at women passing by, or telling incoherent dirty jokes, which they followed with raucous laughter. At dusk, just as the rain stopped, a bus pulled up out of nowhere with a bang. Lumpy Ginger got off first. The men could see he was wearing a Western suit and a crooked tie. He was also leading a very young woman by the hand. Or, actually, he was pulling her with one hand and holding her waist with the other. He announced, proudly to all his former buddies, "This is my wife." The idiots were dumbstruck. The girl was pretty, with a clean face and hair combed into neat braids. Well, she was a little short and had a big butt and thick thighs, but you could see right away that she was an honest woman. Lumpy Ginger huffed and puffed, telling them all to come help get their things. That day at noon they held a wedding feast in town. There were cigarettes and toasts, a big party. Later we heard the girl was from Xi'an. Everyone thought Lumpy Ginger was pulling a fast one. He was so old and so ugly, how could this girl, so neat and clean, be following him so willingly?

A few village busybodies complained to the village secretary, who retorted: "Let's see you get a woman like that."

Lumpy Ginger set up a temporary home in a run-down building at the brick factory. The next day he took his wife in to sign the marriage certificate and to ask for land and food. He also visited everyone in the family to ask for furniture and household items. From there he began to settle down. Two years later his wife even gave birth to a fat baby boy, and Lumpy Ginger was ecstatic with joy. That old bachelor—he was over fifty—had never thought he'd have a son one day. By that time Lumpy Ginger had already spent most of the money that he'd brought back. And his wife was a good woman, but she had no sense of household economy. She ate well and didn't work. On the day her son celebrated his one-month birthday, Lumpy Ginger didn't arrange a feast, but he did take his wife and the boy from house to house, carrying a bag and announcing the good news, saying "Here's your new grandfather," or "You've got another uncle." Although the boy was still an infant, his rank in the generations was high, and everyone in the family was supposed to call him by some title. In any case, when they saw Lumpy Ginger with bag in hand, they understood. They had to give grain or money or clothes that their children had outgrown. They also gave his wife some advice about raising a child.

With the new addition, Lumpy Ginger's house was too small to live in, and they were even poorer. So he started to look for a house and some odd jobs. The former secretary arranged a deal. A village family, which had left a long time before, agreed to let Lumpy Ginger live in their house. It had four rooms and was half-renovated, a really nice place, so Lumpy Ginger took his wife and child to live there, and they had a home.

A few years later, in the spring, I came back to sweep my mother's grave for Qingming Festival. Just as I opened the door of our old house, Lumpy Ginger appeared, with a young woman and a three- or four-year-old boy trailing behind. I guessed they were his wife and child, as the boy looked just like a "little Lumpy Ginger." Sure enough, Lumpy Ginger, with great seriousness, introduced them to me. "This is your ninth grandmother and your young uncle." I looked at the young woman. Although she was not pretty, her face was soft, and her hair, as I had been told, was combed into neat, long braids. She seemed easygoing and good tempered. Everyone liked her. Lumpy Ginger looked around the house, and even availed himself of his age to scold me a little. He touched the table and chair, covered in thick dust, and taking down the hoe on the wall, said, "Look it's all rusty! What a shame!" He seemed to like them, so I said he could have them, which made him happy. He had his wife pick up the hoe, while he lifted the table and chair, and with things under both arms he said goodbye, asking me to come pay him a visit. I watched as they walked away and couldn't help but laugh, although there was something painful about it too. I thought of a scene in Lu Xun's "Hometown." Considering a century has passed since he wrote that story, why are scenes such as this still so common?

I went over to Lumpy Ginger's house the next day. He was in the doorway sharpening the hoe. When he saw me coming, he looked surprised. He probably hadn't thought I would come. But he shook it off and happily called to his wife to bring some tea and something for me to sit on. He squatted down by the stove and rolled a cigarette. He seemed calm, like the head of the household—entirely different from the way he acted outside the house. I looked around. Everything was neat and clean. A small television covered with a piece of red velvet cloth was already sitting on the table he'd brought from our house. His wife sat on the side of the bed, knitting a sweater, and there were bunches of red peppers, corn, garlic, and farm tools hanging on the wall, like in most houses. It was warm, comfortable, relaxed, and well-stocked.

At that time Lumpy Ginger made coal briquettes for a living. He earned twenty yuan for each ton. On a good day he made more than thirty. He was over sixty, but he got up every morning just before dawn and went to work in town. At noon he hustled home for lunch; he never went to the restaurants. But he developed a taste for drink. He couldn't afford it, so he asked people he knows for a little glass.

One day I was relaxing by the door when, in the distance, I saw a stumpy figure pushing a bicycle. Wasn't it Lumpy Ginger's wife? I took a few steps and called out—sure enough, it was her. She had cut her long braids, and behind her on the bike was a little girl. Ah, so she's given Lumpy Ginger a daughter. The girl had a bow in her hair and a little skirt, and her hair was nicely cut. And she didn't have Lumpy Ginger's "lumps." A flowered parasol over her seat protected her from the sun.

Young Ninth Grandmother spoke to me more that day than she ever had before. She wouldn't stop talking about how her son misbehaved and wouldn't study and how the family planning office was giving them all sorts of trouble about making them pay a fine. Then she complained about how Lumpy Ginger loved to drink. As I listened, my sympathy began to grow. How much longer could she put up with it? Or perhaps it wasn't so bad? Rural people have confronted difficult problems for generations. They do what they have to do. It is all part of ordinary life. They always suffer through it.

These thoughts become a kind of prophecy. A few months later, Lumpy Ginger dies. His wife ends up with someone else— there had been signs of it already that summer. He was young, a little over forty, another village bachelor. He had been away working for the past few years and had some money in hand; it's not clear when they started to spend time together. In the village, when there's an older husband and a younger wife, the bachelors are known to flirt. She'd been asking for a divorce, but Lumpy Ginger wouldn't agree, so his wife ran off with the man. One winter night, after he'd been drinking, Lumpy Ginger was hit by a car. In town there's a sharp corner, and every few years someone in the village is killed there. When she found out Lumpy Ginger had been killed, his wife, grief-stricken, came back to arrange his funeral. Someone in the family tells her that the man who killed him had paid a 20,000 yuan fine, that the money was with the village branch secretary. But if she wanted to spend it, she would need approval from the family. She took the children with her and left.

There's some talk among the family about having "Little Lumpy Ginger" come back: after all, he's Lumpy Ginger's seed. But if he comes back who will take care of him? No one wants to be saddled with that, so the matter is dropped.

Qingdao

After we get up one morning, Qingdao calls Father to say he's been to market and he'll start cooking soon. He says come over early. Qingdao says that he's got to do something to celebrate my return.

Qingdao's home is near the highway. It occupies nearly four parcels of land. In the '80s the village's biggest factory, the Liang Village Coal and Construction Corporation (which we called Coal Construction for short), was close by. When it was at its most productive, people from the surrounding area would come haul coal, and every day large transport trucks would race in and out, competing with row after row of wooden wheelbarrows pushed by ordinary rural people. For us kids, its large courtyard was the best place to go when we weren't in school. The tall, black mountains of coal had a special attraction. We would watch the huge machines lifting and shoveling; watch people's white towels turn black with a single wipe; and play hide and seek, getting dangerously close to the coal itself. Around Coal and Construction there were a number of small businesses, restaurants, general goods stores, public baths, and so on. Without a doubt the places that did the best business were the restaurants. That was when Qingdao learned to cook.

In the early years, there hadn't been any houses here nor were there fields—just the large pond. Every year, as summer changed to autumn, it would fill with dark water chestnuts, sweet and plump. Then, slowly but surely, the lake transformed into a landfill, and when it was filled, row after row of houses were built upon it. Of course not just anyone could fill in this valuable land. The houses belong to Qingdao, an accountant and the squad leader, as well as businessmen. Qingdao used to be village secretary, and the spot he occupied was without a doubt the best in the village. He painstakingly filled in the lake with truck after truck of sand and dirt. The coal factory went bankrupt long ago, and there is no trace of its large courtyard. Now Qingdao's house appears to be off in the middle of nowhere, neither here nor there; only the size and quality of the gate hints at its former prosperity.

When we arrive we greet my aunt, a woman with clean features but clouded eyes, who is in the back courtyard making tea. The year before last she had breast cancer, and both of her breasts were removed at the hospital where my older sister works. When women go there, they push aside their clothes to look; they don't care if strangers can see. Aunt still has her trademark long, thin braids, but her hair has thinned and yellowed, and together with her uncontrollable blinking and weeping eyes, she seems old in a way that is both tragic and comic. Their general store is in the courtyard in front of their house, but the few goods that remain are covered in dust. There are loofah gourds growing in the courtyard, sprouts shooting up all around. Next to the well is a natural wetland filled with chickens and ducks. In the stifling summer noon, a faint smell permeates the courtyard. A dog's bark echoes, scaring the chickens into flight, their feathers fluttering down to the ground. The kitchen, in the corner of the courtyard, is open, its stove low and covered in a jumble of water jugs, vegetables, flour, and other odds and ends. The chickens and ducks could jump up on it if they wanted to.

Qingdao has us look at the lunch he is preparing, deep-fried pieces of fish, chicken legs, and green peppers stuffed with meat. There are little meat pastries and things to go with the eight different meat dishes. Everything is fried, so they can be simply reheated when it's time to eat. This is the expectation in the village for hosting guests. There are also about ten vegetable dishes, already prepared, and cold dishes that are waiting to be placed on the table. I can't believe he's prepared everything so quickly, but Qingdao just snorts. "Don't look down on your younger brother, Dao. To set a few tables, to host thirty or fifty guests—that's no problem. The day before yesterday I hosted a three-table feast, an engagement party in the village." Off to one side, Father mentions that this is Qingdao's main source of income now, otherwise, where would he get money to gamble with?

"Where would I get money!?" Qingdao says in a sharp voice, "I have three poultry farms. I sell a few eggs. I sell a few chickens. That's where the money comes from." Father retorts, "There are three poultry farms—but are any still yours? You may have started them, but I'd like to see you take a single egg from any of them now!" Qingdao falls silent, but after a while, he replies, sullenly, "This year I'm going to raise more chickens."

Then I understand. Qingdao has three sons, three daughters-in-law, and five grandchildren. When his sons were first married, he gave each a farm. One per family. But as to the size of the farms, and the relative merits of each farm's location, all the daughters-in-law had their opinions, and they fought between themselves until they weren't on speaking terms. Qingdao had given up control of the poultry farms and so had lost his source of income along with his right to say anything. His daughters-in-law are always glaring at him, but he can't say a word.

In the back there is a small two-story building with a total of twelve rooms. Qingdao told me proudly that he had designed it himself. He has three sons and each son has two rooms; no preferential treatment. But all six rooms are empty. No one has come to live there. On one hand the family conflicts mean the daughters-in-law don't want to live there. On the other hand, the poultry farms need people to look after them, so the sons' main houses are at the farms. So the "castle" Qingdao built lies deserted.

Be that as it may, Qingdao is still very proud. He gave his sons this family property. He asks Elder Sister and me to go around back to see his eldest son's poultry farm, pulling up a few ripe vegetables as we pass by.

The poultry farm is on the cropland that leads to the river-bank. When we get close, the air fills with the smell of an enormous pool of chicken droppings, a poultry by-product. The pool is covered, but there is no way to block the smell. Qingdao said the manure is worth a lot of money—there are fisheries nearby that fight for it—but for some reason fewer people have come for it recently, and the pool is growing.

Truth be told, it isn't a bad rural poultry farm. There are three or four large sheds, where the chickens are raised in long narrow baskets. They are fed food and water that contain anti-biotics to prevent illness. The cement beneath them is washed clean. But it seems like a terrible place to live. The owner's house is in the middle of the farm, and two large dogs are tied up at the door—to prevent theft, they say. The owner's two children are playing amidst the stink. His wife is at the well by the doorway washing vegetables and clothes and letting the wastewater splash into the chicken droppings, which dramati-cally increases the smell. The vegetables that Qingdao picked were grown in this muck: when you step in it, reeking water wells up. I quickly jump away. At lunch we eat these "seasonal vegetables," but luckily they don't taste of chicken shit.

The "castle's" toilet is built in a corner outside the courtyard, in a very low, very small earthen structure. You have to stoop to go in. There's a short plastic curtain in the doorway for privacy, and if you squat down you can see the people inside, but since it's mostly for family use no one seems to mind. The hole is lined with brick, and two bricks serve as a place to put your feet, with the requisite maggots crawling around. Every time she goes, my sister sighs about how dirty it is, but for the village it isn't bad.

When I think about it, the worst part about northern rural villages is the toilets. The side-walls of every family's house are natural toilets. Only the more prosperous and particular families, like Qingdao's, have toilet holes. Most people don't bother and do their business by the side of the wall, letting it all dry in the wind.

Of all the disturbing memories I have from my childhood, nothing is worse than rainy days. The earth next to the walls became squishy, and excrement was everywhere, so there was no place to walk. Even if we were on our very tiptoes, we would always step on a "bomb." It wouldn't be taken care of until there was a marriage or some other major event. For the village houses facing the road, the space between their low, shoddily constructed courtyard walls and the walls of the house was always a toilet. People walking by could see the heads of others squatting, and talking over the wall was common. But by far the most awkward moment was when someone from a different generation walked by, because when you stood to pull up your pants, your bare body was exposed. For a young girl coming into adulthood, that kind of embarrassment was something you never forgot.

I must admit that, being accustomed to city life, I can't use this kind of toilet. Yet there is no way to avoid this gap between the urban and the rural, especially because these little differences in lifestyle can lead to real conflicts between family members.

The morning's meal is indeed rich. It is a taste of childhood, although it is too oily, too salty, and too spicy for me. Qingdao is full of stories and jokes, and everyone laughs loudly. The two eldest sisters-in-law are there to help with the guests, and they easily divide up the tasks. One washes the vegetables and the dishes and watches the stove, while the other is responsible for preparing the food and carrying out the platters. She is also in charge of pouring the liquor and taking the dishes to and from the kitchen. For the most part they don't talk to us, and when we meet their gaze, they quickly look away, their faces almost expressionless. Rural women do not usually reveal their feelings to outsiders. They hold everything in, and occasional visitors have trouble understanding their relationships and conflicts. In reality, conflicts among them can turn ugly quickly, even if they are the most kindhearted of people, and they will fight ruthlessly. But when they appear together in public, they will work in concert, presenting an image of harmony.

After the meal, tea is brewed. Qingdao is half drunk. His naturally purplish face has turned completely red, and his eyes wander as he laughs and laughs, his cheerful, optimistic nature shining through. I ask Qingdao to tell one of his stories with the rhymes. I'd rather learn about this former political figure's feelings and life stories than listen to him talk about politics.

You say you want me to tell a rhyming story? Little Sister must be teasing. Here I am, Liang Qingdao of Liang Village, drunk as a skunk, causing trouble. If that gets into the history books we'll all lose face—they'll say you're taking the piss.

During the second year of the grain tax, I got along well with old Cui, the head of the Grain Office. When I'd go over to the Grain Office, we'd always get a little rowdy. One day, at noon, the work was finished and we had lunch there. After we were finished, I made up a little ditty to tease him. I said, Brother Cui, the past two days your reputation has been hurting. You haven't listened to the masses. They're all saying:

The head of the Grain Office in our town,
Deals in grain tax like you won't believe
When they go to pay, the report to South Du
Good or bad, it all looks fine.
For North Du, though, they always say
Good or bad, no one will eat it.
When Liang Village brings in a report,
If you sign without checking—that's no good.
Now, you could provide for all the folks in old South Du,
Because they've cheated all the people in Liang Village.

When he heard this his face turned red. He ordered some good cigarettes and liquor, and smoked and drank and drank and smoked, and when he left he made up a song to piss me off.

When it was time for the grain levy, some higher-ups decided to come inspect things. When he heard this, he got anxious and started barking out orders. I said, Brother Cui, you said you won't curry favor with higher-ups, but this morning you looked like a lackey to me, that doesn't square. He got mad. He said, Liang Qingdao you're spouting nonsense again, when they come by I've got to pass out cigarettes, right? Just then he heard that the mayor had entered the courtyard, and he went rushing out, ordering Jindian to tell the cripple to stop the scales, not to slip up. Jindian said, the grain just came in, how can we stop the scales? I laughed at them: "You all should watch out. You'd better knock the clay off the scale weights." When Cui heard that, he got jumping mad, he said, "piss off, you fuck, since when is there mud on the weights, see if I treat you to so much as a drink of water ever again." Actually I'd made it all up, just to rib him. I just wanted to play a game on him, play him for a fool.

After that, Jindian became the office head, and a few troublemakers said that I should make up a song for him.

I said I wouldn't, but then:

Old Cui retired and was replaced by Jindian, and Liang
   Village grain surpassed all other years.
In the past, when Zhuang Village handed in its grain,
   they knew it was poor before the tester was out of the
   bag.
This year when Zhuang Village handed in its grain, every
   single household passed muster.

They all chuckled at how I'd praised the new head; looks like I made up a song after all. Was Jindian any better than the old guy? Hell no, they're all just screwing around. It was just a joke.

That year there was also the business with the power management station. Everyone says, "The Party is the father, the government is the mother, industry and taxation are two wolves, and the tiger is King Power." In the village we were all busy fighting a drought when the transformer burnt out. I went and bought a new one, but that offended the people at the power management station. You're supposed to buy through them, so they can get their cut. The Station Master said that if we didn't buy through them, they wouldn't turn the power on. I went to find the Station Master to talk some sense, but Mr. Yang Shumin talked in circles and gave me nothing. I said, "You've got a monopoly, but you charge what you like. That's not fair. Don't think rural people won't understand what you're doing. The station manager goes visiting, and maybe the villages don't all treat him the same. If he feels like he's been treated bad at lunchtime, come afternoon he shuts off the power. Isn't that unconscionable? We take time out of fighting the drought to come kiss ass, and still, as soon as we turn around, you turn off the power. When we come to ask you why, you say let's see how you treat us next time we visit the village." When the Station Master heard this he was so mad he spun in circles. He said, Go on back; we'll give you electricity later. So I went to find the Bureau Chief; he also told me to leave. He told me he'd call the Station Master.

I said, I can't go back. The people are all waiting at the village entrance with bricks in their hands. If we can't fight the drought, they're going to beat me. Later I thought to go to the CCP county committee to see what I could do about it. When the Bureau Chief heard he immediately picked up his phone and yelled at Yang Shuming; he didn't care what the reason was, that power needed to be on. He said, When you go back, thank the Station Master. Thank who? Isn't this his job? Why would I thank him! Before I got home, they told me that Yang Shuming was already waiting in our courtyard, hopping mad!

Let's not talk about home life. Even an upright official can't handle his own family. I've been village secretary my whole life, but I can't manage things at home. Tell me, is that galling or what? Some people say I've been secretary my whole life, but haven't done any good for Liang Village. That's bullshit: everyone's living their two-story dreams now, I'm the one with nothing. I've drunk a belly full of liquor, but my hands are empty. I've managed to make a little money these past few years, by collecting manure.

If you're born and raised in the countryside, you will find that those who seem simple, slow, and inarticulate often possess an amazing sense of humor. Indeed, you find humor and wisdom everywhere: At the lunch spot beneath the pagoda tree, among those who gather at the teahouse to idly drink tea, or even as people greet one another while they work the day away. Frequent bursts of candid, knowing, wily laughter will echo across the sky, bringing a measure of vitality and force to the silent village. That's the kind of person Qingdao is.

Qingdao talks for three hours straight, and as he recounts his rhymes—especially his political rhymes—he gets especially worked up. He takes his understanding of village life and politics and turns it into something like art, bringing laughter and curses together at will, forming a coherent whole.

This popular way to express opinions on politics and government, while it may be funny and witty, also implies resistance, which gives it extra strength. However, whenever something involves a specific individual, such as the situation with the current branch secretary and village head, or his uncle who does the village accounting, he always promptly cuts himself off. Another table had been set up as Qingdao talks, and someone who seems to have been connected to the accountant waits there. When we talk, he keeps himself busy outside, doing this and that. This is a common sight in villages; in the branch secretary, accountant, and village head's homes, there are always people helping out.

Qingdao stands up, stretches his waist, and looks at the card tables, rubbing his hands together. He takes a couple sips of tea and heads out to the toilet. He's getting ready. He's already persuaded father, who had a little nap while we were talking, to stay. Now he's refreshed. I know the war will go on at least until evening.

That night Father plays until midnight. Elder Brother calls several times before he comes home. Father's health won't permit him to stay up all night, but he's addicted to cards, and once he gets in front of the table he won't get up. But that's nothing compared with Qingdao. Father says Qingdao is the "General of Loss." Everyone knew he likes to play, but he often loses, so people trap him. He goes every time, and every time he loses. He takes it all in stride.

Father tells me a story. Not too long ago Qingdao had a fight with his wife, and then with his third daughter-in-law's family. So he went out to sell eggs and disappeared for a few days. He didn't answer his phone, and his wife couldn't find him anywhere. On the fourth day they came over to ask Father, afraid he couldn't hack it. What would they do if he'd killed himself? When Father heard that he burst out laughing. He said he would never do that—if Qingdao couldn't hack it, who could? On the fourth day, Qingdao appeared at Father's house. He'd just gone to play some cards. The first two days he won; the second two days he lost and even owed a little. When his wife complained, Qingdao pointed at her and her long braids and shouted, "I just went out to sell eggs, but you went around destroying my reputation."

6

Rural Politics Under Attack

In 2000, statistical data from a sample investigation into seventeen villages with 9,181 households and 39,104 people revealed the following: Those engaged in collective farming earned 26,890,000 yuan, for an average of 393.7 yuan per person; family businesses took in 14,8210,000 yuan for an average of 2,170 yuan per person. Property assets were valued at 3,848 yuan, while gross per capita income was 2,607.55 yuan; the average net income was 1,989.39 yuan; the average cash income was 1,495.54 yuan. By 2006, the rural per capita net income was 3,647 yuan. In 2019, the average discretionary income of urban and rural residents was 22,070 yuan, an increase of 9.5 percent over the previous year. In particular, discretionary income for urban residents was 31,315 yuan, an increase of 7.6 percent over the previous year, while that of rural residents was 16,673, an increase of 9.8 percent.

—Rang County Annals Revenue

Politics

Even though he has been going to bed late, Father is still up by 6 am, walking around the courtyard singing Chinese opera at the top of his lungs. "Hu Fenglian standing in the skiff, sighs in sorrow, her family gone away; she calls, Young Master Tian, listen closely to what I have to say . . ."

To this he adds the occasional hacking cough. For dozens of years it has been his habit to clear his throat in the early morning.

The tune is slow and mournful, the voice smooth and sad, the story a tragedy. Father has sung it so many times over the years that my sisters and I know it by heart.

> I live on the river, where my mother birthed many boys
>   and girls,
> Only I, Fenglian, remain. I suffered misfortune, I lost my
>   mother,
> and my father and I, over the difficult years,
> Fished in the river.
> My father went to the market at the break of day,
> Young Master Lu took our fish but didn't pay;
> When my father complained,
> Young Master Lu beat him, broke his legs,
> Beat him forty times with the lash,
> Soon my father breathed his last,
> And departed for the Yellow Springs.

Father has loved to sing Chinese opera all his life. Once he told us proudly that when he was a boy, he almost ran off with a traveling opera company. They liked his voice and stage presence. Only his father's strong objections kept him from leaving. When I was young, we would go to bed after dinner on cold evenings. In the yellow light of an oil lamp, Father would lie at the bottom of the bed, warming Mother's ice-cold feet. My sisters and I would huddle close together for warmth in the other bed, covered in a thin, tattered quilt. Then my father would slowly start to sing, "Hu Fenglian, standing in the skiff . . ." In our old house's eastern room, with Father and Mother's bed on the back wall, and my sisters and I in our bed beneath the front window, the clear, cold moonlight would pour in, and tragedy would flow into our hearts, filling us with a mixture of comfort and sadness that is hard to convey in words.

After breakfast, at Father's insistence, we sit down to talk. He has found what has emerged from my interviews extremely interesting and tells me over and over where I should go and who I should talk to. He even asks about the project's ultimate goals. I suggest he talk about his political struggles, which are, after all, also a part of village history.

You tell me what politics is. I've never been an official in my life, but politics has followed me everywhere.

In the twelfth month of 1966, the Cultural Revolution finally arrived in the village. All of us, young and old, became Red Guards fighting the capitalist roaders—production team cadres and people in high positions. Cadres all ate and drank on public money, and we thought we had to fix them up. But who wanted to be in charge? No one. The villagers all said I should do it—they chose me to be the Red Guard Group Leader. Later, I became a production team Cultural Revolution Committee Member. When something happened in the village, I had to struggle against people, like storekeeper Liang Guangming, for example, but my struggle sessions were all genuine. That guy was bad, he should have been struggled against long before. He beat people and embezzled grain. One day, the accountant Liang Xingjian hurried over and started kowtowing. Why? He had written something incorrectly on a small red flag: "Chairman Mao" was upside down. It was just a mistake, but people said he was against Chairman Mao. I was still in bed, but he was in front of the house on his knees. He begged me to forgive him.

In July 1967 I was overthrown by the "new Cultural Revolution," a newly formed group in the village. They said I was protecting the Imperial Clique and the cadres. They started struggling against me; it was all totally fabricated.

So finally I left and went to a construction company in the county seat, the Xiancheng Construction Company. I found your uncle and asked for some sort of job. Some of the young people at the construction company had formed a 7/1 Brigade to harass all the former workers. The workers saw I supported justice, so they talked it over with me, and we formed an "8/1 Brigade," under the leadership of the Destroy-Capitalism Headquarters. I was 8/1 Brigade #1, and my main job was to lead everyone in the revolution. There was another group called the 8/1/8 Brigade. They opposed us. We fought, shooting blindly at one another, but no one died. In the end, the 8/1/8 Brigade won, so I was in the wrong party again. Then I was struggled against by the 7/1 Brigade, so I took off. Later they sent my documents to the village government. They wanted me to be sentenced. From then on I was always trying to escape.

In 1968, after the February Black Wind, your fifth uncle and I went to Hubei to make cotton quilts. We came back in June. We returned to the construction company and then joined some others to build warehouses in another location. People thought we were trying to get away. While I was there, I ran into someone from the village. I treated him to a nice meal and lots of liquor and made him promise he wouldn't mention that he'd seen me when he got back to the village. Well, when he got back he reported it to the Revolutionary Committee. At that time, Liang Xinglong was a battalion commander, and he sent someone right over to capture me. I couldn't escape in time. They tied me up and escorted me back. We had to pass by your mother's family home on the way to the village, and luckily it was July, so as we went by, folks saw me. They said to my guards, come have some tea, and then they quickly hid me in your grandmother's house. They couldn't find me, so they reported to the production team branch secretary in your grandmother's village that a counterrevolutionary had escaped, but he didn't care. The folks in your grandmother's village said, don't bother looking for him, if you do we'll beat you to death, you bastards.

Since I was in hiding I didn't dare go home during the day. Sometimes I would go sit in a tobacco field, and sometimes I would sit in the shade of a tree, far from the village, and other times I would run over to a relative's house. It was midsummer, and you couldn't escape that heat, especially in the tobacco field. In July and August, the tobacco was particularly dense and half a man's height. It grew thick, and there wasn't a breath of air. In the morning it would be relatively cool, but by 2 or 3 pm, it was hot. I would sneak back in the evening. Your third sister wasn't even a year old yet. Chunsheng saw me and reported it to the production team. Liang Xinglong sent some people over to capture me; they blocked the corner by the Wang house and the road to the vegetable plots, places I had to pass if I was going to escape. I took the road from the Han family house to the northern hill and from there went over to the main road, where I saw seven or eight Red Guards. They were waiting for me. This time there was nowhere to run.

On July 3, 1968, I was captured and returned home. I remember it clearly—I'll never forget it. Liang Xinglong's people said, there will be a struggle meeting tomorrow afternoon at the school playing field. A report will be given to the chairman, and you'll have to answer our questions clearly. They were afraid I would escape, so I was guarded closely. Why did they have struggle sessions in the afternoon? What they really wanted was to wait until it was dark, and then they could beat you up. Your elder sister remembers it well. They tied me up in the meeting place, and the production team activists and core members sat close together. A few of the village ruffians sat in front, and Liang Xinglong sat to the side giving orders. Your first uncle later told me that Liang Xinglong told them they could beat me to death if they wanted. The first charge was raiding an arsenal. The second was insulting Chairman

Mao. The third was supporting Liu Shaoqi. All were punishable by death. They asked me to kneel, but I refused. I knew something bad was going to happen; I said Chairman Mao forbids feudalistic superstitions, but that didn't go over well. Then I said that I was the scum of society and I asked the higher-ups to deal with me. Actually, I didn't admit to any of the specific charges. Li Xueping is a relative of ours. He took the Red Book and beat me with it until blood ran from my head. I was bruised from head to toe. At first it was the activists who beat me, but later things got messy and everyone was beating me. I couldn't even see who it was. The clothes I was wearing were torn to shreds and covered in blood. When I returned on the road, people followed at a distance, and at the fork I could see your mother waiting for me. When she saw I was covered in blood she began to cry. She said, I rolled out some noodles; you eat them, I'll be back in a minute. She went to find Xinglong's mother, and she said, Fifth Mother, we're all Liangs, no more than five generations distant, you go tell my Seventh Brother, don't beat him so hard. Just then Xinglong came back, and Fifth Mother told him, she said when we had nothing, when there was nothing to eat or drink, Guangzheng's family sold bread and an oil press, and they helped us. This business about Guangzheng, you can call it whatever you like, just try not to beat him so hard. Xinglong said, we're going to beat him to death to show our strength. Don't talk to me about the past, it has nothing to do with me. Xinglong hadn't seen your mother sitting there. When she came back her body was trembling with rage.

The next evening they started again. This time they were going to settle my guilt. They took me to the wall surrounding the school, where a large crowd of students and children threw bricks and tiles at me. When they took me back to the field, someone shouted, "Down with Liang Guangzheng!"

and they told me to confess. They found witnesses who made up all sorts of stories that I'd insulted Chairman Mao on such and such an occasion. They said when Liang Guangli was building a wall, I'd cursed Chairman Mao and the schoolchildren had all heard me. Afterwards, they put out the lights, and the bricks and tiles started hitting me, on my chest and face, it hurt for months afterwards. Then Li's mother said, Liang Xinglong, that's not right, the wall was built at night. The children get out before dark, so how could they have heard Guangzheng insult Chairman Mao? This isn't right. Xinglong didn't know what to do, so he said, we'll discuss this later. That was the end of it that night.

So that's why I have you all visit Li's mother every year at Spring Festival. The year before last she died, and your sister came back with two hundred kuai to do a proper funeral.

This happened in July 1968. After that last session they stopped for a bit, and all sorts of people came to ask me what had happened. At the end of 1968, they started purging the work team of class enemies, and the production team said, you'd better get your situation squared away. But by February 1969, I was a target again. From February all the way until the wheat was tipped with gold, they kept me shut up in the town high school. Everyone there had to bring our grain to the Xu house and cook collectively.

The investigation went on for months, but in the end settled nothing, and I got another "we'll discuss this later." Even after you were released they would still come get you. I was beaten twice. And I was struggled against in one way or another dozens of times. They hung a sign on me that said "Counterrevolutionary" and "Rebel." Later they said there was another movement, and I'd be given hard labor to do. In October 1969, I took your eldest sister and fled to Xinjiang to look for your eldest uncle. I came back in December. On the second day after I came back, I was taken to Zhi Diao reservoir to work. I was also struggled against there. To make the reservoir we were supposed to dredge the Diao River and divert it, but it didn't work. At this point it has all been demolished, but the ground still isn't level. The fortunate thing is that, since I never admitted to any wrongdoings, things got easier for me in the '70s.

In March 1970, because I opposed Guangjie, Guangyong, and Guangming's tyranny, they took me behind our house and beat me until I was bloody. In 1975 we made a kiln. In 1977 we built a house and your younger sister was born.

I wasn't rehabilitated until 1978. That year something major happened. On the 15th of November, Liang Xinglong blocked the road in front of our house. Your second aunt had already sealed off the road to the left because we always went to the right anyway. But if you blocked the road to the right there wasn't any way out. How were we supposed to live? I took a hammer and smashed the wall down. After that we came to blows. Your elder sister and brother remember it clearly. I took a vegetable knife, and your brother had that iron ball and your sister an iron hoe. That was the first time that iron ball came into its own. They reported us to the commune and the commune secretary said that he was definitely going to tell the production team secretary that I was a serious counter-revolutionary and was fighting him tooth and nail. I heard about this, and when the commune secretary held a meeting I went over to have him settle things once and for all. He got fed up with the whole thing and said he'd take care of it that very day, so he sent the deputy secretary to take care of it. Liang Xinglong said, have Guangzheng come over to my place, and I'll take down the wall. I said no way, he should come to our place. He cut us off from the road, which keeps us from earning a living—why should I come to him and apologize. Later he said he would only let people go by, not vehicles. I wasn't having that either. It wasn't until Tomb-sweeping Festival of '79 that it was finally resolved.

Me, I can't abide injustice. What I can't abide, I deal with. People call me a troublemaker. When we were "getting rid of the old and bringing in the new" we chose a new village secretary, and a few families in Liang Village fought hard over it. Liang Guangwang was a close relative on the male side, he counted as "bringing in the new." To protect him, I went around from morning 'til night, looking for others in the village who would work with us. I thought it was something for the clan, a kind of loyalty. No one thanked me. Your mother said, "He's always harassing us, he nearly killed you, and still you're working with them. Have you no shame?" She was really angry. She went to her parents, and I had to go after her several times before she would come back.

Your mother got sick in 1980, on the 16th of November. It was because of the irrigation fields. Xingzhong waterlogged our fields, and your mother fought with him. Xingzhong pushed her to the ground, and she hurt her hand. Between her temper and being pushed down, she had a stroke that paralyzed her. She was only forty.

From then on I carried your mother on my back everywhere, looking for treatment.

Father uses a lot of jargon like "State Purchase and Marketing Monopoly" and "February Black Wind," terms I'm not familiar with. But for Father they come naturally, making it clear how deeply the politics of the time permeated the lives of ordinary people. It's just that Father's role in the movement was as a "saboteur" or a "target of the struggle." I imagine Father hiding from capture, sitting in that enormous tobacco field hour after hour, surrounded by nothing but silence, with the blazing hot sun shining down on him. How did he feel? How did he endure the hunger? The thirst? The heat? In the '60s and '70s, the village was entirely engulfed by politics, but it had its own logic that was fundamentally distinct from politics. The village households' grievances, power struggles, and relationships were all part of this. They decided one's attitude in the struggle sessions and the fate of those being struggled against. In the end, the case against father was determined by an elderly woman who challenged the case and its preposterous logic.

Father has always been a village man who "doesn't know his place," and that's how he has participated in modern political history. Although nothing truly earth-shattering ever happened, politics has affected his life and family in direct and absolute ways. He's belligerent, and he's not afraid to "meddle." Mother and the rest of the family bore the brunt of this. His history of being struggled against is our family's history of suffering. Mother's illness and early death, above and beyond the physical causes, were a result of constant fear. Whenever we criticize Father for this, however, he swears in rage, calling us selfish.

He has, however, to a small degree "lost his virtue in old age": he has finally been accepted in village power circles and is quite proud to have been received with courtesy in the former and present secretaries' homes. That being said, if he notices any misconduct, such as problems with the village's finances, or a family treated unfairly, no matter if they're part of the village, if he knows them or not, his "gusto" returns, just like when he was younger, and he starts rushing around on behalf of other people.

As I remember it, Father has always filed lawsuits for other folks, and people were always coming around to consult him. When I was in my second year of middle school, some children lived at our house for around two months while a family member filed a lawsuit. At that time, we could basically only afford one meal a day. Mother was paralyzed in bed, and Father wasn't working because he was going with the family member to see the judge, or he was giving them emotional support, or discussing the case with close friends. In the end, they lost. When you bring this up Father starts swearing again: Could I just stand by and do nothing? These people were bad through and through. We had to punish them. I've heard these words so many times over the years.

Father has never admitted that there's anything wrong with his behavior; indeed, he doesn't think there is. Disregarding his identity as my father and considering him as he is, I see a man filled with passion for the "political," a "thorn in the side," a "troublemaker," "a meddler," and it is he who has preserved justice and morality in the village. People like Father play the role that would be given to village intellectuals. They have knowledge, experience, and an innate suspicion of power and those who use it on their own behalf. They aren't afraid to help out when injustice rears its ugly head.

The Former Branch Secretary

Liang Qingdao, the former branch secretary of the village, is fifty-seven years old; he has a broad, purplish face, and eyes that sparkle with sharp intelligence. A self-made man, he is an outstanding chef and an astute strategist in village politics. He's a fast talker and often comes up with funny bits of doggerel. He's also an avid gambler and can't control his daughters-in-law.

I asked him to speak about the nature of politics and power in the village over the past thirty years.

Rural policy's different: it's really only progressed in the past fifteen years. Before that, there was a bit of doggerel that summed up the situation clearly:

The team leaders walk loudly; the accountants wear blue khaki. The team leaders have power; the accountants have money.

Those in charge are stuffed to the gills; the commune
members starve.

Now young people today, they may seem short on brains,
but they're earning money as soon as they leave the house.
The least successful earn 10,000 or so, and those who find
favor can earn 20 or 30,000. I'm mad I didn't retire earlier.
I just retired a few years ago. The leaders took care of us
and helped our eldest become a village functionary. So that
burnished my reputation somewhat. After decades doing
this, my only real accomplishment is to drink. Fuck, I could
have done a lot better trying to get a job. Do I have a
pension? Yes, yes, I do, but I won't tell you how much or
you'll laugh. Ask them what the pension is these days. It's
200 kuai. I've retired, and I get 68 a month, and with insurance it's a grand total of 116.

The individual household responsibility system was a
disaster for the countryside. If they kept it up like that,
there wouldn't be any more village cadres. In our administrative village there were more than 2,000 people, and each
had to pay more than 100 a year, while every year we needed
to turn over 28,000 yuan to the county government. We
also had to charge people specialty-product taxes; if you
grew peppers or tobacco, you had to pay a tax. Village
expenditures also had to come from the people. Private
teachers' salaries, office expenses, entertainment expenses,
all came from the soil. We had no industry, it all came from
the earth. Each *mu* of land was taxed, otherwise there
wasn't enough for the village's collective expenses or for
central government taxes. Originally, whoever farmed the
land would pay; later, if the land was in your name, even
if you didn't farm, you had to pay 50 yuan a *mu* [666
square meters]. In many families the husband and wife
were both away working, and they clearly weren't coming
back. If the cadre asked for the money but the villagers

resisted, in extreme cases there could be real conflict. That's when relationships with cadres were the most strained. It just worsened step by step. Sometimes you were able to explain that it's government policy, nothing to do with the cadre personally, but sometimes you couldn't, and some of the cadres were taking the opportunity to collect their own extra fees. So people hated cadres with a passion. They said, what are you good for, besides taking our money! Especially after 1997, when state-run teachers' salaries also had to be paid locally. Teachers went on strike in the towns and villages, and the villagers caused trouble, so county cadres had to take out emergency loans. If that policy had lasted another two years, who knows what would have happened.

Now the villages all have a lot of debt—they owe hundreds of thousands. The major deficits are due to levies and fines for exceeding the one-child limit. The levies have never been fully collected, so the village has to advance them. Birth policy fines are levied according to population, and every year our village hands over 30 or 40,000 yuan. The villagers should pay it, but they're all somewhere else, they never come back, which means we have to advance that money, too. The villagers mock us, saying the village functionary's job is to "Claim grain, demand funds; order miscarriages and abortions." This old man was mortified when he heard that.

Most of this depends on private loans; the banks won't lend a cent. The loans are high-interest, 1.8 or 2 percent, and they're repaid if and only if the levies are collected. This leads the villages into debt, which piles up. Some credit unions will lend, but you know what that means. They won't lend to the collective, you have to have an individual's name on the loan. The branch secretary has no choice but to borrow as an individual. In almost every village it's the branch secretary who collects, borrows, and lends. He completes the transactions and deals with the expenses. He bears the debt. There's no way around it. And he can't quit, either—if he's in the job, he at least might find a way to repay the debt. If he quits, it's all his own responsibility. How can you live that way? There was a village secretary last year who wasn't able to borrow, and then he wasn't reelected. He went to the County Party Committee Secretary and said, if you won't let me do the job, I'll hang myself in your doorway.

I was determined not to go into debt. What I could collect I handed over; what I couldn't, I didn't. Our village doesn't owe money. I passed my responsibilities down to the production team and told them to figure it out. At harvest, sell your produce and pay it. They had a hold on the land and charged 100 yuan per *mu*. If you paid it, you could farm. If you didn't, you couldn't.

We live in a poor village. In other places they might spend a few million to attract a village head. Here no one would do that. There's nothing to be had from a poor village like ours, no matter what you do. Elections are held every three years. Democracy is democracy. Sooner or later it turns into collectivism. There is also a village committee; the names of the members are posted and there's a system for elections, but it's only for show. It's not that it isn't a good system. Village autonomy is certainly a good thing, the problem is, who's left to govern? The young people have all left to work, and those people don't participate. You could offer to pay candidates and still wouldn't find anyone. We administer more than 2,000 people in the village and not even 200 people come to the meetings. We just go through the motions. In this economic society, rural people only think about money. No one wants to compete for leadership positions. It's their jobs that bring them income, the collective is just a shell, so no one wants to be a part of it. In some villages the meetings are more active, and the candidates pay for their own campaigns, so they call for people to come back. That's because there's profit in it. There are also a few villages that don't have elections. Nobody would take the position. It's better to go work than to be a village secretary!

But that being said, a majority of people still want to do it. There are little benefits, and also the political reputation. It's a kind of admission that you're a capable person. That's all just vanity. Some people say, Qingdao, you were village secretary your whole life, but you didn't really do anything for the village. I say, what the hell are you talking about, everyone around me got what they wanted, I have nothing. These years I've managed to scrape a bit together by gathering manure. I drank my fill, but I'm empty-handed. On the other hand, my neighbors have nothing to do with me as branch secretary—they've all left to work. Those who haven't gone to work, they're doing poorly. They only own two *mu* of land and can hardly feed themselves.

When he talks about his own poverty, Qingdao gets pretty emotional. But Father lets out a loud laugh and says, "Kid, don't put on airs. You talk as if you're the victim, but if you weren't the village secretary, you would never have been able to build that house by the main road. You raised three sons and have three poultry farms! Don't play the poverty card. You've also had your share of liquor. And gambling, where does the money come from when you lose?" Qingdao is part of our family, and a close relation, so he and my father insult each other all the time—they don't stand on ceremony. Father can't help himself when Qingdao tries to paint himself as an innocent.

Well that's true, I've got something out of it. But when I was doing the job, I usually didn't eat out in town, to keep costs down. The village was beyond poor. You can't just eat wherever you want. Who you meet, what you eat, what you talk about: at the end of the month you have to submit an expense report, and everything is thoroughly inspected. It doesn't matter if you're entertaining at home or at a restaurant. There are rules about how much can be reimbursed. If you go over the limit, you pay the difference. I had to keep accounts every day. What I did today; who I ate with. I had to write it all down clearly.

My experience being an official is this: most people are very sensible, but a few are unreasonable and try to find fault with everything. They look for problems with the cadres first; they don't look for them with ordinary people. Ordinary people are sensible 90 percent of the time; it's you, the official, who didn't explain things well. During the years when we submitted grain tax, some refused to pay. I would go over three days in a row and talk until my throat was hoarse. Some had other complaints and were using the tax as an opportunity to get it off their chests. Cases I could settle, I would settle. Cases I couldn't settle, I would explain clearly. But the grain tax was for the national government; you need to pay the tax first, and then settle things afterwards. Using the payment as an excuse to make a scene—that isn't right. Later, the villagers all said, if you'd said all this to begin with, we would never have refused to pay. Let's resolve what we can, discuss what needs discussing, that's all.

Now the state policies do well by the masses. They subsidize the crops more and more. So of course no land is left unused. Neither the township nor the village governments ask the villagers for money, and with the government subsidies the people don't have any financial obligations to higher levels. If it's a good harvest, you get more; if it's not good, you get less. Now the village cadres' responsibilities are simple. They disseminate the Party's policies, perform their family planning duties, maintain an office, keep the peace, and administer to public disputes. Other than that, they have to come up with ways to lead the masses toward prosperity. Before, the cadres demanded money; now they are in public service. If a family or household can't get something done, he helps them do it.

Some people say that with the new rural policies, there's no need for a village cadre. You can just get rid of the position and be done with it. But that wouldn't work at all; it's not appropriate. The villagers would scatter like dust. There is inevitably a divide between the government and the rural level. The higher levels of government wouldn't be able to resolve local disputes. For one, they wouldn't understand the circumstances.

Relationships between people in the village, issues between one family and another, and the history of events are extremely complicated. Somebody from the outside wouldn't understand what was going on and would have a lot of trouble resolving it. Second, it's hard to judge the true from the false. The township government simply can't operate at this level. If you got rid of the village level, the local people simply wouldn't hold together. You could reduce the village-level staff, but you can't remove the structure. That would be tantamount to breaking the binding thread. In a village there are a thousand or so households. The government can't work directly with each one. They wouldn't be able to get any of their own work done.

I really admire our current County Party Committee Secretary. The first time he held a third-level cadre meeting, after it was over I said, it's settled, there's hope for our county. He works with facts and with what's really happening. In the meetings, if you dropped a needle, everyone could hear it. From people on the stage to the people below, it's completely silent. Theory is connected to practice; it's sophisticated and multifaceted, and he explains the complex problems in simple terms. To make a joke about it, at other meetings all you want to do is sleep. It's all clichéd, meaningless. At his meetings you don't even want to go to the toilet; you're afraid you might miss something.

I've suffered through five County Party Committee Secretaries, and none of them were on his level. Each new official decided he had to have some accomplishment, but they never thought things through; they eventually screwed things up, wasting labor and capital. Each former secretary had his pet project: One year it was to plant apple trees, so they dug ditches on either side of the highway, but there never were any apples. There were also the "secretarial projects": each township came up with a project, built a big compound, got all heated up and pushed it through even if it was totally impractical. The waste from showing off was in the hundreds of thousands; the waste from incompetency was in the tens of thousands. And, in the end, all that grew was weeds.

Now there's the poplar economy. I think that will work. They started with meetings for the people. It's smart to plant a few *mu* of poplars, after ten years, it is worth more than a small oil press. Before, the leaders all wanted to do something that would set them apart, but they only wasted labor and money. They were backwards economically and culturally. I'm growing fifteen *mu* of poplars. Every year the trees grow an inch. When they're eight inches thick and a few *zhang* tall, say it's 400 yuan a cubic meter and each tree is half a cubic meter, that's 200 yuan. There are fifty-four poplar trees per *mu*. You can add that up yourself. It's better than raising children. If you raise a good kid, how much can he give you? The grandkids are left with you, and at Spring Festival the kids come back and give you a few hundred yuan, and you're overjoyed. Or they don't come back, and a phone call to the old man takes care of it. They don't come back because they miss their ma or their pa; it's mostly for their own kids. If the grandparents don't have any money, the grandchildren won't come running to them. If you have 40 or 50,000 yuan, you can take care of yourself in old age and not bother your kids. Now you can raise some poplars on unproductive land, and your old age is taken care of. I support the program. It's a green bank.

After the national policy changed, at least the land is being put to use. Those with skills keep working outside the village, getting rich. Those without skills work the land and aren't too badly off. In short, it's a good policy. It's benefited rural people, and it's benefited village cadres, and so the relationships between the two are better. We just do good things around the village; we don't have to ask for money. We've never had this kind of policy before; it's a first in history. Now there are fewer disputes.

As long as the country stays strong, this kind of policy can continue. Good policies make the people believe in the Communist Party, and the Party is cohesive. It shows that the country is growing stronger and stronger. In the past there was a period when the Communist Party's prestige sank low, but now the people are benefiting. Whatever the country calls for, the people are willing to support.

Of course there are still problems. Even the best societies, with the most perfect policies, still have problems. Distance learning is so-so. They give you a television, but it just gets stuck at the production team headquarters, and there it stays. You can set it up, but no one goes to watch it. Older people farm in their home villages. They watch their grand-children. They don't get a moment's rest. Everything's okay as long as nothing goes wrong. But if something happens it's all over, they can't handle it. Your fifth grandmother still cries every time her grandson is mentioned. The grand-parents are looking after the children, but the children don't listen. There aren't very many who want to go to school. The villagers don't have the energy; they're exhausted. Now when someone dies in the village, you have to get people from two production teams before you have enough to carry the coffin. That's a problem.

There's no hurry, I suppose. The country has to come along slowly, Rome wasn't built in a day.

Actually, Qingdao didn't have a strong political base in the village. His father was an honest, well-meaning old man. He never held an office in his life. When the former branch secretary, Liang Xinglong, was stepping down, the villagers didn't want his son to become secretary, so they were adamant about Qingdao taking the position. He had never offended anyone, and no one had anything to say against him. After he took office, Qingdao demonstrated his dedication and his ability to govern. He handled relationships well. He even treated Father and Uncle Laogui, both "thorn-in-the-side" types, with respect, having them over for a meal from time to time to consult with them about things. This was his way of "inflating" a few old men—making them a little giddy. He also arranged for Xinglong's son to become village head and for the former storekeeper's son to become head of public security. Those positions were, in a sense, their "inheritance."

Qingdao seemed proud when he said this, satisfied with what he'd done. Although ordinary village folks disapproved, they'd never held positions like these themselves and weren't entirely clear on the benefits, so they just grumbled a bit in private. On top of that, Qingdao was "fair and square," so there weren't any major actions against him.

Over the past decade, the government has continually adjusted policies in rural areas. It hasn't always been easy. Rural policies have now been completely reformed, and investments are increasing in both effort and scope. On the surface, conflicts between the government and rural people, between cadres and the masses, seem to have decreased. But this hides many funda-mental problems, like democratic process and village autonomy. Although they've been talking about this for thirty years, the ideas are abstractions and still very strange to inland villagers. Because China's farmers have never been the masters of their fates, terms like government, power, and democracy seem to have little to do with them. In addition, basic interactions between the government and the people—interactions based on mutual understanding, respect, and equality—are lacking. Over the past thirty years, rural people have not only *not* become the rulers of the country, on the contrary, they have become, in the popular consciousness, synonymous with burden, darkness, and backwardness. They are the negative side of modernity, the main impediment to reform. The high migration rates among rural populations are a fundamental obstacle to the progress of democratic politics. Principal family members don't live at home and are losing their connection to the land. What matters is making money. The earth is no longer an important source of income. It's no longer their "lifeblood." All the government's flip-flops are simply a matter of whether or not to collect taxes and how much to collect; there's nothing to keep people there. At the same time, as basic, living entities, the villages lack both plans and potential. They simply don't have the cohesiveness to bring their members together and make them part of an organic whole.

The Current Village Secretary

I thought it would be easy to arrange a meeting with the village secretary, but after more than a month, I still hadn't had the opportunity. When I asked the former secretary about it, he shook his head and said that in the past the secretary would spend all day wandering around the village, but no one knows where the current secretary is these days. He's with the higher-ups and won't check in here. One day I went to the township to see if I could better understand what was going on. At lunch, I mentioned that I wanted to see the village secretary, and the township Party secretary said he could arrange a meeting. Not long after, a man came back to say that the secretary was in town drinking, but he was resolving a village dispute, and since he'd put in a lot of effort to get the two parties to talk to each other, he couldn't leave right away or he'd have to start all over again. The township Party committee secretary didn't seem at all offended by this; in fact, he seemed used to it. After about an hour, our village secretary, Han Zhijing, finally came in. He seemed slightly drunk, and when he saw the township Party committee secretary, he greeted him with a joke. It was immediately clear that they were on excellent terms. He looked surprised to see me and came right over to shake my hand. He said again and again that he'd heard from my brother that I was back and that I should tell him when we could get together for a meal. He seemed to have a strong performative streak.

Han Zhijing is around forty years old. He's tall and thin in a short-sleeved collared shirt, the kind intellectuals wear. His eyes are small, but they flash with intelligence and he seems to be an old hand at dealing with political situations. He speaks very straightforwardly. He's been in the position six years already. He was in the food purchasing business before, and now he runs a side company repairing roads and bridges. He also has some cement trucks that he rents out.

Actually, I imagine you already more or less know what I'm going to talk about. I won't say a lot about the larger administrative village, just our local Liang Village. If you add up all the families, there are 1,300 or 1,400 people in 300 or 400 households. There's less than one *mu* of land per person. In economic terms, the bulk of the income comes from people working outside the village. What industry do we have? There are two private factories that started out producing mud bricks and now do cinder blocks. Han Yunlong has a pig farm, which for years was a disaster. Recently the government policies and market prices have been good, and he insures his sows for 60 kuai each. He pays 30 and the government pays 30. The insurance company will compensate 1,000 kuai. The family has more than forty pigs. They eat pig feed—feeding them hay is too slow and no one has time to cut the hay. Why do they raise so few pigs? Because it's not worth what the family puts into it. The elderly have to look after the children, so despite the subsidies, very few do it.

Now we're a poplar tree economy, right? Around six or seven hundred are growing on the village riverbanks. I also planted fifty or sixty *mu*, and the thickest are already twenty-four centimeters. You fertilize them each year, which costs about 250 kuai per tree per year. You end up earning about as much as raising crops, it's just that the revenue comes all in a lump, at the end. The way things are going, in ten years we'll be able to sell them for 300,000 kuai. That would mean 100,000 kuai in profit. It's like a fixed deposit. You'll have money for old age.

Now farm work is basically mechanized, and fewer people are needed. The rural work force is used to having to leave to earn money, and they rarely come back. Now the government isn't collecting taxes on crops, and is even offering subsidies, and that's a good thing, but it won't cause the trend of people returning to the village that you're talking about. What good is that little bit of money when you want to build a house and pay your children's school fees? You still have to depend on the people who leave. But there is another new development: people who were letting others farm their land now want it back, to raise some simple crops. You might not earn much, but you don't have to pay tax or hand over grain: what you earn, you keep.

According to my analysis, in the future we'll still have to follow a collective path. It's better to be united than dispersed. It's too inefficient for each of us to work a tiny bit of land. When we farm collectively, the costs of overhead and manpower are reduced, and large equipment can be fully utilized.

People here still don't have a head for business. The money they earn stays in the bank, waiting for when they build a house. Their only fear is not having money, and they keep a lot in savings. They build houses that no one ever lives in. They don't care if they throw it all away in a house. In the south, there are all kinds of products, and the markets are developed. At the very least, each individual family can work in manufacturing and also maybe get together and start a business. Some young people work together and talk business plans, so if they suffer some losses it doesn't matter. But here it's another story. People aren't the same. They don't cooperate, and they start fighting before things have even gotten off the ground. Every time a few families work together, things start off well, they're on intimate terms, but every time they end up as enemies. Others hoard quite a bit of money. They're tired of leaving for work; they'd like to get something going here in the village, but they look around and can't decide what to do. They're afraid to lose money. After a while, they end up leaving again.

Now being a village cadre is the hardest job. The village doesn't have any money, but commune members have to be paid. For example, take raising poplar trees. Every village has its quota, and the branch secretary is personally responsible for it. We're only reimbursed at the end of the month. The village has advanced 30,000 yuan. It's a good thing to do, but if requirements are too rigid it becomes a bad thing. They tell us only to grow them in the irrigation ditches, but in some villages, in order to reach their quota, and also to save trouble, they ruin their arable land by forcing people to plant there. A good thing turns bad. Being a rural official is just a political label. We're here in the spirit of sacrifice. When our village was working on the village-to-village construction project, we employed twenty or more people. All of them needed to be paid. I had to advance all that. And for what?

Rural official work simply cannot be done according to the books, according to the codes and regulations. But there are lots of ways to get things done within the range of legal policy. A production team cadre's salary is 30 or 40 kuai a month. Mine is 168; basically we're doing this work as a favor. To be an official, you have to be able to get things done. Like land allocation: you try to allocate fairly, but you get pushback, so you have to curse and cajole to get it done. There are also second-level township cadres who come around, but they stand to one side and don't get involved. After a month the land's still not allocated. They call that their "grassroots experience," their "rural experience." Now today, at lunch, why did I stay for that meal? We had a spell of heavy rain, and some houses' foundations stones were washed away. They couldn't tell whose was whose and the two families started fighting, no one could resolve it. So I needed to get to work: I asked the team leader to set up a meal and to find someone in the village to be an intermediary, someone with prestige who could bring them together and get them to make concessions. It takes at least two or three meals. That's how it always is in the village. People are always taking a stand on things, and if you want to talk them out of it, well that depends on who's talking. It has to be that guy. Otherwise, even things that could be resolved won't be. Sometimes they cause trouble during the meal. At first everything seems fine, but then one side threatens to bring in outside muscle, and the other side hears that and says let's see you try, I'm not going to let you, you think you can put me in jail? And it all goes down the drain.

Disputes over residences are frequent. There are always new directives, but it's hard to carry them out. Say I build a house according to the directives, but that means I occupy a bit of your ancestral plot. Our two families need to work it out ourselves—if we can't, then it's completely hopeless. The new directives are hard to carry out. We're supposed to tear down the old and build the new. But everyone's only building the new, not tearing down the old. The regular people get their way these days—let's see you try to change me! It's obviously wrong, but what can you do? Yet leaders have their duties that have to be fulfilled. Being secretary is an honorable position. All families have their weddings and funerals, and you get the seat of honor at each. But if you don't give a gift, you're done for. Every day crowds of people come to my house; I can't afford all the tea and cigarettes. Sometimes, I just want to disappear. They treat me like the brick you stick under the short leg of the bed. Being a village secretary is all thankless effort. People always sum it up, how does it go: "When you've left home for work, they ignore you; if you have ready money, they won't leave you alone; if something happens, they'll come for your help; if you can't help them, they curse you; if they're angry, they'll sue you."

If you can handle this village stuff, it's not that bad. If you can't, you work yourself to the bone and no one gives you any thanks.

You also have to keep track of all the petitioners, and that's enough to kill you. Some are reasonable, and we have to take care of them. Some you can tell at a glance are totally baseless, but still we have to accept them and treat them respectfully; but they'll come again next time. How much do the village, the town, and the county pay to deal with this kind of trouble? We secretaries know exactly how much. If you ask me, we shouldn't be accepting these letters—let them sue! If they've got a real case, what are we afraid of? If we're afraid of them lodging complaints against us, then maybe there's something wrong with us. Are the problems going to resolve themselves simply because we treated them respectfully? Everyone's got their own two legs; how can you control them? I think there are major problems in governmental policy in this arena. If they're not resolved, something bad might happen.

Now the "village-to-village construction project" is a good thing, but there are also hassles. For the part of the road in our village, the costs were divided between the government, the village, and individuals. But some families don't live here and don't use that road, so they didn't want to pay, and they really didn't want to have their land confiscated. The primary road is finished, but they didn't do a good job with it. The ditches are uncovered, and in the summer after it rains, they fill with mosquitoes and stink to high heaven. There are all kinds of things that need fixing, and the crux of the matter is that there isn't any money. The government didn't allocate enough. And you need to know people to get anything done. If you've got contacts you can get a little money to work on the roads and ditches. But on the other hand, it's already a huge improvement that the government has these plans at all.

You're asking about the sale of the village road by the river? I know that people are talking about that, but I'm not afraid, not a cent of it ended up in my pocket. The road was sold for 174,000 kuai [more than $25,000], so they could run sand mining trucks on it. The mining companies were happy about it, and we made some money. The large trucks can easily damage the roads, but if they do, they can be fixed. And we built more village roads with what was left; that's a good thing. The villagers only care that we made money; they don't care that we spent it.

Now there are quite a few subsidies for irrigation works and the diversification of rural production. I went to the county level to get some projects going: digging wells, building power stations with distributors, running high-voltage lines to the wells, setting up the irrigation and magnetic cards for billing. The farmland is now 100 percent irrigated. I got the projects approved, but the money was earmarked for particular uses. I had to chip in my own money for cigarettes.

More than 90 percent of adult labor is outside of the village. Over the past two years the price of grain has risen, so some have come back to raise crops, but not many. These individual subsidies are good, but they're not enough to make a real difference.

In my personal opinion—I could be wrong—if you took all the individual subsidies—forty here, fifty there—and you gave them to the collective, you could really do something to rebuild the countryside

Now, for example, with the 2,680 *mu* in our village, we receive 100,000 yuan or so under the current subsidies program. If that were used as a lump sum, we could do a lot like fix the roads or build sewers. That would be better than distributing it to individuals.

You can talk all day, but in the end the problem is simply that our country is too big, there's too much countryside. It can't be helped.

As Han Zhijing talks, the county Party secretary interjects from time to time, especially when he comes close to contradicting the Party line. For example, when Han is talking about letters of petition or complaint, he suggests that the current policy has problems. There the county Party secretary interrupts him before he finishes, saying a lot of the complaints come from slick old foxes, who complain day in and day out about the tiniest things. They're not quite right in the head, and even if you settle their problems, they aren't satisfied. They just want to freeload. I don't disagree with the county Party secretary—he must have seen plenty of examples of this in his time—but his disdain and contempt are hard to accept. And although Han promptly changes his tune, he doesn't seem like a complete "yes-man." They act almost as equals, which makes me curious about their relationship. From the way they greeted and joked with one another, I got the sense they don't interact as superior and subordinate, but rather with a kind of brotherhood that is personal, not professional.

In the Chinese system, village secretaries hold very ambiguous positions. They are not government cadres and can return to being ordinary farmers at any time, yet they are also responsible for carrying out state policy. Village secretaries are not quite "officials," yet they are "major figures" whom people seek out for matters large and small. Although the village secretary relies upon the county Party secretary for his position, if he ever decides he doesn't want the position anymore, the latter can't do much about it. In other words, the county Party secretary controls whether the village secretary stays or goes, but he doesn't have unconditional power, because he doesn't have the ability to promote the village secretary. If he wants the village secretary to be more obedient or to force him to do something, he has to rely on other, more ordinary means or promises of profit. One must admit that this kind of unofficial pressure is not very reliable, and if one side doesn't fulfill the other's demands quickly, it can lose its effectiveness and create instability.

While the village secretary's complaints only serve to paint himself in a more positive light, it is true that some haven't carried out the reforms well. The higher levels want them to implement governmental policies and economic imperatives. Yet if farmers have grievances or problems with them, they have to seek out the very same men for help. If they are incompetent, or if they rely too much on their clan's influence, it can be hard for them to complete their responsibilities. The village secretary gets emotional as he speaks: "If the government wants to weave together 1,000 threads, it must depend on the village secretaries to be the needles." It's like he's finally found someone who really listens, someone to whom he can tell his side of the story, how he has endeavored to benefit the village and to resolve difficult situations.

When I ask about new policies regarding village secretaries, like letting them enter government administration, with a rank and a cadre's salary, Han doesn't wait for the county Party secretary, he just blurts out, "Oh, that is just a formality. At most the county has one or two cases like that, and they are most always from wealthy villages, or from villages near towns. They never choose an ordinary village secretary." Only then do I realize that the village secretary from northern Wu township who became a civil servant must have used his connections. Even though Han seems completely disgusted, the county Party secretary only smiles. He doesn't look especially displeased, either, nor does he try to stop Han from talking. He's more like an older brother watching a younger sibling who has had a bit too much to drink. This is a kind of tacit admission of their connection. At the same time it is a confirmation and display of his own superior position.

When I return to my brother's house that evening, I chat with him and Father about my impressions. My brother says, "That guy has the balls to get things done. He's aggressive and isn't afraid to lay down the law, to spend money or to use his contacts." Father spits out an indignant *pei*. "You've got that right," he says. "He takes the people's money and spends it without a second thought. Don't listen to him praising himself. If the job was as hard as all that, would he still be that enthusiastic about it?" My father's face turns red and his veins start to stick out. "The villagers are pissed about it. Uncle Laogui and I have been talking it over. We have to get rid of him. The village will never get better while he's around." This ill-tempered old man has never given up his country habit of finding fault with village cadres.

It's obvious that even if the village secretary does expend a lot of energy and care for the village, the villagers won't be grateful. This is because the cadres enjoy certain privileges, which they use to seek out personal gain, just like any other official. When all is said and done, if this isn't changed, the conflicts between cadres and administrators and the people in China's rural areas are unlikely to be resolved.

The County Committee Secretary

The Rang County Committee Secretary has been very supportive of my work in the village, and my discussions with him have given me a better understanding of many of the government's policies and overarching views, which in turn broaden the scope of my investigation to include many different levels and points of view.

The county secretary began his career as a rural teacher employed at the local level, and he has the air of an educated man, an intellectual official. Regarding the economic growth of China's countryside, he has his own expertise and opinions. He worked his way up from the lowest level and has extensive experience and understands the conflicts between village problems, policy, and people's livelihoods. He's willing to express his opinions and has the literary aspirations, as well as political aspirations, particular to those who live in China's central plains. You can sense his desire and determination to reform present rural conditions both in what he says and in his county policies. I have heard his governmental and academic reports, and they are rare examples of work that is not filled with empty jargon; they demonstrate both analytical awareness and modern concepts. He has transformed urban areas, created an ecological economy, restored villages, and implemented new working practices. Not only has he transformed Rang County's natural environment, he has increased the people's political conscious-ness, and, on the most basic level, is slowly modernizing people's ways of thinking. But long-established practices run deep, and ideas are liable to change as they're put into practice. Many of his plans have been prevented from bearing fruit, and many of his projects, visions, and programs are impeded by different factors, so much so that eventually they change until they become unrecognizable. But the secretary is a tenacious man, and as he puts it, little by little, step by step, we'll get things done. There will always be results.

For clarity, I present our conversation as a Q&A session.

As someone who worked for a long time as a grassroots level cadre, what are your thoughts about reform and opening up and its effects on rural life over the past thirty years?

Without exaggeration, one can say it caused a turning point in China's rural villages. Taken as a whole, it all started with the rural villages and the division of land and house-holds. Collective production teams, the organization of production teams, people's communes—all that fundamen-tally collapsed. Hao Ran's literary work *Golden Streets* is a typical example of people's communes being "large in size and collective in nature."

In 1980, '83, and '84, rural production capabilities were opened up, and people were able to eat white bread on a regular basis. The Central Committee published three top-level documents, liberating rural people and spurring their enthusiasm for production. It sounds strange to say, but Father Heaven also helped: during those years, the wind was sweet and the rains temperate—good years for farming. There were bumper harvests year after year, and the rural people, on the whole, didn't have any heavy burdens. Later, some problems arose. The public services of the collective period were slowly dismantled. Collective irrigation facilities and tractors were all sold. Then the government began to speak of developing rural enterprise and permitted a small amount of commodity production, increased the purchase prices of food goods, expanded privately owned businesses, and further strengthened the collective–individual household-responsibility system. In this system "collective" means the land is collective and the system of ownership cannot change; "individual" means the land is contracted to individual families who operate it. In practice, we saw that in many places collective capabilities were weak and individual families were stronger. Conflicts between small-scale production and the demands of the marketplace increased every day. A typical case was when everyone stopped buying Luoyang tractors for a time. All of the sudden people didn't know what to do.

One could say that the '80s were a transitional period for rural policy. From the late '80s until the end of the '90s, Deng Xiaoping said the nation's market economy was gradually taking shape, and industrial infrastructure and forms of employment were greatly altered. Before, land had always been the most important. Now, leaving home was most important. And that caused great social upheaval, huge changes. Leaving home to earn money left families smaller and more dispersed.

In the '90s, burdens on rural populations increased daily. For example, take the "three collectives and five plans." The three collectives are wages, official reserves, and public subsidy funds; the five plans are road building, family planning, rural education, militia training, and disease prevention. The Central Government set the rural per capita income tax at 5 percent to resolve the "collective" aspect in the integration of the "collective" and the "individual" and mandated the number of days of farmers' obligatory labor.

Later, they ameliorated this with the payment instead of labor option, but the result was that farmers had to produce both payments and labor. There were also regional agricultural taxes, taxes for butchering pigs, and so on, which gave cadres more pretexts to demand money. Meanwhile, there were fewer and fewer restrictions on their power. They could do as they wished, and the demands upon farmers increased layer by layer. In those years conflicts between the people and cadres were intense, and every year, in every part of the country, there were reports of cadres seizing illegally held grain and money and farmers drinking poison or hanging themselves. Rural circumstances deteriorated, and in many places there was mass resistance. Or else people just left without a trace.

Throughout the '90s, the impact on farmers gradually increased in severity. In 2004, when I first arrived, I did some research and found that in this county, a dozen villages and townships hadn't contracted out all their land. The people said that when it came time to plant, the secretary would charge them for it, 120 yuan per *mu*. Most people gave up farming so that they wouldn't owe money. They could just leave to find work. When I went to one village to investigate, a fifty-year-old woman grabbed me by the hand and said, "Secretary, if we keep farming this land, we'll farm ourselves right into prison." She said, "Think about it, we have a lot of land here, three *mu* for each person, but for each *mu* we have to pay 150 kuai; that's 450 kuai for three *mu*, and five people would have to pay more than 2,000. It's like a money tree for them. They can come and ask for money at any time. If we don't have any money, the village secretary takes our seals over to the credit union and takes out a loan in our name. When it comes due, and we still can't pay, the credit union sues us. Then the people in the courts and the local police come over with handcuffs and say, if you don't pay we'll take you away. Isn't this farming ourselves into prison!?" So for a short period of time, a lot of the land was left uncultivated, because to farm was to lose money, and no one was willing to do that.

From 1992 until 2002, the burdens on farmers, and the conflicts between them and local officials, were at their most intense. On the one hand, there were all sorts of demands for money, and on the other there were continual calls to improve the farmers' plights. It was contradictory. Every year horrible things happened, and the investigations would reveal the cadre's responsibility. Once an inspection leader came to investigate, and I told him that we must consider why all the nation's lowest level functionaries are committing the same offenses. From Manchuria to Hainan, from Henan to Hunan, why are there conflicts between them and farmers? They grew up with the farmers' grand-fathers, and young or old, there should be emotional connections. This is not a local demon. If things don't change, Heaven itself won't be able to set it right. To be honest, during that period of time, the only cadres who actually protected the interests of the farmers were the old and backwards ones. The cadres winning all the prizes were the ones who extorted the farmers so exorbitantly.

Looking at it now, rural policy during the '90s was a failure. The Three Rural Issues Policy was like a train stuck at the station, sounding its horn, going nowhere. Lots of documents were published, but it didn't do any good. The farmers' problems were not alleviated; they only worsened.

In 2002 they started to raise the issue of tax reform. At that time, I said that it wouldn't be carried through, because previously, on the whole, Central Committee plans were basically "a liter of water and a liter of mud." How much you brought in determined how much you could spend. For poor counties like ours the reforms would never work. The farmers often said: The halls of power and the courts conspire, just to collect their 4.8, meaning the tax on tobacco. They come down and force us to grow tobacco, because then they could collect the specialty production tax. It was a "solution" that would never solve the problem.

Under the new policies, the government offers many rural subsidies. This year they've contributed more than 380 billion to rural farming. This has never been done before. It's a fundamental shift. If they continue like this, after five years, the relationship between the Party and the farmers will be as good as it's ever been. Before, when I went to the countryside to observe and study, the township Party committee secretaries would block the roads. They were nervous, afraid that the people would expose them. Now it's a lot better.

What view do you have of rural policies that were implemented around 2003 and their impact on life in rural villages? What is their significance?

If you look at the trends from approximately 2000 until now, it was disastrous for rural villages. It's hard to imagine; it might have led to real crisis. The villages were on the point of collapse. Farmers were heavily burdened and conditions were worsening. People were really angry. But the Central Committee policies were adjusted in time and now things are much better. There are no levies or taxes, and there are subsidies for growing crops.

After 2004, the country's large-scale plans underwent fundamental changes. Especially with Hu Jintao's Scientific Outlook on Development. Rural areas and people benefited the most. On the whole, in Chinese rural culture, people follow their instincts. Take the performer Zhao Benshan, whose "Three Whips" obliquely criticized grassroots level functionaries. Although it's a historical play, it also eluci-dates the mindsets of rural people. Literary and artistic works explain life, and this work reflected a certain style of contemporary official. Just as, when heavy rain comes after a long drought, we say Father Heaven is good; or, if there's been continuous rain, we say Father Heaven is bad. Rural people are very direct. If today someone does me right, I say he's a good guy. If he does me wrong, I say he's a bastard.

The present policy, along with a real grasp of local situations, has quickly resolved many practical problems for the rural population and changed their living conditions. Problems that we'd been trying to solve for years were finally resolved, step by step. I have said this before: the construction of a new countryside must not be idealized. In talking about the new countryside, we cannot paint images in farmers' minds of European villas, blue skies, white fluffy clouds, a car for traveling, everything sparkling clean. It's easy to idealize a new-style village. The problem with this is that it demands quick fixes, and in rural work we often commit this mistake. For example, if you talk about the people's communes in '58, or the Great Leap Forward, or even the Cultural Revolution, those were all highly idealized. But when one replaces practicality with idealism, it can turn absolutist, with imposed uniformity and a kind of empty formalism. Many problems in rural economic and social development come from idealism. You must have ideals, but you can't have idealism.

I have another opinion: There must not be idealism in rural policy, but there mustn't be a laissez-faire attitude, either. The state policy on new rural construction is a fifteen-word dictum. "Produce development; live comfortably; keep villages clean and rural manners civilized; and administer to democracy." The premise behind these four phrases is growth. It suggests the possibility of comfortable livelihoods. Why did the Central Committee establish these provisions? They didn't want to give the new rural villages concrete standards, because in practice, things start off in a hurry but end up slow; the beginning is easy, what follows is hard. What you begin with is what follows. Idealism often turns into formalism; and laissez-faire policies often drag on with no results. If you let things progress naturally, no one knows what to work for, and the results will be like the lyrics of that song, "The stars are still the stars; the moon is still the moon." Rural areas do not yet enjoy the benefits of modernization. And new rural construction must begin with changing rural production activities, concretely, piece by piece; this will allow rural people to experience actual change.

Progressing project by project, village by village, starting with the peasant's most direct and concrete concerns, the things they care about most: electricity, drinking water, transportation, village appearance. This can be done step by step. We cannot first imagine the rural population's prosperity up to a certain point and then get to work, because development will always proceed unequally. In the past, though no one talked about a new countryside, there were always some people who lived relatively well. But if you don't work on basic infrastructure and improving basic living conditions, you might build a house, but it will be in the middle of a swamp. It might be a good house, but you can't go anywhere.

This is a crucial point for rural reform. It is also time for rural restoration.

What are the most critical issues regarding the construction of a new countryside?

In the midst of this major shift, rural culture is also being affected, and this is creating a new state of affairs. First, rural children have no hopes of a postsecondary education. It's not like the '80s, when people did all they could to go to university, because if you got into a school you could move to a city. Now schooling provides no real way out, and it doesn't seem very useful. They feel there's not much point in going on from high school to college. Even if graduation rates are high, students' aspirations aren't high. Second, because people are away working for long periods of time, there is little education through the family. Third, there is a crisis in new beliefs—people are at a loss concerning religion. Fourth, more and more long-term workers are failing to adapt to the world outside their villages, and their job training is not especially good. Because rural people do not have access to technical skills, they remain at the lowest standard of living. Fifth, the rural infrastructure is deteriorating. Sixth, as things are going, we should be addressing the personal character of low-level cadres. At present, the emotional rapport between the people and the functionaries has improved somewhat, but this is due to the comprehensive policies. If, after a few years, the cadres do not improve personally, if they don't approach their work with new philosophies and ways of thinking that are conducive to this new rural reality, a crisis could arise.

At the same time, under these new policies, many of the tasks of low-level village cadres is to carry out Central Committee policies that are beneficial to the people. For example, they are supposed to help the rural population earn money. But this opens the door to ethical problems. It can lead to new kinds of corruption and social conflicts and cause general discontent. For example, subsidies could be directed to one's own family members, or fraudulent quotas could be given. These should be for the collective good. If the cadres handle things unfairly and don't use these policies to benefit the people, new flashpoints will be triggered.

In the academic world, it is a commonly held view that the urbanization of rural areas will be the inevitable solution to rural problems—it's a done deal. What are your thoughts?

In and of itself, this viewpoint isn't wrong, but we can't simplify or idealize the situation. Many scholars advocate urbanization. But if things are simplified too much, they'll become disconnected with China's reality. In my thinking, China's future rural problems could be resolved through small- to mid-sized cities, small- to mid-sized enterprises, small- to mid-sized banks, small to mid-sized incomes, and the middle class. I'll focus on the following two points: the first is small- to mid-sized cities. China now has a typical case of "urbanization indigestion": cities are overcrowded and the rural people who gather there are without a steady source of income. This causes them to become drifters, without resources, a huge problem that easily produces slum areas. This is a necessary evil of urbanization. Second, we have to develop small- to mid-sized enterprises in order to create local employment. We are used to a centralized labor model for enterprise. That's a fact. It's also a condition particular to our country. Some people say we make low-grade industrial products and are calling for change. Actually, there's nothing wrong with this, we have the advantage in terms of population, and it's part of the development process. This kind of centralized corporate model is necessary for China's high-level development.

What is urbanization? Is it living in a large city or an urbanized life? I think that, first and foremost, urbanization is a lifestyle; if you get a job and earn an income in an urbanized way, only then can you say you're urbanized. Can you flush the toilet? Can you take a shower? Do you take a car when you go somewhere? That is urbanization. I went to Korea to do some research. Most of the Korean professors live in the suburbs, but every amenity is available. This is also urbanization. If what urban people enjoy are the achievements of modern culture, rural people should also enjoy them. And besides, according to new organizational models, lifestyles that rely upon cooperation between specialized fields are also urbanized. Within Rang County, we have established a four-level system that develops the functions of towns and villages. Beyond the towns and villages, we have created locations for commercial centers, which will be just as successful as those in the cities. To a certain degree they almost feel like the small towns in foreign countries. In addition, some traditional market locations are becoming logistical hubs for the circulation of goods from several villages and in a way act as small towns.

If rural development is good, rural people won't need to leave their hometowns to obtain an urbanized lifestyle. This can also alleviate problems in the cities. At this point, rural areas have been restored to a good condition. There are roads, and you can leave home when it rains. There are supermarkets nearby. There is running water and solar energy. You can take a shower, and it's easy to visit your friends and family. Everyday comforts and conveniences are the same as in the cities. What is lacking is information. When the problem of information circulation is resolved, what won't you be able to do in the villages?

How influential do you think local, traditional culture is for rural people?

A few village girls go out and earn money doing bad things. Then they come back and build a house, and they appear very honest and pure, no matter what they might have done while they were away. But you can still more or less tell what they've been doing. Rural culture and village life possess very strong purifying capabilities.

Rang County has woven together scholarly and farming cultures. We are both industrious and frugal. We are also relatively traditional. This all has an invisible effect on people's behavior when they are away. When I worked in other counties, I would often go to teahouses with friends.

217

But in Rang County, I don't go at all. We've been in here talking half the day, and soon word of this will get out, and become news, and it will be news of a negative kind. This is an example of differences in local culture. Regional culture and regional xenophobia and conservatism are very strong. They are resistant to other cultures.

Simply put, culture is customs, habits. It has a solidifying effect, it locks things in place. When customs are made philosophical they become religions; when customs are idealized, abstracted, and made immaterial, they can create religion, art, and literature. When interpersonal customs are solidified, they become culture. The more reified a culture becomes, the more xenophobic it is. After a regional culture takes shape, it shifts away from modern life. This is one of its inevitable effects. For example, when people visit Rang County, you might ask them to sing karaoke or go dancing after you eat, but the people might think Rang County is boring because the whole family comes along.

In your opinion, given the development trends in rural areas postreform and opening up, which aspects of local culture are under attack?

Current attacks on local culture consist of two major elements. One is building homes alongside highways. This is a blow to the former village structure, and it has a concrete impact on village culture. Before it was 30 *mu* of land and one cow, a wife and children on the *kang*. We have a proverb here: "When the milling is done, the bamboo garden is behind the house." In the farming life-style, baskets and sieves were all woven by hand, and everyone was self-sufficient. Villages formed within a culture of mutual aid, cooperation, and sharing. Although neighbors might be at loggerheads with one another over ancestral plots, in the long run they would join together as

part of a culture of mutual assistance. Even when they
clashed, there was mutual aid and interdependence. Later,
when people became wealthy, they began to build houses in
a row along the road. As a result, the village couldn't share
equipment or facilities. There is also the loss of other
traditions. In the past if you lent me something, you could
just pass it over the wall we shared. This is slowly changing
and has led to many "hollow villages." We've been working hard over the past several years to transform the
villages, to make the roads better, to provide running
water, to encourage those who have left to come back,
mostly with conveniences. Second, because of changes in
employment opportunities, family structures have disappeared. Problems arise between the young and old because
Chinese culture has hidden generational divides.
Grandparents spoil their grandchildren—they don't provide
true discipline. And for children there is the long-term loss
of parental love, which is harmful to the children's growth.
This is another blow to traditional culture. Never mind
external pressures, these two factors alone have created
tangible problems in the villages. The Phoenix Channel
from Hong Kong came to film here, and I just said one
thing: Only culture has no rival. Culture is very strong. It
has a fixative effect, and that's true of both virtue and vice.
For example, in villages near the railroads, individuals steal
and strip railway cars. I don't know how many people
we've arrested and sentenced for this, but they still do it.
Moral degradation is also a kind of habit, and it, too, can
gradually solidify and eventually turns into culture. Culture
is like a rubber wall—you can only make a hole in it if you
poke it with a knife. You can also throw a stone at it, but if
you throw it lightly, it will only make a dent, and if you
throw it too hard, it will bounce back at you and you'll end
up hurting yourself. And, in the end, it will return to its
former shape anyway.

Deng Xiaoping has said that the greatest mistake in reform and opening up is education. This doesn't just mean education in schools; it also includes moral education and views about shortcomings in traditional culture. We haven't been able to resist Western thinking, and many feudalistic elements are popping up again.

As someone who must put theory into practice, how do you implement policy? At what level do you begin?

You must carry out the Central Committee's policies that benefit farmers one by one. You must study them thoroughly, fight for them, and implement them completely and well. For example, the introduction of solar energy affects farmers directly. This is an important change in quality of life. They had to learn to take showers. This is a major psychological change. We'll promote construction of teahouses as well as the projects that connect villages and bring modern culture and lifestyles to rural people. It's a gradual thing. You've got to start with the very basics of their lives, their homes. At the very least you need to protect and develop the traditional cultural structure of the village. Local cadres need to be responsible for bringing all the various fruits of modern civilization to rural people, and for helping them develop their own capabilities. We cannot say that they are backward. Telephones, cell phones, televisions are universal.

Modern civilization is entering farmers' lives at a faster pace. They have increased access to information, and their horizons are constantly expanding. However, has individual capacity been developed? This is an important question. I think individual development should happen in three ways: First, in new employment and career capabilities. In the current climate, rural education should emphasize profess-ional and technical education; it should not simply follow a college track. Rural education has been marginalized, and we ought to define concrete, professional skills. Second, they must be able to assimilate into modern life. On one hand, the rural population earns relatively little, but on the other, they don't spend anything. They don't know how to adapt to modern life.

The last thing rural college students want to hear is "you're such a peasant." This is because of the schism between the urban and rural. Third, we must raise rural political consciousness and protect political rights. Rural people don't know to protect their own political rights. The right to information, the right to participation, the right to vote, the right to self-expression, and the right to appeal. Lower level cadres often see these rights as causing trouble for themselves, and they interfere.

Another place where work needs to be done is to make lower level cadres use new methods, new modes, and new lines of thinking to respond to new problems. For this reason, Rang County implemented the "four plus two" work method. The Central Committee has given its approval, and it has now been written as a Central Committee document and extended to the entire country. "Four plus two" means "four comments and two disclosures." It is a sequence of work provisions for lower level functionaries to use. All important rural matters must go through four steps: First, the Party Branch must propose it; second, the village party branch and the village committee must discuss it. Third, there must be deliberation among a Party general assembly. Finally, there must be a resolution from a general meeting of village delegates. Both the resolution and the results of its implementation must be publicly disclosed; these are the two disclosures.

This way of working, both in theory and in practice, is worthwhile. From the theoretical perspective, according to the Central Committee overview and scholarly generalizations, they tie together the Party leadership mechanisms, the two village party consultation mechanisms, the mechanisms that ensure the democratic privileges of party members and the village autonomy mechanisms. From a practical perspective, four plus two offers us several lessons. It teaches low-level cadres how to consult and compromise. Indeed, consultation-based compromise is a foundational aspect of democracy. It teaches low-level cadres how to practice procedural decision-making. Without these procedures, there is no democracy. It teaches the common people that the minority must defer to the majority and that the minority benefits when it does this. This increases the democratic conscious-ness of low-level functionaries and their sense of the legal system. It also gives regular people a greater understanding of present conditions, and thereby they learn how to inte-grate these conditions into their daily lives. At the same time, it ensures the villagers' voting rights, their right to information, their right to expression and to control in public decision making. It also develops their political consciousness.

When peasants' voices are ignored, they're sure to end up apathetic to politics. When an individual doesn't have a position within the collective and cannot participate in public affairs, he's bound to be apathetic. When he comes to feel that he's an indispensable part of the whole, then he will naturally become more proactive.

7

Trials and Tribulations of the "New Morality"

In 2006, 151 Christian churches as well as multiple simple activity halls were established in Rang County. Members include three church elders, 184 pastors, and three new seminary graduates, as well as 40,000 believers. Most churches have an educational and administrative group numbering between five and seven people, responsible for implementing a regulatory structure and the patriotic pledge. Religious life is common.

—Rang County Annals, Religion

Grandpa Ming

Grandpa Ming is fifty-eight years old. Many years ago, when he was a handsome and confident young man, he served in the army. After he returned to civilian life, he continued to keep his khaki military uniform well ironed. He was well-groomed and imposing, one of the better known men in the village. For a while he worked in transport, but because his wife often traveled for her church, he had to give it up to stay at home and run the household. In the '90s he earned some money repairing bicycles in Beijing. When he came back to the village, he bought a house and opened a small bicycle repair shop. On a good day, he can earn about twenty kuai.

My life has had its twists and turns: I could talk about your eldest grandmother's [Grandpa Ming's wife] beliefs for

223

three days and three nights and still have more to say. I feel as if God has robbed me of my life. In any case, he sure ruined the family.

All your grandmother's fellow believers call her "Sister Linglan." My two kids have always been smart, and college was a real hope. But when I left to drive trucks, your grandmother left to become a believer, and she sent the kids to your old third grandpa's [Grandpa Ming's father]. Sometimes she didn't even send them to school. She'd take them to church instead. So their grades suffered. There weren't any church buildings then, but your grandmother can sing, so she would travel to different counties and be away for ten days or two weeks. I said, if your church is so great, how come not one of Han Liting's kids are believers? [Han Liting is a church elder.] I said, go ask old Diankui how Liting and the others cheated him. He'll tell anyone who asks: now I see clearly, they asked me to print flyers, print flyers, print flyers, but they never gave me a fen. Now they all have large courtyards, eat good food, and drink their fill. They're just a pack of liars. They cheat the foolish. If you have eggs, they take eggs. If you have grain, they take grain. We were pathetic: while they were getting rich, we were losing everything. When smart people believe in God they get rich, because there are so many fools to give them money. The church elders, their kids all drive cars. Where do the cars come from? Where does the money come from? Donations! You know they spend your contributions, right! You know nothing, you only know to keep donating. Some people sell their own family's food to make donations.

When it first started, I would swear at Eldest Grandmother, but she ignored me. She had such an elevated awareness, she wouldn't stoop to my level. After that I cursed God. I said God has done you wrong. It didn't touch her if I swore at her, but if I swore at God that stung her to the quick.

Who's going to give you a fen, except what you earn yourself? She didn't take care of the kids; she didn't take care of the house. After the kids grew up, they were really angry about it. Once your grandmother beat my daughter, and my daughter went and knocked her own head against the wall, crying. It broke my heart. She had been such a good student, but the problems at home never stopped, and it interfered with her schooling.

I don't know what God is. A few years ago a woman was drowning. I jumped in and saved her, but she didn't thank me, she thanked God. Fuck your mother. I just don't get it. This really happened: in a village there was an old woman who had her two grandchildren with her because her daughter and son-in-law had left to work. She was also a Christian. One day at noon, she saw two children floating in a pond, but she was in a hurry to get to church, so she didn't say anything. It wasn't until she came back that she realized they were her own grandchildren. These lessons are written in blood. Believers should wake up. It's not right to be so rigid. If it's a Sunday, they must go to church, no matter what. It's not humane. It shouldn't matter if they are your grandchildren or not, if you cry out, some kids have fallen into the pond, and then leave when you see that people are coming to help, wouldn't that be just as good?

I can't control your grandmother at all. When I try, I just make myself angry. One time, we were putting up the beams for the new house. There were dozens of people around, everyone doing something. But the church called your grandmother and told her she needed to come teach the choir. I said, you can see how busy we are, can't you skip it for once? She said, I'll go teach and then come back. I was furious. I said, no way! If you try and leave, I'll break your legs. Your sisters know you're building a house, but did any of them come to help? They're just lazy. How many believers have clean houses? But your grandmother went anyway, leaving all her work and all the people who were helping, and me with my hands full. When I think about it, I still get so mad my chest hurts.

In our village, Pingzhan's family, my fourth sister-in-law, Lame Chang's wife, and Baogui's family used to be believers. Later, they left the church. God just wants money. It's all a scam. Your grandmother holds a relatively high position. They all respect her. I said, respect is respect. I have none around here. We argued about divorce for years, and finally did it, but it hasn't amounted to much. When she comes back, she still lives here. Where else can she go?

When I was in Beijing fixing bikes, I was often angry. My daughter had a child and asked her mother to come and take care of him. But she always wanted to return for church. You know how far Beijing is, and how long it takes to get there and back.

I didn't buy this house until I moved back from Beijing. Your grandmother had planned to live with her sisters, but in the end she came back, too. For a little while, I went with her, I wanted to see what was so great about God. I had nothing to do, and the village roads are bad, all ruts and potholes, and I could at least help her walk. Pastor Liang's sermons at the general church meetings weren't bad. They weren't all miracles and revelations. They aimed to change your way of thinking. These people are just people, but some of them make out to be gods. What the Pastor Liang used to say made sense. But what your grandmother and her friends were hearing was a pack of nonsense.

Later the local church chose a leader, and your grandmother became assistant leader. I was completely against it. I said, you can't be leader. I am the head of the household. If you become head of the church, you aren't welcome here. How many good people are there in that church? The church accounts are a complete mess. They want you to sign for expenses, but if you make a single mistake, you'll have to take all the responsibility. I know how you are, you can't even do the household expenses, you're going to end up personally responsible. Those other people are no good. They say, Eldest Grandmother, you have such high moral virtue, you have to do it. I said, if you're assistant church leader, you have to make it clear: this thing might end up in Timbuktu, but you won't be held responsible. I said, Linglan, you've been a group leader, how many good people have you seen at church? You can't count on any of them.

Grandpa Ming's bike repair shop is in a remote part of the village, but it still looks like a proper shop. In the front is the main building with two floors and two rooms. The kitchen is in the back stairwell, but it's covered in a thick layer of spiderwebs and the coals are ice cold. It doesn't look like anyone has started a fire there for a long time. I ask, Grandpa Ming, do you cook? He says, in the morning I eat a bowl of noodles, and at lunch I eat cold bread. I drink water, and in the summer eat cold noodles and bread. All I need is a full belly.

Grandpa Ming is Father's best friend. In my childhood memories, the two of them would often sit up through the night; for a time Uncle Yuan was with them. Sometimes they would come over after lunch, go home for dinner, and then come back after dinner again. In the summer, they would sit in our courtyard, waving their leaf fans. In the winter, they sat in a corner of the west room, burning corn stalks or tree roots, still sitting there after the fire had gone cold. What were they talking about? I have never known. Perhaps family matters. Or maybe things that were happening in the village. When they discussed the wrongs being done, their voices would suddenly grow louder, and they would start to curse. Often they wouldn't talk at all.

They would just sit silently, staring into the fire, watching it slowly grow dim. This is rural companionship. Even its silence is deep and rich.

When he brings up his marriage to Eldest Grandmother Linglan, you can tell that he remains deeply perplexed, despite all the thought he's given it. He doesn't understand how she can remain so deeply immersed, how she can so lightly discard decades of family life in favor of God.

The sky has darkened; the lights at Grandpa Ming's are all low wattage; the room is dim and gloomy. Father teases him a bit, saying, Your Grandpa Ming's monthly electrical bill is less than one yuan, he drives the electricity guy crazy. When Grandpa Ming hears this he lets out a laugh, *Pah*! Fuck his mother, they're just out to charge you fees, I won't give them the pleasure. In any case I don't work in the evening. And I don't like to watch television. I sit in the courtyard and enjoy the cool. In the winter I like to go somewhere and chat, and when I come back I go to bed. What do I need electricity for? I thought about when he was young, how he would wear his khaki military uniform, handsome and confident. Back then Grandpa Ming was filled with mettle. Now he's become a "stingy" old man. It's both funny and a little bit sad.

Huge mosquitoes buzz by our heads and bite our legs. Wherever I slap there's a little spot of blood. Grandpa Ming takes out a small fan and turns it on me full blast. The mosquitoes spin dizzily around the light and fan. It's quite a sight. Grandpa Ming takes out a little bottle of green menthol ointment from beside the bed and has me put some on. It doesn't help a bit. I can't imagine how he gets through the night.

After dinner, we move into the courtyard and continue our conversation.

Back when I was driving long-distance, I went to Yunnan and some old army buddies of mine said, there's a girl here who was sent down from the city. She's really pretty, nice

228

and tall. Let's go have a look. So we did. She really was good looking. Me, at that time, I was good looking, too. That's a fact. Your dad knows all about it. She was willing to go with me, but I wouldn't accept. You've got to have morals. Do I regret it now? What is there to regret, it's your fate. In any case your grandmother wasn't a Christian then, and she was pretty good to me. Right after I was discharged, she was really good to me. When I came back from working in the fields, the children would be eating soup noodles, and she would give me a large bowl of noodles with an egg at the bottom. My clothes were always clean. She washed everything. She would say that a man's clothing is his wife's face. I remember that phrase very clearly. Sometimes I would get so angry with her, but then I would remember those tender words, and I would forgive her.

Some people say I should just let her believe what she pleases, it's a good thing. All that matters is that she's happy. I say, it didn't happen to your family, so don't go running your mouth. If your wife ran away and didn't come home for three days, I'll be damned if you didn't fight with her! Over this question of faith, I went to her family's home, and I said to her father, can you please try to persuade her, for the children's sake? But her father said, Christianity is a good thing; the Party supports it. I support it.

Motherfucker, what was there to say to that? After that I didn't go over to her family's house anymore. After your Eldest Grandmother became a Christian, she slowly began to forget her family, and it really hurt our daughter's feelings. We fought about it in Beijing. My daughter said, Ma, if you get a divorce and remarry, I'll disown you. At our son's wedding, your Eldest Grandmother suggested they become Christians. My son said, become Christian, not a chance. Any young person who becomes a Christian is bound to be a small-minded tightwad. I have three conditions for a wife: that she isn't a Christian, she isn't an official, and she isn't rich. The first is the most important.

A few years ago, my son sent me a television. My sciatic nerve was bothering me, and I couldn't walk. I said to your grandmother, can you call to see if it's arrived, and if it has, if someone can go pick it up. But she was involved with a church performance and was gone every day; she wouldn't help at all. So I limped over, and the pain brought tears to my eyes. Afterwards I said to my two kids, your ma gave birth to you, but your dad raised you. My son and daughter are both married and are very filial. They said, neither of you have to work, we'll send 600 kuai every month. I said, it's better to work, who wants to be idle? But even easy business I can't do, not all by myself. Your ma might leave at any moment, we can't get anything going.

You wanted me to talk about family things, fuck, I won't ever finish. In the Liang family, your dad has had it the worst. I've had it the worst in the Han family.

It's a kind of tradition that the Han family doesn't work together. When Mother Jiunan died, her sons held separate funeral feasts. The *suona* players showed up early, but no one received them, and they didn't know which house to go to. Those who have left to work don't send money home. There's just no love. One year Wan Jinling went to Xinde's to borrow some money because her husband was sick. Her husband is Xinde's nephew. Your Third Uncle Xinde sat on his settee for half an hour, refusing to talk. He gets a salary, and his family is fine. Of course he's got money to spare! I couldn't stand it, so I told Jinling to come over, and I gave her 200 kuai.

I've tried to be upright all my life, but everyone I see is a crooked tree.

After the Great Sichuan Earthquake I was going to the phone company to pay the phone bill. I took fifty with me, but only put thirty toward the bill, and then directly donated the remaining twenty. Later, the Party members were asked to donate, so I donated another fifty. I gave my daughter a call and asked her to donate; you didn't want your workplace to have to scrape it together; it's a question of morality. That was such a critical time, saving lives. I heard there was stealing in the disaster area. Fake emergency trucks would go in and take things. This is what society has created; it's not that people are bad. It's all society's influence. Look at how rotten the kids are these days—who knows where society will end up if we don't whip them into shape.

The social atmosphere is bad in general. In Ding Village there was a child who died saving someone's life. His family wanted their child to be remembered as a martyr, but they said they couldn't do it, because he wasn't eighteen yet. I couldn't stand it, so I went with them to the county administration, but no one did anything about it. You see, these fuckers, they can't see what really matters anymore. Chairman Mao once said, it's not a matter of doing something great, but doing something worthwhile.

After talking like this for a while, Grandpa Ming turns suddenly to Father and says in a mysterious voice, Guangzheng, I have to tell you something, and you tell me what you think. I don't know what I should do about this. I was going to come to town and ask you. A young woman, twenty-seven years old, divorced with a small child, a high school graduate—she speaks Mandarin really well, she said she dialed the wrong number and reached me. You know what, we seem compatible. Her family runs a small sweater factory, and her father is difficult. She wants to come live with me. I didn't ask her to come. But she says, she's afraid a young guy will look down on her, she wants an older man.

Father says 85 percent of the time these women are homing pigeons. They go right back where they came from. They're tricky. Hasn't this happened before? In Hepo Village, there was an old man who married a woman from Shanxi, who also brought her child. They had a marriage ceremony in the village, and while it was happening she said something had happened in her family, and she had him send over some money. Ten days later, when they were on a trip and staying in a hotel, she ran off. The man lost 10,000 kuai.

Grandpa Ming doesn't think she's lying. If she tried it, he'd know. Clearly, he's got his heart set on it. Actually, though he and Grandma Linglan are divorced they still live together, but this year during summer vacation, when she came back from Beijing, she stayed at her family's home instead of with him. Maybe that has something to do with it. Frank, firm, irascible Grandpa Ming has suddenly become lovesick as a teenager, flushed and excited.

It's almost midnight when Father and I finally head home. Grandpa Ming walks us to Elder Brother's house. He and Father keep whispering to one another behind my back; I imagine Grandpa Ming wants Father's opinion.

In the black sky, the stars shine all the more clearly. The small town has fallen completely silent. Occasionally a car passes by, like a flashing meteor, and then the town falls silent again.

Linglan

I make an appointment with the president of the County Christian Association. He proposes that we meet at the town's church and also arranges for a few church members to join us. The president holds the highest teaching and administrative position in the county church, and he's also a clergyman. He's not particularly well spoken and has trouble really opening up. He chooses his words carefully, perhaps because the county Party secretary and other local cadres are in the room with us.

I have been a Christian for twenty or thirty years. When the policy on religion opened up in 1978, I became a believer. Suffering brought me to the faith. My family struggled to survive, so I chose this road. After I started believing, I felt spiritually changed. Before I had been too focused upon material gain in my interactions with others. After I became a believer, my heart and mind became stronger. I felt I could do good, that I could be a good person. From a cultural standpoint, it's a form of self-cultivation; religion benefits society. Churches began to form earlier but were only officially accepted in 1978. In Rang County there are 152 places of worship and around 30 or 40,000 believers. This is more than in other counties, mostly because the base population is large, which is an indication of the policies of religious freedom. Once the gates are opened, it's not only those who have suffered who believe, it's also those with spiritual needs. In the past we thought people believed because they were stupid or ignorant, but now all kinds of people, from all levels of society, are believers. Many retired officials believe. They are transforming themselves. They have come to think and act as one.

In the villages, most believers are female, very few are male. Many are elderly. This is because most of the young people have left. In addition, in accordance with national policies, those under eighteen years of age are not permitted to profess a faith. They're also not allowed to join the Party, so that's fair. Over the past few years, the number of believers has continued to increase. People aren't running around in private like they used to, and they're not allowed to worship at home. You must gather at an officially sanctioned church.

During the interview, the town church leader listens carefully and notes everything in a notebook. I ask about the relationship between the church leader, the town church, and its believers.

Between four and five hundred people come to our town's church services on a weekly basis. We're in charge of eight administrative villages. That's according to regulations, you can only go to the church that serves your area. Most often husbands and wives come together. Young men come least often, they've all left for work. The countryside is run by the 3860 team now. The "38" means women, because Women's Day is March 8, and the "60" is the elderly. Some have had fallings out; some are weak; some are strong, and they have different degrees of understanding. Their faithful souls learn gradually, as they reach toward perfection. The scriptures are beneficial, but what you get out of them depends on the individual. It's a question of continual refinement. So they're permitted to be bad people. Why do we work for six days and rest for one? The day of rest is the day of self-transformation. Those who have just found faith are like small children. Christians commit very few major sins, although they do have minor faults. We are human beings, not gods. Christians are people too, but people who seek faith. For example, if you want to steal, but don't, that is a kind of sin because you had the thought. Religion is a supplement to law; it is practical; its goal is to control the spirit. If you do not try and improve, that is a sin.

One must obey those in power; they are God's servants, the ones God has chosen.

Jesus was a loving man. He called people to do good deeds. For example, the Bible says, all of you, from the high to the low, must serve the country. Officials are also God's servants. Those who believe are always at the vanguard. Some might not understand. People mock us and say, it's not raining today, can you say a little prayer and ask God to make it rain. Whether it rains or not, that's God's plan. As for those who become officials, it's the same thing; it's God's plan, they're there for the public good—to teach ordinary believers to obey society, to set a good example, to do good deeds.

Religious belief aids the government. Each person makes church contributions as they wish; whatever they give is enough. Most of it is used to build churches, to buy teaching materials, and sometimes when there is a national disaster, to respond to the country's call. No one is corrupt or accepts bribes. Everyone's trying to give as much as they can. One more believer is one more good citizen. To lose a believer is to lose a good citizen.

In our interactions with others, we would rather be at a disadvantage. In Chenji, east of the river, there was a large canal that made it hard for children to go to school, so some Christians took the initiative to raise money to build a bridge out of prefabricated wood. The Christian way is one of good deeds. In so doing, they also reap good. There are even some converts, who, when a church is opened, kill a family pig to share with everyone. They love their country and their church.

The clergyman and the church leader are trying to make connections between faith, patriotism, and politics, and they make it clear that they are in keeping with government policy. As they speak, they observe the Party committee secretary's reaction out of the corner of their eyes. The atmosphere is very delicate.

I also ask an elderly woman who has been serving us why she believes and whether she knows Eldest Grandmother Linglan and Grandpa Ming. To my surprise they actually know each other well. They've been church sisters for more than ten years. In fact, she is one of the church sisters that Grandpa Ming was so upset about. When I bring him up, she simply shakes her head.

I have been a Christian for more than thirty years. I believe simply because it brings me peace. My neighbors were

Christians before I was. They would talk about the benefits of religious belief and how it's good for society. You do charitable deeds, good deeds. You don't do ill. And you improve your temper. A believer must control herself. When you're angry, you look to the words of the Bible, and your anger fades away. My husband doesn't support me, but we've never fought about it, either. I work hard six days a week, but I keep one day a week open for church. He doesn't say anything. If something really comes up, I don't have to go. God doesn't like it if you insist. God is pleased with the work of your own two hands.

You don't know how irritable and violent Ming can be. He's always criticizing Linglan for this or that. Yet Linglan has never said one bad thing about him. You can see the extent of God's grace in her family. Their daughter and son both have homes in Beijing—who has that? Ming is not a Christian, but Linglan is one of God's faithful children. She won't argue or fight, so all he can do is yell. Linglan had God's love inside her, but Ming doesn't curse her father or mother, he only curses God. That she can't tolerate. He finds fault with her, it's verbal violence. Actually, it's because Ming is so weak. He doesn't consider her faith, he interprets everything negatively.

Ming is too cruel to Linglan. He hits her; when he's angry he curses her; he won't let her say anything in her defense. How can Linglan love him? He just makes his assumptions and always assumes the worst. He's never able to see things in a good light. He says Linglan sneaks off and does bad things. Linglan also has her faults. As soon as he hits her, she leaves. He says she doesn't take care of the family, but that's just an excuse. The faithful don't go to church every day, just Sunday. Besides, now they don't have so much to do, and they don't have much land. And in the busy season, in addition to the combine harvester, they have temporary workers.

Again I ask the church leader, are there some who don't take care of their families? Or some who are sick but won't take their medication? The church leader says, some are confused in their beliefs. There are some who don't care for their families, who don't work, who become professional believers. In the end they become cultish. Eastern Lightning is a cult, for example. There are very few who won't take medication. But it has happened that some, whom doctors have diagnosed with terminal illnesses, have been cured in church. He then adds, in a meaningful voice: Religion can sometimes be supernatural. This is what makes it a religion. As for Grandpa Ming and Eldest Grandmother Linglan, as he sees it one is a Party member, one is a Christian. Those are two different forms of faith, so conflicts are to be expected. But at the same time, they are both laborers.

In the village there's a sort of universal contempt for believers, and their words and behavior are often mocked. Father, for instance, thinks that all believers are stupid, lazy, and poor. They don't understand anything—they just follow blindly. When I ask our current Party secretary if he would let his wife become a believer, he says, very bluntly, "No. I wouldn't. I don't want to be a laughingstock. All the believers are old women with nothing better to do. It's just a kind of moral support. No one really knows what to believe. And as a cadre, I could not allow her to be a Christian, we have to belong to the mainstream." The driver who has been accompanying me also can't help saying what he thinks: Christians are ridiculous and a little dumb. As he puts it: Fuck, where do they get all that gusto? A group of fools, kneeling down and mumbling stuff. They're just people with nothing better to do. But at the same time he has a definite respect for them, like when a bridge collapsed in his village. When the Christians saw it, they talked it over, and each one went to get stone or wood or to mix concrete, and in a few days they had fixed the bridge. He says, they really work together, much more so than your average work unit.

We also can't simply label Grandpa Ming's attitude toward Eldest Grandmother Linglan's beliefs as "ignorant." This touches upon the reality of village productivity and questions of traditional beliefs and the rural approach to spiritual questions. In this society, husbands and wives work together. Shared labor within a household is a basic premise of life. If you don't do your share but spend your time on spiritual activities instead, survival can be compromised, and the family can fall into harder circumstances, like what Ming and Linglan are now facing. From a cultural standpoint, in rural areas, especially in northern rural areas, "elevated" activities that encroach upon the secular are typically unwelcome. In other words, things that are not considered part of the community's heterogeneous culture are considered "other." Many who take part are described as having some sort of "mental illness" or to be "abnormal" or "peculiar." Grandmother Linglan is an example of this. Strong-minded and ambitious Grandpa Ming did not want his wife to become a village laughingstock, so he did his utmost to prevent her from becoming a "believer." His stated reason is that she doesn't help him earn a living, but, in reality, he is deeply ashamed. He feels like he can't hold his head up. A village is an organic, living entity, in which each person has a position, a role to play, a certain image. Everyone is conscious of this, it informs your self worth and self image. If it is damaged, it can affect you psychologically.

In addition, most of the rural converts have an incomplete understanding of the religion they believe in. (The phenomenon is quite common. I was talking with a few relatives who are Christians and asked them some questions about the Bible and Christianity. Often their answers made me want to both laugh and cry.) But in religion they have found dignity, equality, and respect. They find inspiration and spiritual sustenance in saving others. As rural Chinese women, these are things they've never had before. So while they may not have a deep religious understanding, it is an important refuge from life's oppression and spiritual impoverishment, which may also be why there are more female converts than male. They don't dare express themselves openly, to say what they feel, because they are generally considered to be lazy, a bit touched in the head, or even just a bunch of fools.

Actually, most of the time, there need not be a conflict between faith and productivity; those involved can sometimes exaggerate religion's effects on labor and daily life. Chinese rural culture remains deeply pragmatic. The most important thing is to live a steady life; for this reason, individual spiritual needs and affection between husbands and wives are often distorted and handled through ridicule, mockery, and avoidance; rarely does anyone speak directly or earnestly about these subjects. This kind of oppressive, twisted psychological environment doesn't only exist within households, between husbands and wives, parents and children; it's also the fundamental mode of interactions between neighbors, which creates all kinds of problems.

Old Daoyi

Old Daoyi ("Old Mr. Righteous") was one of my uncles. Why "Old Mr. Righteous"? My uncle may have been the first person from our village to go to college. After he graduated, he taught high school at the county seat, and after that he facilitated the construction of a new school in town, where he was asked to be a head teacher. Although he was well liked by students, he wasn't always loved by the administration. He was for reason and rationality, stubborn and frank, and his mantra was that a person needed integrity and righteousness. If the school cafeteria food wasn't good, if students were charged unreasonable fees—even if the school sidewalks were being invaded by plants from the teachers' gardens—he'd go straight to the administration. If they didn't respond, he'd go straight over to the local education department or even all the way to the county. He'd see it through no matter what. They couldn't stand him at the school or at the county, and eventually people started calling him "Old Mr. Righteous" behind his back.

My uncle didn't have a good relationship with his sons. His youngest went to college, and the other two, after graduating from high school, became private teachers. In the early '90s, many private teachers were given official positions, and his sons were perfectly qualified, but every year there was a quota, and the teachers were ranked, and you often had to do a little extra to be chosen. Because he wanted to be "righteous" about it, my uncle refused to use his connections, to talk with people or offer gifts. When his sons suggested he do something, he was furious. He only worked according to his conscience. In the end, his sons weren't selected. Later, private teachers' positions were eliminated, and they had to return to farming. For a few years, they wouldn't even speak to him. Only after my uncle retired and came back to the village did their relationships improve a little.

When I go to my uncle's house, my elder cousin Wanhui is watching television. His family still lives in the village, in a three-roomed, gray brick house. It used to be one of the best houses in the village, but now there are large, overhanging eaves in the front, and the courtyard is woven with brick paths. My uncle's portrait hangs in a black frame with a black silk bow in the central room.

Your uncle died in 2004. He had emphysema. If he hadn't died, things would be a lot better. He could watch the house, and I could go out and earn a little money. He was sick for six or seven years; his health had never been good. After he died, we kept him in the house for two days, waiting for Wan'an to come back for the funeral. Your aunt and I had different opinions about whether we should cremate him or bury him.

In my opinion, both are fine. The person is dead, and if you were filial while he was alive, that's good enough. But your uncle had some final wishes. He didn't want to be cremated. He always grumbled about how much it would hurt. When the village secretary came to see him, he told him, too: I don't want to be cremated, even if it costs a little bit more money, that's okay. Villagers fear cremation. They want their bodies to be buried intact.

It's common now for people to be buried in secret; you can pay 2,000 kuai and have it done. One way is to go directly to the village secretary and pay, but you can't do it too openly. The other way is to bury the person in the middle of the night. But then you can't make a sound. The children are there, but they can't cry. Before it was an event, you would have gongs and horns as you walked to the burial site. This way you give the village secretary a little money, and he gives you the nod, and then in the middle of the night you take the coffin, the sons following behind, filled with grief, but afraid to breathe, because they can't cry out loud. Of course everyone in the village knows, they're perfectly clear on what's happening. You tell me, won't you be buried one day?

But some are unlucky. Zhou Baoliang from our village, they didn't cremate him, they paid off the village secretary and he said they could bury him. But just as they put the coffin into the grave, before they even had time to cover it with dirt, people from the civil administration showed up. They didn't dare say that they had already paid off the village secretary. So they had to pay another 1,000 kuai, and that took care of it. To be honest, it's all about the money. The policies may be good, but you've got to look at how they're carried out.

As soon as I brought up cremation, your aunt started to cry. But during that period of time, the rules were being strictly enforced. We were a model village, and everyone was watching us. The secretary didn't dare take money. He only said, cremation isn't a big deal. Later, Wan'an came back from where he was working. I guess he's got a bit of a position, and a few people from the county know him and came with him, so there didn't seem anything to do but cremate him.

But what could we do? We couldn't go against your uncle's final wishes. Finally we thought of an idea: Before he was cremated, we would have the geomancer cut his finger and toe nails, and set them aside. After he was cremated, we would arrange his ashes into a human form in the coffin and place his nails in the correct places. Then we would have the complete form of a body, a whole person. Of course, the moment we picked up the coffin, the shape would be lost. But what can you do? I guess it's the thought that counts.

His sons-in-law had arranged drums for when we left to take the body to be cremated, and firecrackers were set off as we left the village, as we, his filial sons, kowtowed. I guess that counted as a send-off. Now they've started to do this in the village. Even with cremation there's a ceremony. People with money will even arrange a small car to carry the relatives. When they come back, there's the burial and a meal. It's tantamount to paying twice, for two different things.

I'm still not happy about it. I know that when people die, they're gone. But there's always a thread of hope, and when I think how we had to cremate him, I feel awful. Before he was cremated, your uncle was lying there, his head covered with that kind of yellow paper we use here in rural areas, and I don't know why, but it fell off. I picked it up and put it back on, and then, a little while later, it fell off again. Then later I saw his arms were stuck underneath him. Was he in pain? It was as though he were trying to tell me. So I started to cry. I knew he didn't want this to happen. I rearranged his arms and said, Dad, there's nothing I can do, this is government policy, please understand.

After they were done, I went to collect the ashes, and they were all white, just like the beanstalks we burn at home. Even though a body gradually rots underground, you can still think, there's a complete person there. But now, he's just a heap of ash. Your aunt cried until she fainted.

After all that, we still had to bury him on the sly. We had already dug the grave, and the relatives had gathered, his sons were kneeling and the other guests were there. We had the relatives come kowtow for the rites, but we did it very quietly, and we didn't dare cry, we held it all in, only wiping away our tears. Think of your poor uncle, he suffered his entire life, and when he left his sons and daughters and relatives couldn't even see him off properly.

When will cremation become the norm? It's hard to say. There seem to be as many graves as before, the only difference is that the people in them have been cremated. Originally the production team said, we'll find a piece of land, raise a building, separate out the various villages, and when the urns come back we put them in according to the order of death, each person in their own alcove. But that was years ago, and where's the building? That will never fly, not here in the countryside, not in a million years! It's not our custom.

For a few years there, there was plenty of ruckus around burning bodies, too. You probably haven't heard this, but Hua had some affairs outside the village, and it drove his wife crazy. Later she drowned in a pond, and they buried her in secret. But somehow they found out about it, and dug her up again. It had been more than two weeks, and the body was starting to rot, so the authorities came and used an iron hook to pull her out. Her buttocks had softened, and when they pulled her out, her body was misshapen. Hua didn't have a home, and her siblings didn't care, so all they could do is take her to the city and cremate

243

her. Later her son came back to collect her ashes. He was so disturbed. People driving by stopped and stared.

The more Wanhui talked, the quieter he became. There was none of the elegant manner he had had in years past, when he was our teacher. He and his brother Wanming, whom I mentioned earlier, were highly regarded private teachers then. They'd graduated from the former high school, and they were in their prime, filled with energy and drive. They could teach and were responsible, and their efforts made the Liang Village students among the best in the area. He's deeply resentful of the current burial policy and rural conditions in general. But he only talks about it; he's deeply dispirited and hardly wants to think about the problem. You can see that having to return to farming had a huge impact on him.

Later I go to the county seat to meet a friend. He tells me this story:

This is a true story. It was in 1994 or '95. One day, I suddenly got a note telling me to go the countryside and bring a mask. I found a whole group of people watching, just throngs of people. We were in the village to exhume a grave. They had just implemented the cremation policy, and the idea was to make an example and scare people a little. In rural areas, it's bad luck to exhume a grave; it's considered immoral. Hardly anyone would do it, so they had to find some lowlifes, some guys who had been released from prison or labor camp. They did the work, and someone from the government watched them. We were a team of five. I was team leader.

The woman hadn't been dead long, and when she was disinterred her body had just begun to swell. Her face was pale and swollen, and there were some maggots crawling around. It was horrible. We pulled the body to the side of the grave, and no one wanted to touch it again. So we put some gasoline on it. We'd already decided who would light it; it would be those lowlifes. In the end they didn't use enough gasoline, and she only half-burned, then the fire went out. You can't imagine what an awful sight that was. So then they went to light it again. Around seven or eight people had been buried recently in the cemetery, and we cremated them all that afternoon. There were flames everywhere, and the smell, when I think of it now it still makes me nauseous. After the fire was relit, and we saw that they were burning at least a little, we left. We didn't care how it turned out.

It was quite a sight, and there were crowds. Some people couldn't stand the smell and left. But they came back after a while, wanting to see what was happening. The families had cried and cursed and tried to block the way in the beginning, but they were pushed aside by the police. When they'd burned gravesites in other communities there had been conflicts, so we had arranged for a large police presence. Later, when the smell was really overwhelming, even the family members didn't stay. They left, too, sobbing. They would return and weep some more, and then leave again.

Now it strikes me as extremely disrespectful. At that time, many people were arrested because they resisted the disinterment and burning. These past few years it hasn't been as strict. You simply pay a fine, and especially those who have money will just go ahead and bury their dead, although it's all done covertly. Half of the time, people cremate first and then have a burial. As long as you cremate and pay the fine, no one cares if you have a burial, they turn a blind eye.

Huan

It has rained for two days straight. The open land is clean and fresh, and the leaves of the trees and the crops in the fields are green and glistening. Above, heavy gray clouds seal off this vast and quiet world. The rainy season has come. Even though we're in a northern region, there are always a dozen odd days of continuous rain. Actually, I love this kind of weather, with rain rushing down, but not gloomy or gray. The sky glows majestic and solemn.

The woods on the riverbank were only planted a few years ago, and the grass still isn't thick enough to cover the ground. As we walk barefoot in the sandy soil, the fine pebbles hurt our feet, yet they also tickle in a pleasant way. The river bubbles past, filled with force and yearning. The giant reeds, scrubbed clean by the rain, rustle happily, filled with life. Mist rises from the river and reaches out across the horizon.

Scattered along the riverbank are small huts for those who tend to the watermelons and peanuts, which grow best in open sandy areas. From time to time silhouettes are visible bustling among the watermelons, checking them over; this kind of rainy weather isn't good for them. We glance into a small hut and see a middle-aged woman doing housework as a three- or four-year-old girl plays by her side. When they hear our voices, the woman turns and my elder brother lets out a laugh. Isn't that Sister Huan?

Huan, who looks as if she's in her early forties now, dated a young man from the Zhang family when we were young. She would come hang out in the village, and everyone thought she was gorgeous. She caused quite a sensation. A country girl, she worked in the fields all year long, but her skin was still fair and her eyes bright and clear. Her long hair would float in the breeze, like a movie star, and she sashayed when she walked. Her only defect was her nose, which was too straight and short, disrupting the harmony of her face. But it gave the impression that she was someone with a strong character and her own ideas—which turned out to be the case. After she married, she and her husband left to work and to have a child unofficially. First she was an unskilled laborer and carried trays in a cafeteria. Then her husband learned to make noodles, and after a few years of careful economizing, they opened a noodle shop outside Tianjin. Business was really good, and they earned quite a bit of money. They built a house by the main road in the village, one of the few that has three stories.

Her only regret has been that she never had a boy. The Zhangs are one of the families in the village with only one household, and although they had three boys who started three families of their own, those families have only had girls. We call this "ending the line," and people find it humiliating. Huan's husband is the eldest. They got married more than ten years ago, and they must have had five or six girls, but to this day they haven't had a son.

The girl playing next to Huan is her youngest daughter. I look at Huan again; her silhouette is the same. She's still pretty, perhaps just a bit thinner and darker. Actually she looks a little haggard. We ask why she's here, didn't they open a restaurant in Tianjin? Huan smiles, she's been back ten days or so. She came back to see a doctor. She has lower back pain, along with some dizziness. The doctor says she has a slipped disk, so she's taking medication, but it will take a while for it to improve. In a few days she'll head back to Tianjin, it's busy, and it's hard for her to be away long. This is her mother-in-law's melon patch, and she came to see if she could help after all the rain.

After we talk for a while, I ask, as tactfully as I can, if I might ask her some questions. She listens closely to what I have to say, nodding from time to time. After I'm done she says she's willing to be interviewed. It might do some good. When she has a moment to think about her life, and this problem, she isn't completely sure whether her choices have been right or wrong.

Sitting on a little stool by the door, she embraces her little girl, who sparkles with intelligence and charm, and she tells us the story of her children.

I want to have a boy. In the larger Zhang family, there are three sons, but none of them has a boy. It isn't right, for the family, I've got to have a boy, no matter what, I must have one.

I care deeply for my daughter. She's precious, as close to me as a quilted jacket. I'm devoted to her. But I almost didn't keep her. When I was five months pregnant, I did an ultrasound, and when I saw she was a girl, I thought I should just be induced and forget about it. I had given away another daughter just after she was born. You can't imagine how I grieved. But this one, I hadn't even seen her face, I might as well not have her at all. The doctor was a distant relative of mine, so every time we went, I would ask her to check the ultrasound. She said don't get rid of it. Find a good family in town, and when you want you can go and see the girl in secret. I thought, a girl is also a living thing.

When I induced labor the first time, it broke my heart. It was at five months—I've heard their faces and organs are all fully formed, but I already had two, and I still wanted a boy, and I couldn't have another. So I induced labor. My heart was broken, but there was nothing I could do. The next two, I didn't even think about it, I just got rid of them. So this time I planned to give birth, although my husband opposed it. One, I would be pregnant for several more months, and two, he was afraid I wouldn't be able to part with her when the time came. And once you give her away, she isn't yours. Why go to the trouble in the first place?

When the doctor put it that way, I was moved. I asked to see the head of the adoptive family, the married couple, and they were very accomplished, only a bit older than me,

248

still pretty young. They worked in the government, and their son was already a college student. I was pleased with what I saw, so I decided to have her. But they wouldn't agree to let me see her afterwards. I thought it through and decided it was okay, to be able to give my daughter to a good family was enough.

As Huan spoke, she looked tenderly at her daughter, who was gently stroking her face. She continued: She was born early, more than ten days before her due date. It was in the evening, and my belly suddenly started to hurt. We hadn't even been at the hospital thirty minutes before she was born. The midwife didn't have a chance to let the adoptive family know. Originally, I hadn't wanted to see her, I would just give her away and be done with it. I was afraid that if I saw her I wouldn't be able to do it. But there she was, crying and crying until her voice turned hoarse, and the family still hadn't come. I was afraid she would hurt herself with all that crying, so I had the nurse bring her to me, and I spoke quietly to her. And who would have guessed, but as soon as I held her, she stopped crying. I opened up the blanket; she was pink and white; her eyes were wide open, looking at me. And in that instant my heart melted, and I decided I wouldn't give her away. The couple came later and when they saw how pretty she was, they really wanted her. They gave me gifts and said they would recognize me as a relative, but I said it didn't matter. Her midwife was furious, because the family blamed her. But you can see how fortunate it is that I didn't give her away. This little thing is so precious to me. She understands everything.

Truth be told, I know that when I'm old, it will be these girls that I'll count on. Girls are good, they're considerate. After they marry they still take care of their own parents. What's so good about sons? I'm clear on this. Look in the village, which sons still take care of their old mothers after they're married? It's not that they're not filial, you can't abandon your own family, but at most they give their parents a little money to spend. But the ones who really love their parents, who sit by their sides and say more than two sentences, that's the daughters. This is clear in my mind. And yet I still want a boy; we must continue the family line.

My husband also wants one. He is the kind of person who keeps to himself; he doesn't say a lot, but he's seen my suffering over the years; he knows we're not going to succeed in having a son. But sometimes he will give a sigh and you can hear his despair. When we come back for New Years, the way they look it's like we owe them a son, I hate that look. Everyone knows we want a son, and they assume we're worried there will be no one to inherit the money, the house, but that isn't actually the case. We're just thinking there ought to be a boy—three sons and not even one grandson, others will laugh, and it doesn't seem right.

Has all this damaged my health? No, it hasn't; our own mothers would have four or five, and it wasn't a big deal. For women to have children is natural. On the other hand, I'm getting older, and I'm starting to have little ailments. I'm careful not to tire myself out. I have three girls. The two oldest are in junior high, their grandmother helped take care of them, and now they live at school and come home on Sundays. This little one is with us in Tianjin, she's no trouble at all. Usually, I ask someone to watch her. My job is to take care of the money and make purchases; it's not tiring, but I have to be there.

About a decade ago we were poor, and when we had our second daughter the family planning office was very strict; many people who were about to give birth were arrested and labor was induced. Wanming's wife was only twenty days from her due date and assumed there wouldn't be a problem, but who knew: she was arrested, and even though she was about to give birth, you can't think they would be so heartless, but they were, they took her to have the operation. It was such bad luck. When she thinks about it she still cries: a perfectly healthy child, killed. We've been to places all over—Xinjiang, Gansu—we've been there. My man Zhang, he had left to work, and I was in a small rented apartment, not daring to go out. At home they arrested my mother-in-law and held her for several days. We couldn't pay the fine and almost had to sell the old house, but in the end we borrowed money from my family. Only then did they release her. It was really hard! Things got more stable after we moved to Tianjin. And the rural policies are more flexible now; they let you have a second one. To tell the truth, not so many exceed the birth policy. The cost of raising a child is so high now, if you have another one you can't afford to raise it, and you don't have the time, either.

There is one other thing I want to tell you. When I came back I went to a fortune teller. He said there are seven little angel girls in my destiny. Only after I've gathered all seven will I have a boy. I thought about it; if you add the ones I induced, wouldn't that be exactly seven? If I get pregnant again, shouldn't it be a boy? I'm thinking of trying one last time—I'm older now, and if we delay any longer I won't be able to have another. If it's not a boy, I'll just give up the idea for good. What do you think? Should I try again? I still haven't told Zhang.

Looking at beautiful, calm, candid Huan, I am bewildered. Here is a woman with understanding and experience. This is clear in the ways she gets things done, in her opinions and her knowledge about the world today, including how she talks about business in Tianjin. Yet this matter of having a son makes almost no sense at all. She says over and over that she wants a son, not because of some sort of backward ideology, but simply because she wants one.

I calculate it in my mind: Huan has had seven girls altogether. She has three, she induced three, and she gave away one. According to a modern way of thinking, the educated, urban point of view, this is a kind of cruel war on reproduction.

Rural women are no longer the "hero mothers" of the 1950s; reproduction now takes place amid an atmosphere of contempt and disregard for life. When the repeating cycle of pregnancy and abortion becomes the norm, motherhood begins to lose its overtones of heroism and joy, and in the end what was forced becomes voluntary, heartbreak becomes numbness, and finally all this is internalized as her own desire. It's as if her life will not be complete, her duties undone, until she reaches this goal.

The situation is slowly changing, however. Births in rural families are gradually decreasing. According to Qingdao:

> If the firstborn is a boy, most families aren't in a rush to have a second, or they might adopt a little girl. If the second is also a boy, everybody cries. They get really upset. What will they do? They can't afford to raise him. If the first is a girl, then 99 percent of the time, they still want a boy. They don't want it to be the end of the family line. Practically no one has a third. If you really want to, and you can pay the fine, then you can. The family planning policy doesn't have much binding effect. It's economics that restricts people's decisions.

Sometimes it's unbelievable how resilient people can be. Huan is now healthy and cheerful. She has coped with her pain and suffering on her own—either that or she's repressed it. She asks my brother which boarding schools in the city are good and which teachers are best. Her daughter is already in the eighth grade, and she wants her to test into the best high school in the county. She has high hopes for her. I ask if she knows the "migrant policy" in Tianjin. All you have to do is buy a house there, and you can have a *hukou*, and the children can go to school and take the college entrance exam there—the competition in Tianjin is less fierce than in Henan. She's really surprised, is that true? She never knew. She's up at 5 am and never in bed before 11 pm. Every day is so busy; she only rarely has the chance to watch television or read the paper. I think that maybe even if they did see the news, they wouldn't think it had anything to do with them; even though they live in Tianjin, they and the city are two entirely different entities. Their focus never strays from their hometown. Hearing that a house in Tianjin would probably cost between 400 and 500,000 yuan, Huan seems relieved. All the money they earned went to build the house. Now they only have around 100,000, and there is no way they can afford a place in Tianjin. Her expression makes me a little sad. She's relieved because she can't afford it. She won't have to "overstep her bounds."

It's almost noon, and there's still a misty rain. Huan locks the door and she and her daughter walk us back to the village. The little girl is really very well-behaved; she has a pair of big black eyes that never stop moving. They watch us closely, as she holds on tightly to her mama's hand. I think of when she was first born and how she suddenly stopped crying when Huan held her, a clever little sprite. Perhaps she had a premonition that her mother was going to give her away, and she used her cries to save herself. She succeeded.

When we get back to my brother's house, we find the rain rolling in majestic waves on the road; the sewers aren't working, and with nowhere to go, the water overflows across the roads. Even a town like this still doesn't have a complete sewer system; there are just some shallow and narrow drains, with stone slabs thrown haphazardly across the top. They're often blocked with household garbage, sewage, silt, and stones. This always happens when it rains. On the surface, trash and filth float along, stinking to high heaven.

Qiaoyu

Han Qiaoyu and Liang Wanqing ran off together. In Shenzhen, she found factory work that paid by the piece; he drove a pedi-cab. Others from the village worked there, too, but they weren't ashamed; they lived together anyway. Qiaoyu's husband Ming, whom she left back in the village, ranted and raged; he cursed her from the east side of the village to the west, from the north to the south. After a few months, he and some family members went to Shenzhen, planning to bring Qiaoyu back. A couple of weeks later, they returned without her, grey-faced. I heard Qiaoyu helped pay for their tickets home.

Han Qiaoyu isn't actually a Han. When she was three, her widowed mother married into the Han family, and she took the name. Her family story is heartbreaking. Her stepfather was the infamous Old Lumpy. He was withdrawn and couldn't earn any money, and there was never enough to eat. They all depended on her widowed mother's side business with the bachelors in town for food, ration tickets, or money. Although it was secret, everyone in the village knew about it, and Qiaoyu's family didn't have a good reputation. They all—especially her mother—actively avoided people. She wasn't well spoken, and when she met someone on the road, she would shoot a glance from a distance, her expression grim and vigilant, and then she would continue on with her head lowered, not saying a word. When I was young I thought they were strange. People hardly ever mentioned them. It was as if they didn't exist at all.

Qiaoyu grew up quiet and obedient. She was tall and well developed, with slender eyes that suited her long, good-natured face and gave her a certain radiance and gentleness. That plus her habitual nervous, hurried energy, as if she didn't know what to do with herself, made her strangely endearing. Han Ming began to pursue her. Ming's family is well known and prosperous. His father was a village cadre, his family had flour-milling machines and oil extractors, and they were also distributors. After Qiaoyu dropped out of school, she started helping at the mill, and every month they would give her a little money and some wheat bran to take home. According to the villagers, it was because Qiaoyu's mother and Ming's father had something between them that his father gave her the position, to help her family indirectly.

But Ming's father was firmly opposed to the match, and for several years he would hit, curse, and punish Ming to show that his mind was firmly made up. For Ming's part, he showed his determination by arguing or running away: If it wasn't Qiaoyu, he wouldn't marry at all. In the end, they married at a house on the east side of town without his father's blessing. Only Qiaoyu's mother quietly helped her daughter prepare some bedding and kitchen essentials. This was big news in the village. They were from the same village, and they were even both Hans. But then again, Qiaoyu wasn't really a Han. For a while everybody talked about it, but after the villagers got used to seeing them together, they were accepted.

They had a son and a daughter and even built a new house. And despite Ming's fiery temper and the fact that he beat her, they seemed to get along well enough.

I don't remember when exactly this happened. For a little while, my younger sister and I would often go to Qiaoyu's house. Her kind face, narrow eyes, and warm smile were deeply inviting for two people who no longer had a mother's love. She would always take out some snacks and pour some tea. She would sit in the main room on a traditional Chinese chair and chat with us. Because she was so tall she was always a little hunched and seemed even more so when she was sitting down. Her hands were large and broad, and as she raised them they would somehow draw us to her side, giving us a surprising sense of security. I don't remember what we talked about. It's funny, really, a woman of about thirty with two children, a woman who worked in the fields all day—what did she have in common with two adolescent girls? All I remember is that we would always sit for a long time, and eat a lot, and that sometimes we would even eat lunch, and then afterwards, happy, we would walk home as if in a dream. When I think of it now, I am filled with happiness and a sense of safety all over again.

No one knows when the relationship between Qiaoyu and Wanqing started. My cousin Wanqing, like most other men, didn't live in the village. He only came home during the busy season and at Spring Festival. Later his wife fell sick and died, and he left to work less often, so that he could stay at home and take care of his two kids. Wanqing is smart and loves to make jokes; he's a real smartass. He's an active figure in the village, too, while Qiaoyu is retiring and very rarely goes to public events. When did they even have a chance to meet? No one knows when they would have set eyes on one another. Villagers would go over to Qiaoyu's to play cards, watch television, or drink and chat. But after serving food, Qiaoyu would always stay in the kitchen. She very rarely spoke to the men of her own accord. She's not like the other village women, who like to joke with the men.

After a few years Qiaoyu and Wanqing's relationship became more or less overt. How many beatings did Qiaoyu endure during that time? Countless. The villagers were used to hearing shouts and screaming every ten days or so. At first people swore at Ming and some even tried to intervene, but by then all they did was shake their heads and smile bitterly. More than once they brought up Qiaoyu's old, declining mother, and that old adage, "Like mother, like daughter."

Qiaoyu and Wanqing put down roots in Shenzhen and didn't come home for a few years. Later, Qiaoyu's grown daughter and Wanqing's two children even went to Shenzhen to work. They all lived together like a regular family. Ming knew where Qiaoyu was and knew his daughter had gone to live with her, but the strange thing is, he never went after her again. Time passed and Ming started to look depressed; his hard, fiery temperament gradually turned silent and uncommunicative. He immersed himself in farming work. And, one Spring Festival, he and Qiaoyu finally went through with the divorce.

Two years after the divorce, Ming was diagnosed with a blood clot in the brain; a stroke left him bedridden. On the very evening of the day her son called with the news, Qiaoyu and Wanqing bought train tickets and returned once more to Liang Village. They hadn't come simply to visit, but to live. They began to care for Ming. Qiaoyu lived in Ming's home, where she took care of him and the housework. Wanqing went to live in his own home, and he worked both families' land. During the off-season, he would do temporary jobs in town. When Ming needed an injection or to visit the doctor, Wanqing would push the pedicab while Qiaoyu walked alongside, and together the three of them would go into town; sometimes they took a car to the county hospital. For a while, the three of them became part of the landscape, and people talked about it all the time. A year later Ming died, and Wanqing fixed up his house, and then invited the Liang and Han family elders to a meal. The point was to reassure everyone that he wasn't taking over Ming's house or the ancestral plot, something everyone had been speculating about behind his back.

In this ancient, rural land, so long as you do virtuous deeds, people will overlook your other problems. Early on people made comments behind Wanqing's back, suggesting that the only reason he returned was to take over Ming's house and land. Some people also suggested that the couple felt guilty, because Ming fell ill from rage at their behavior. But in any case, for a year they had taken care of a man who stunk of illness, someone who was no longer their concern, and that wasn't easy. Qiaoyu's sincerity and quiet nature gradually restored her reputation, and for the adept and fair way he handled everything, Wanqing, too, was quickly forgiven by the Han family. Finally Qiaoyu and Wanqing received the village's blessing. They are now a proper married couple.

As night falls, the heat of the summer day subsides, and a breeze picks up. I walk by my aunt's door and hear her loud laughter coming from inside. I follow the sound, and, quite unexpectedly, find Qiaoyu and Wanqing inside. Apparently Wanqing's son is getting married, and so they have returned from Shenzhou for the ceremony. Qiaoyu's hair is as black as ever, combed back and fastened with a clip, like a housewife from the '50s or '60s. She has always worn her hair like this, even when she was young. I only learned much later that there's a patch on the back of her head with no hair. It's a trace her former husband left of his temper, something that happened soon after they married.

Qiaoyu's cheeks are red, and she looks at me with pleasure. She sits on a far stool, hunched as always. She looks at me as if I were quite a stranger, although pleasure remains on her face. She seems a little shy, and the way she rubs her two large hands together betrays her nervousness. She really does seem very happy to see me, but for some reason she doesn't dare or is too embarrassed to display further enthusiasm. She just keeps looking at me from a distance. I ask when they returned, and how things are going, but she doesn't reply, and instead she turns to my cousin to indicate that he should answer. It seems he normally does the talking. I tell my cousin that I've heard he has an unusual job in Shenzhen. He helps people play mah-jongg and even substitutes for them, but whether they win or lose, he gets paid for his time just the same. At first it was only an occasional thing, but since he's so good it's become his full-time job. He starts to laugh. Who made that up? It's only because I have a good sense of humor. If I really played well, would I still be pulling a pedicab? But the flash in his eyes makes me wonder. Everyone who works outside the village has some kind of secret.

Qiaoyu, listening closely to Wanqing, is still warm and kind, her hands still large and bursting with strength and energy. All this is hidden by her unassertive nature, and only those who are close to her, who love her, know and appreciate it. I am so moved that I want desperately to give her a hug, but I, too, repress the urge.

Aunt Zhao

I am chatting with some elderly folks at the edge of the village when Aunt Zhao and her husband come by pushing a stroller. Inside is a little granddaughter, just ten months old. Two other grandchildren, around four and seven, come trailing up behind. Some diapers on the handle of the stroller blow in the wind like flags. Maybe she just wet them? When Aunt Zhao sees me, she shouts, What are you doing here? I see you everywhere I go. I laugh and say Aunt Zhao, I never see you working, you're always just walking around. I hadn't even finished speaking before she interrupts me, Not working, you think I don't work? I'm practically sixty and raising three little bastards. Don't work! Do you want to give it a try? Her husband doesn't say anything; he just stands to the side smiling. My impression of him is that he's never spoken. He worked in the village brick factory. He's a thin man, with a face that has been darkened by worry. I ask Aunt Zhao if she's exhausted, and how they feed the little girl in the stroller, and then, without further ado, my brisk and chatty Aunt Zhao is off:

> I never take what you city people tell me to feed them too seriously. Before they were six months old they ate corn noodles, wheat noodles, pumpkin. They loved it. Their ma would call and tell me don't do this, don't do that, she's learned it from city folks. She talks the talk, but she's not the one raising them. They can't see me, and I do what I'm going to do, I don't listen to them. If you did it the way they told you, it would never work. Before, when we had you young ones, when you were sick we'd get you down in the dirt. You'd roll around and came out just fine. How does that compare with what you do now?

259

So they've earned a bit of money—so what? If it wasn't for us free babysitters watching the kids, they damn well couldn't leave. Add it up: they wouldn't be able to make any money. I'll do the math for you. My oldest and his wife work in the same factory and earn more than 3,000 kuai. They rent a place to live, and food and lodging cost 1,000 kuai. The two kids live with her aunt in town where they go to school. It's a few hundred kuai per month, if they get sick it's another 100 or more. At most they have 1,000 left over—our monthly babysitting fee. My second son and his wife live in two different places, and they both live and eat at their different factories. They have about 1,000 left over per month, too, but my daughter-in-law guards that with her life. She has her heart set on building a house; she doesn't have any to spare for the two of us.

Do you think they thank you? Thank you, my ass. Why not? The old folks take care of the kids, but they can grow crops on your land. This seems like a fair trade. They don't care if it wears you out or not. They figure that letting you use their land is payment enough. They don't care if you earn money or not. So many who have left send their kids home but don't give you a cent. There are some old couples looking after a whole bunch of kids; the mothers are practically competing to leave their kids behind. If you don't, you're giving up an advantage. They even fight over who leaves more kids behind, like they're determined to eat us old folks up.

Look, do I have an easy life? Am I not pitiful? I'd only just brought my own up, and now I have to take care of theirs, too—I won't have a day of peace until I die. You say, well then don't take care of them. But how can you not help when you see what a hard time they're having? There's no hope here in the village, and if you don't let them go work, the daughters-in-law will hate you. Who in the village would dare say they won't take care of their grandchildren? These days if you don't help out, you're taking a serious risk. Don't you want to live into old age? In the neighboring Li Village, an old couple, over seventy, had four sons and two daughters, but not one of them would take care of their parents. They went from house to house but no one let them stay. Finally they took their sons to court. If they hadn't reported them, maybe they could have gotten a bowl of food, but after they did no one would even give them that. Their second son threw money in their faces and said, Isn't that what you're after? Take it: from now on, we'll just tend to the water in our own well. Then he turned and left. The eldest son is a cadre, at least, but he doesn't know bad from good and isn't likely to do anything. He managed their money, putting the money from the judgment into an account. He sent someone to deliver the bank book, he didn't even see them face to face. He was angry his parents didn't give him face. Now they cry every day and can't regret it enough.

And something like that happened in Wang Ying, too. A widow brought up three sons and divided up her house and lands to give to them. But none of the boys wanted their old mother to live with them. Each had a reason; they said the mother favored one or the other. The one who'd gotten two extra years of schooling and spent the family money, he should take care of her. Or what about the one who had wanted to get married against the mother's wishes, so hadn't had as much for the celebration, or the one who had built his own house without any money from the mother. It was just shameful, all their talk. The mother was ashamed of them, so she tried to drown herself in a well—she'd just die and be done with it. But someone saved her. The sons treated her better for a few days, then went back to the way they were. Finally the production brigade branch secretary said just take it to court. And so they did. The court decided the mother should take turns living with each son, one month at a time, and when she was sick they all had to share the costs. At her second daughter-in-law's, she'd taken care of her daughter-in-law who'd just given birth, and she went out for a bit. While she was gone her daughter-in-law took her things and threw them over the wall. She wouldn't even let her come in the door. She said she was no longer welcome. Said sue us again if you can. She didn't dare sue, and now she's living in the city working as a nanny. In a few years she'll be too old to work. Who knows what will happen to her?

The world has changed. It used to be that daughters-in-law were scared to death of their mothers-in-law. Now there's no mother-in-law who isn't afraid of her daughter-in-law. Which is easy to get along with? Which doesn't press you for the last drop? You go to all that work to raise them, but they'll still fight with you if they feel like it and abandon you if they feel like it. If you mention how well you're taking care of the kid, they say, Hey, it's your grandson, you can starve him to death for all we care. That's a mean thing to say.

Are the children estranged from their mothers? That's impossible. She's still their mother. You've got to hand it to the little bastards, five minutes after their parents are back they're as close as anything with their mother and follow her everywhere. You love them like crazy, you work yourself to death for them, year after year. But that's nothing compared to a mother who only comes back for a few days a year. I have two other grandchildren, you know, they live with their aunt in town. They've tired her practically half to death. Me, I have to make steamed bread and noodles for them every week.

Life is great for those who left to work. These young married couples, they go to work, come home and eat, and then go to sleep—what leisure! We old folks at home are the ones who take care of the kids. They can't afford kindergarten, and they don't have a *hukou* so they can't go to school. Plus, who would take them there and pick them up? And the factory work, that's no joke. You're so tired you can't even move, and you don't want to deal with the kids. Your nephew works at a glue factory. It's so hot that by the end of the day he's in pain. He's always coughing, the environment is so bad.

You see, that's my second grandson; he's always angry. It's really strange. He wants to go to his aunt's, but she's only just got some peace in her own home and doesn't want to have him. This little girl, her mom left five months after she was born. She hasn't been back since. We'll see if she comes home this year or not.

Even as she "yells" at the kids, she gently rocks the stroller, reaching inside from time to time to check the baby's diaper. The lives of these village elderly are nothing like those of the elderly in the cities. In the cities, there are problems of loneliness and isolation; here it's always a question of money.

What are the costs for a migrant worker? Zhao has done the calculations for us. If the elderly weren't working as free babysitters, then their wages would simply not be enough to cover the cost of living. On the other hand, the elderly don't dare complain too much, because of the question of their future care. All rural elderly think about the eventuality of being bedridden, unable to move, unable to work for the family. Who can you rely on then? They have no pensions; there's no social security system. If you don't help take care of the children, if you don't work hard to make a living, then when that "eventuality" comes you might be stuck. Here the view is: if the old folks don't take care of your children, you won't take care of them, especially when leaving home is the only way to earn money.

In these circumstances, sons and daughters very rarely feel that their older parents should have their own lives. So it is natural that they ask for their parents' assistance. In any case, they don't really have a choice. Only their parents would agree to be free babysitters. If you have more than one child, your parents will have a hard time of it. There's also the problem of "keeping up with the Joneses," as Aunt Zhi and Aunt Zhao mentioned. Everyone's "competing to leave their kids behind" because if you don't, you'll be worse off than the others. Even so, as Aunt Zhao tells it, there's not a single old person in the countryside who insists on a leisurely life, having a little glass of something or practicing taiji, and who could see their kids in need and not lend a hand. Aunt Zhao is relatively young. Many over seventy are still working hard to support their children. They might complain, and their children might feel bad about it, but they haven't thought about how to do it differently. They'll just keep at it until they can't anymore. Indeed, to ask "what is an individual's life?" or "what is individual freedom?" is so unrealistic it's laughable.

Aunt Zhao enthusiastically invites me to her home. From the outside, her house looks completely ordinary, but inside, you can tell that careful attention was given to details and that it was built to be lived in until their deaths. You can see this from the bricks to the rafters to the course, rounded, wooden beams, and the finely woven bamboo mats spread above, which are there for structural purposes, as well as to prevent dust from falling from above. The cement between the earthen bricks on the floor is smooth and neat with no gaps to trap dirt. The house is bright and well furnished, the clean home of a well-to-do family. You can happily spend your days in this home. As I praise the house, Aunt Zhao remarks sadly that "people" want to tear it down! "People" being her younger son and his wife. Her elder son already built a two-story house by the road, and because the younger one gave him some money to do so, this house and the ancestral plot will go to him.

When I ask who they will live with later, Aunt Zhao gives a cold smile. With who? Nobody. You can't expect that because you took care of "people's" children, in the future "people" will take care of you. Not a chance. But we don't worry about it. Old Zhao and I can still go back to our first house and grow old there. When the kids feel like it, they'll come and see us and give us a bit of money. If they don't, well, so long as they don't curse us, we'll be fine.

Only then do I realize why, at Spring Festival, the Zhaos had been at loggerheads with their youngest and his wife. The reason was this house. It represents all their effort and love; it symbolizes their worldly possessions and authority as the heads of the household. Old Zhao worked half a lifetime in the village brick factory, and brick by brick, tile by tile, beam by beam, he assembled the materials to build his own home. He spent eight years just getting the bricks and tiles together. When his bricks came out of the kiln, he ducked behind the others and wept. The house was built in 1993. With its completion, the miserly Zhaos killed chickens and a goat and bought strings of firecrackers to set off. They finally had a proper home and were a proper family. Their daughter had just graduated from the teaching college and recently come back to teach, and while their two sons hadn't tested into higher levels of schooling, they had both finished junior high and were planning to leave to find work. It seemed that good times were just beginning.

In Aunt Zhao's mind, they would leave this house to their youngest son, and they would live with him. Indeed, while he had given some money to his elder brother, it wasn't even close to the amount the house was worth, but their elder son had agreed, because he thought their parents would continue to live in the house. If he inherited a little bit less, that was as it should be.

But at Spring Festival their youngest daughter-in-law had again brought up the idea of a new house. In addition, she had hinted that they shouldn't have to assume full responsibility for the old folks, because Aunt Zhao was taking care of the elder son's children. This destroyed the previous balance and led to some nasty remarks between Aunt Zhao and her sons and between the two sons themselves. According to Aunt Zhao, although her daughter-in-law mentioned a new house, what she really meant was that she didn't want to take care of them. If she tore down the house they built, then all the proof of their effort and value would be destroyed. And when the real argument started over who would take care of them, they wouldn't have a leg to stand on, because they were living in someone else's house. Uncle Zhao interjected to disagree. He didn't think their youngest daughter-in-law was that malicious. Maybe she was just jealous that her brother-in-law was living well, in a good house he'd built. It was fashionable now to build concrete houses, one or two stories, and even if their old house was a good, tile-roofed house, it was still a tile-roofed house.

I know this sort of thing often happens in the village. If there are two sons, you usually want to divide the family property into two, and because land is in short supply, one usually receives the land, while the other is given some money to make up the difference. Yet, this is tantamount to saying that, in the end, the parents have neither roof nor room. They have to depend on their sons for everything. In contemporary society, this approach is mostly unimaginable because it strips the parents of all their rights. But in rural areas, this is still the most common scenario. In most cases, when the sons and daughter-in-laws are gone, they need the parents to take care of the children and the house, so there aren't any problems, but as soon as they come back, problems start to occur, and the parents' fate often starts to look extremely precarious.

As far as the elderly are concerned, they don't dare ask for what is within their full right. They can't even remind their sons, with full confidence, of their traditional filial duties, such as respect or letting the parents live with them. This is because the parents no longer support their sons economically. Their sons left when they were young; they got married and built homes with the money they earned working outside the village. The parents no longer have any right to control them. The deterioration of family structures, the weakening of public morality, and contradictions between national law and family tradition mean that sons, and particularly daughters-in-law, are free to disregard the parents. Sociologist Yan Yunxiang has called this phenomenon "parental status and the secularization of filial piety." Traditional cultural mechanisms are breaking down. Filial piety has lost its grounding in culture and society. Sons and daughters-in-law are treating their parents according to the new morality of the market economy, and, more and more, their relationships are based upon a logic of exchange. The two sides must consider one another as equals, something that this generation of rural parents is simply unable to do.

At the deepest level of Chinese culture, there is an essential deficiency, namely the loss of the individual. The demands of society, economy, and morality put enormous pressure on individuals. They cannot express their convictions or feelings, their needs or wishes. Everyone seeks to sacrifice themselves for their family, but this sacrifice is unhealthy. Sacrifice is the basis of their emotional connection, the basis of the family. If at any moment they falter in the spirit of sacrifice, or change their minds, it will result in conflict and rupture. In addition, in daily life, family members don't communicate with one another. They remain silent and isolated, in a kind of ignorant, primal state.

This is not to suggest that they aren't aware or that they do not experience suffering, but rather that they are all bound invisibly and cannot talk about it. When conflicts break out, they are often destructive.

The strangest thing is that in all of Aunt Zhao, Grandma Wu, and Zhi Shen's complaints, you can always sense their deep love and tolerance for their children, a keen sensitivity to the difficulty of their lives away from the village and to the grandchildren who have been left behind to interrupt their golden years. They may worry about their future, and they may worry about their daughters-in-law's behavior, but mostly they just watch carefully over their grandchildren and take on all responsibility. They don't express this, not even to their own daughters. It is buried beneath the surface, hidden as deep as can be, until they themselves are no longer conscious of it. Village life requires tenacity, as does every kind of survival in the natural world.

Aunt Zhao's kitchen fills with the good smell of newly cooked salt rice. She fries up some meat and celery, adds a little water and then some rice, cooking it over a low flame. After twenty minutes she turns off the gas and lets it sit for a minute longer. Then it's ready—and it's delicious. When I was a child, we only had this when we were trying to do something a little special. A family could afford it only two or three times a year, which is why the smell evokes such a particular memory. By now, it's been common for many years. The smell of cooking smoke floats through the courtyard, up above the village, weaving its way through the housetops.

8

Where Has My Hometown Gone?

By 2006 Rang County had begun to see the effects of new village construction. All county administrative villages had fuel lines, and active effort was given to bringing villages into good condition. About 910 kilometers of roads were constructed; 179 ponds were administered; and 118 village-level swimming facilities, 300 cultural teahouses, and 3,800 methane tanks were built. Cable was installed in 5,700 homes, as were 8,700 solar water heaters. With an investment of 34 million yuan, solid progress was made in creating information villages, of which 330 were built. Village-level nursery schools, sanitation units, commercial networks, public security units, and village activity centers, as well as other public service systems, were progressively and comprehensively coordinated. Villages have been changed beyond recognition. Great efforts have gone into the establishment of 12 "Million Project" model villages, putting into motion programs focused on "Three Cleanups and One Reform" as well as the regulation of village and household appearances, resulting in major improvements to rural appearances.

—Rang County Government Working Reports

Swamp

Morning arrives, and I'm feeling heavy and weary. Rural life is a swamp. Back less than a month, you feel submerged. Not as if an external force is pushing you down, but as if you are falling against your will. Your mind grows heavier and heavier, more and more scattered. You can't touch bottom—how far is the fall? It's a feeling that continually circles back around. Every year before I return, I make a firm resolution to stay a little longer, but then, every time I live in the village for a while, I want to hurry away.

I have concerns about the efficacy—and even the possibility— of my research. How to put it? I didn't leave home, didn't leave the countryside, until I was twenty, and in the time I've been back I've been continually speaking with the former village secretary, the accountant, and other villagers, yet I sense in my gut that I cannot access the village's deepest structural layers. We don't speak the same language anymore. The village secretary and accountant might reveal vague hints or sly glances that spark your interest, but when you try to pursue it, they change the subject. Rural life is like a vast web. There are so many knots and holes that you don't know how to take hold of a single one.

Speaking with Aunt Shen, Gramma Wu, and the others, I have come to feel that their inner hearts are impenetrable castles. They naturally treat me—an outsider, and someone with certain goals—with silence. We have little emotional connection, and our points of view are not the same. Given this, I sometimes don't know how to return to the subjects at hand; it's almost as if I lose the ability to speak. To the women, to myself, I am no longer a villager. My ideas and their ideas are never aligned.

One day we are at Aunt Shen's house. Her five-year-old grandson is playing next to the pond, which is filled with trash and algae. My son starts to whine that he wants to go too, but I tell him no, in no uncertain terms, and pull him back. As I do I see the knowing smile on Aunt Shen's face. She clearly under- stands, and suddenly I feel ashamed. You may wish to "return to the land" or "go back to the village," even to go back and be one of the villagers again, but you can't. You can't help your sense of superiority or the disdain that arises from differences in rural and urban lifestyles.

Many national efforts and policies are focused on rural areas. For example, we now have compulsory education, tax breaks for farmers, and other subsidies. The government is trying, but that only makes the crisis, that black hole, even bleaker.

Compulsory education has finally been implemented, so rural people no longer have to worry about tuition and other educational costs. When I was a child, students were often driven from the classroom because they couldn't afford the fees. Every year, just before classes began, you could see my father's figure, going from door to door, borrowing money for our school fees anywhere he could. But just as it's become easier to go to school, the students' enthusiasm for it, and their parents' dedication to helping them, is waning. Middle and elementary school enrollments are decreasing. This is, in part, because the population has decreased, but another major factor is declining cultural aspirations. Children have no desire to study; they expect to find jobs as teenagers. This creates a paradox: Rural people work as hard as they can to make money, hoping their children will receive educations that will lead to better lives, but the children don't want an education, they just want to become workers.

It also leads to another phenomenon: marriage rates among young village people have fallen. Many families fear their children will end up badly; they fear they will fall in love with someone from another place. There's not just the difficulty of visiting relatives to consider; all sorts of conflicts would be hard to resolve and would likely end in divorce. The few young village couples who have divorced did so because of long-distance relationships. The couple have a fight and split up just like that, then each returns to his or her own hometown where it's unlikely they'll ever make up. Thus, parents often look for help from relatives in the area to find partners for their children. The couples usually get engaged and marry quickly and then leave together to find work. No one really considers differences in temperaments or feelings. For example, my elder cousin's son was working as an oil technician in Jiangxi and fell in love with a girl he met there. When my cousin heard the news, she hurried to Jiangxi and forced her son to come home. She wanted to make sure he was engaged to someone who lived close, and even forced him to marry before he left again. When I saw the young man at Spring Festival, fresh from the city with a fashionable haircut, he told me his story. He had really liked the girl, but his mother didn't leave him any options. And he understood where his mother was coming from; she was just being realistic. She had already set up an engagement for him, a girl from the other side of the river. He thought she was good natured and not bad looking, so he decided to forget the girl from Jiangxi. After Spring Festival he took his new wife somewhere else and continued his work as an oil technician.

Although there's no longer a farm tax, my father still keeps accounts. You might not pay a land tax, but there are the costs of fertilizer, seeds, and labor, which keep increasing; you can grow crops for a year and still end up back where you started. There's no profit. So people who left aren't very enthusiastic about coming back and farming. They just do it to amuse themselves for a while.

My elder brother's clinic is empty all morning; I ask if it's because the houses on either side are being renovated. My sister-in-law laughs and says no, there are never any patients. The village has implemented a cooperative medical treatment program, in which the government reimburses part of the cost, so now very few people come to these rural clinics. Some people with connections got the cooperative programs to move some treatments to their clinics, and they can keep themselves afloat. Others have partially closed, and young people like my brother are looking for other ways to make money. But not even those directly affected by these changes have complained too much, because everyone knows these cooperative medical programs are hugely beneficial to ordinary people.

Chinese rural people are easily satisfied: do a little something good for them, and they'll remember it forever. While I was chatting with some elderly folks, we talked about the cooperative programs, the cancellation of taxes, and the subsidies, and they were ecstatic. They said these things had never happened before in all of China's dynasties. One said, "Now we dress every day as if we were going out visiting. No one looks ragged anymore, and we talk and act differently. Sitting at home, we know all about what's happening in Nanjing, Beijing, inside the county, or internationally. We can learn and see all kinds of things on the TV. Of course we're happy."

Construction is still going on just outside my brother's door; the workers are men from the Wang family. Looking at those familiar faces, I heave a sigh. There are also a few women, one of whom is the best-looking young wife in the village. She has a lively, round face, with dark cheeks and sparkling eyes, but because she's married a Wang, no one pays her any mind.

I am flipping through the Chinese-American sociologist Yan Yunxiang's book *Private Life under Socialism: Love, Intimacy, and Family*. Yan's book avoids structural observations of a sociological nature and instead recounts the emotional issues of the village. From this angle he examines familial relations, changes in interpersonal relationships, and deeply rooted connections between the traditional and the modern. This was the first example of a rural sociologist "turning inward," and its presentation of the village people's rich and subtle emotional lives is enlightening. Yan, however, remains a sociologist; he emphasizes larger macro changes as well as conclusive findings; it is an integrated and systematic work. As a literary scholar, I'm afraid I don't have the ability to make similar overarching conclusions, and, in any case, I am more interested in shedding light on individual lives, in finding and recounting the diversity of individual feelings: the joys and sorrows, the partings and reunions that belong to them alone.

The Forgotten

Rural areas can offer a warm feeling of comfort, despite the shocking destitution. And while there certainly have been changes, they often seem natural, disconnected from time or tempo and thus free from crisis or anxiety. At the entrance to the village, a few women are playing cards under a tree. Some, accompanied by their grandchildren, have come to gossip and pass the time. Some are working in the fields; the very few young people are busy with their own work. My expectations of the village's emotions—sorrow, suffering, helplessness—and my expectation of its issues—the collapse of the countryside—slowly begin to evaporate, even to be disproven. They aren't problems here. They are only one part of life, taken in and dealt with.

It's as if I've been looking for some "poetic tragedy" or even just to find fault. Yet behind this feeling, a certain perplexity remains, as well as an even larger question: All these rural stories I've told, the individual lives, their conflict, suffering, and challenges—what do they reflect? Is it the suffering caused by social inequality, or something else? For some reason, I'm unwilling to simply assume that their lives have been defined by society or the government. I've always felt that it's much more complicated and ambiguous than that. It's not only the government; it's also tradition, culture, morals. It's this land, this sky, these open plains. It is something that is deeply rooted in the earth of Rang County and in the thousands of years people have lived here, intimately connected to the land. There is a kind of ancient, secret code, a shared unconscious. Contemporary politics and policies and all the changes they have wrought are only one layer, a temporary influence. Should this powerful external force disappear, everything would revert to the way it was.

So I remain hesitant and uncertain. Things are always different, depending on whether they're seen from within or without. When you consider issues from society's lowest levels or highest levels, you get entirely different answers. The problem of the underclasses isn't a simple question of oppressors and oppressed; it is a game of cultural power. This is something I learned from the people who live in the graveyard.

Perhaps we are neglecting the most important issue: Chinese rural indifference to politics. For rural people, society still belongs to someone else; they have no place in it. They passively accept the good and the bad. They may be "rescued," but they are never the protagonists. "Rural China" is not only the countryside in a geographical sense; it is also a basic characteristic of all of Chinese society. In its present iteration, rural people are still seen, politically and culturally, as a burden to society. They are a large burden, which must be faced head on, rather than agents in their own right. If they are not made into socio-political agents, if they are not given the means to participate in political life, then the rural problem will never be resolved.

Someone emerges in the distance, walking slowly along the narrow embankments, looking from side to side. He's holding a black plastic bag. He must be a trash collector. When he gets closer, I can see his clothes are ragged. He's dressed in a white shirt that has turned gray, black pants and the yellow gum shoes that were popular among farmers in the '80s. Could that be Jun? Is he homeless? There was Xing, Jun, and then their younger brother, I forget his name. There were three of them—their parents died when they were young. None of them married, and from what I can remember, they lived in an earthen hut by the side of the road. Xing is a veteran; the youngest brother was smart and handsome, full of energy. Later he became a petty thief. He was in prison for several years and finally died there. How did he become a thief? How did he go from stealing things to stealing women? There are rumors, of course, but his brothers remain silent. Even when they gather with the other men on cold winter nights, they only listen, silently, from darkened corners. I've never once heard them speak. After their house collapsed, they didn't know where to go. I ran into Xing a few days ago, now here's Jun. They must live in the village somewhere.

When Jun sees me his eyes light up a bit, or so it seems. But then he quickly moves away, and his eyes are again those of a stranger. I stop and say, you're up plenty early, Jun, and he stammers out a few words, as if he wants to say something but can't get it out. He doesn't look at me. His eyes wander in the distance, to cover up his awkwardness. He never stops walking and passes me by. I am surprised that he remains so standoffish, as if he wants to protect himself, as if he has no connection to me, to anyone he knows, to the village itself.

How many people are forgotten in a village, in the life of a community? I remember a scene from a Spring Festival at Wan Hu's house. At noon on the second day of the New Year, he carried out a bowl of noodles without a single green vegetable. The noodles, white and disgusting, were topped only by two slices of liver. This was his New Year's meal. The kitchen was filthy, his wife sitting beside the kitchen stove, staring directly at me. She let her bowl fall to the floor without even realizing she'd done it. She had once been witty and beautiful, but one summer she used cold well water to wash her hair, and it had damaged her mind. Wan Hu's two children, their faces red and swollen from the cold winter wind, wearing clothes that hadn't been washed in ages, sat on small stools in the courtyard and inhaled their noodles as if they were delicious. I asked Wan Hu about his wife's illness. He said he'd sought advice all over, but then the money ran out before they found a cure. Now she didn't even speak. Wan Hu stammered a little, his face turning red, and I had to listen for a long time before I understood. He was working at the village brick factory, he earned a few hundred yuan a month, but it wasn't enough to pay for his wife's medication. I asked him about the communal clinics, couldn't he get reimbursed? He shook his head, seemingly confused by my question. But then I realized, whatever was wrong with her couldn't be treated in the communal clinics. It was a chronic illness and didn't require a hospital stay, and thus was unlikely to be reimbursed. Wan Hu, who can't even speak clearly, has difficulty fighting for his rights. And the government won't take the initiative to help them.

How many have been forgotten? Xiao Zhu, Qing Li, Lumpy Ginger, Kun Sheng . . . and, of course, Wan Shan, a cousin on my father's side. When he was young he nearly drowned and ended up with brain damage. Now he must be a little over fifty. For many years he has lived as a vagrant. From time to time he comes back, sneaking over the wall to see his family, hiding in the corner. He greets people politely and seems normal, but after a few sentences, he starts to perform. He will twist his ears and in very proper Mandarin say, "*Ding*, The Chinese People's Radio Broadcasting System starts now." Then everyone gives him some money. It's been dozens of years, and no one even knows where he sleeps. When I ask my brother he says, oh in haystacks or caves or in the fields. He'll sleep wherever he finds himself.

And there was the girl who did acrobatics. Traveling drama troupes would have a few of them. They'd find a place out of the wind, and with a stroke of the gong, the show would begin. "Kachong!" The little girl seemed to have dislocated arms, like noodles, supple, swaying in the wind, her head hanging low, as if she couldn't lift it. Sometimes, for dramatic effect, she would make her arms tremble, as if to show that her arms and body were two disconnected things. This strange trembling and powerlessness made an impression that is hard to forget. When the show was over, they would take her from house to house to collect things to eat, whatever people were willing to give.

Where had they gone?

Where is Xiao Zhu buried? What became of his four-year-old daughter? Who remembers his name, that he once existed, that he was so full of life, so healthy? Xiao Zhu was born the same year as me. We were always especially close because of this.

When we were about seven or eight, someone in the village asked us, which one of you is older, and I jumped in, I'm older of course. I was born in the tenth month. He was born in the fourth. If I'm not the oldest, how could he be? Everyone started to tease me about this, and whenever his mother or someone else in the village saw us together, they would laugh and tell the story.

The last time I saw Xiao Zhu was at Spring Festival thirteen or fourteen years ago. It was the morning of the first day of the New Year. In the village, and especially among the Liang households, that was when we brought each other food. When Xiao Zhu arrived with his dish, it was already 9 am. I was so happy to see him, and I told him to stay with us and eat. So he did. At that time we were just twenty years old. Xiao Zhu was tall, around 1.8 meters, and he had a sort of sophisticated style, not like someone from the countryside. He had been very open and cheerful, but he'd worked outside of the village for a few years and had picked up some city mannerisms. He left at sixteen. He'd been a security guard, done electrical welding, worked in a foundry, and been a construction worker, all in Beijing. That year he'd moved to a jewelry factory in Qingdao, and for Spring Festival he had come back to get married. They planned to go back after the fifth day of the New Year.

No one knows when Xiao Zhu got sick. He'd been in the jewelry factory for ten years and had started to spit up blood the year before last. He'd stayed at the county hospital for almost two months, but they could never stop the blood. Nor could they figure out what it was. In his final months his internal organs were failing, and in the end, even a light cough would send blood spraying out of his nose and mouth. The stench of rot filled his home. In the beginning his brothers and sister had raised a lot of money, but then it was spent, and there seemed to be little hope, and conflicts arose about the money. Before he even died, they'd gone back to where they were working. Afterwards, his wife took his daughter and married someone else. A year later his mother suddenly died of stomach cancer.

Of those who have left—aside from the few who work as oil technicians or who have graduated from technical schools and work as skilled laborers in factories—most work in construction, in jewelry factories, or in high-temperature plastic workshops or in foundries, or else they drive pedicabs. Aunt Zhao's two sons are employed at a high-temperature plastic workshop, where they brought some other boys from the village to join them. According to their sister, it's a terrible work environment. They often faint or vomit, but no one wants to admit there's a direct connection. Even though they all know, they just hope it won't fall on their own head—after all, this certainly isn't the worst place to work in China.

My childhood companions, Qingli, Dongxiang, Duozi, where have they gone? How do they make a living? Are they like Chunmei, holding it together at home, waiting for those few days a year when they can enjoy a little happiness before they must be separated from their husbands yet again? A Wang family girl has been gone since she was a teenager, almost twenty years, and hasn't been in touch with her family at all. Is she still alive, or is she buried in some dark corner of a city somewhere?

Yet it's not all hopelessness and pain. There is always warmth and tenacity. Faint flashes of hope, like with Grandmother Wu, Aunt Zhi, Aunt Zhao, and their daughters. No matter how much they suffer, complain and quarrel, there is always also understanding and love.

Walking down the road, I run into two elderly members of the Han family growing vegetables. I'm not sure how to address them, as the Han family and Liang family generations don't match up; my father says you'd have to count from the generation that emigrated from Shanxi's Hong County, far too long ago. But, in any case, these two old folks and I are in the same generation, so I call them Elder Brother and Sister-in-Law, even though they are already in their seventies. The man is using shoulder poles to carry two baskets of vegetables. He trembles as he stumbles along, bent almost to a 90-degree angle. His wife, holding a handful of vegetables, follows on the left side, also trembling. But they're clearly still in good health, still working in the fields and depending on their toil to cover life's costs.

They still have life within them.

One day I run into my cousin's wife. She and my cousin sold vegetables in Beijing for ten years or so and then built a house and have some savings. She speaks in Mandarin as she expresses her powerful longings, and whenever we discuss major issues, she always has strong opinions. She's critical of city folks because they always haggle over money. And when we talk about the real estate market, she has her own point of view. Even though I find her conceited, I have to admit that city life and her success have given her self-confidence. That day we went to eat at the house of a village girl who had married into the town; I was shocked to see how modern and urban their home was. You could see the enormous effect that money had had on rural life.

But those who work in the cities will always remain country folk. When she came back, my cousin's wife was self-confident and full of vim and vigor, but in the city, she was one rural worker among countless others, just another awkward market vendor. My cousin is a construction worker. Whenever he comes home he seems at a loss and wears a silent, helpless expression that shocks me. He graduated from high school and used to be quick-witted and easy to talk to. He was known in the village for his intelligence. But in the city, he is simply another body eking out a living. In that life, his feelings and intelligence are beside the point.

In so-called "modern society," rural ways of thinking and speaking, their very ways of being, are no longer applicable, because rural society's customs cannot cope with a modern society made up of people who are unacquainted with one another. Untold numbers of workers move cautiously through city streets, wearing shabby clothing and strange expressions. They move clumsily, as if half dead, like fish out of water. Imagine: in the villages, in their own homes, they might be revived, restored to their natural selves, like fish returned to the stream.

New Life

We usually think that economic decline leads to cultural disorder and decline. Cultural heritage requires economic and social stability to fully manifest its internal and external forms. In contemporary rural China, however, it would seem that the opposite is true. When you consider the rural economy as a whole, or the income of rural households, there is real development happening. Husbands and wives can go into the cities to work and earn money, as can their grown children, and regardless of the quality of the jobs, it is better than relying solely on farming. Yet culture in the countryside is in a state of rupture and decline, in terms of continuity, individual spirit, and the thirst for knowledge. We, who represent the national ideology and the intelligentsia, are always using the word "transformation" to describe this rupture, but in so doing we neglect the immense damage caused by the "black hole" of this transformation. What I mean by "culture" is not only traditional concepts, morality, and customs; it is also the practical reality of their lives.

As for Liang Village, its existence as a complete "village" centered around clans and blood relations is gradually weakening and dying off, to be replaced by a mere economic gathering point. As a member of the village's principal clan, I still have a sense of security and control, but that sense has been so weakened as to become negligible. In some other more developed areas, clan forces have more than once risen up to protect their economic interests. In villages in the northern interior, however, clan power seldom brings economic benefit, because there aren't any resources to draw from, and most villagers are working somewhere else.

At the same time, the village structures, and the binds that link village families together, are undergoing changes. The best locations are often occupied by those with the most money, and that has created new bureaus of civil affairs, social classes, and hierarchies. But emotional connections between households of the same clan have been diluted, especially in new households. Everyone lives elsewhere and only comes back at Spring Festival. They don't really care about the village political situation or public works, including elections, road repair, brick factory closures, or new schools.

Changes are also happening within families. Financial relationships are replacing parental relationships, and the knowledge that used to be passed on to children through everyday interactions with their parents is now happening through the efforts of grandparents or relatives. After the closing of the village school—a symbol of the village's mental state—and following the death of some highly respected village elders—often the village's moral compass—village culture began to collapse from within. Only its form remained. The village itself was dead. The implications are this: China's smallest structural units have fundamentally broken down, and individuals have lost the stabilizing force of the land.

This collapse means that its inhabitants no longer have an ancestral home. They have neither roots nor memories; they are without spiritual guidance or a place they belong. It means children have lost their earliest cultural instruction, opportunities to learn by word and example and from healthy and warm human interactions. It also means that the unique character and temperaments of the people have disappeared, because they no longer have a place to exist. The village, in a certain sense, is the womb of an ethnic group. Its warmth, its nourishment, and the healthy functioning determines the physical well being of its future children, the richness of their emotional lives, and their knowledge and understanding.

In these many years of reform and opening up, rural areas have undoubtedly developed to a great degree, but these

changes have also brought about many unprecedented problems. These problems now exist in the environment and run in
the blood, deeply influencing villages' entire existence. To simply
describe all this as "transformation" is entirely insufficient.
Only when we look from an "inner perspective" do we see that,
in the contemporary process of reform, attitudes that are inim-
ical to traditional cultures and lifestyles are being endlessly
exaggerated and politicized, creating imaginary perspectives
that ordinary people and intellectuals too often use to judge
village life.

The Rang County Party Secretary agreed with my observations. And he expressed his admiration when he heard I had
been back for over a month and was living at my former home.
Other scholars had come to do research, but they always left
after a few days, and then wrote a 10,000 character article.
How perceptive can that be? Rural conditions and problems
cannot be clearly understood in a few days. He gave me the
green light to visit villages around the county in the company of
his own secretary. This would expand my breadth of knowledge
and allow me to see rural development in its many aspects.

Our first stop was X Village. It's well known throughout
the country as a clothing distribution market that first developed in the early '90s. It had created an integrated supply chain
of manufacturing, wholesale, and marketing. Every year, for
publicity, village leaders would spend tens of thousands of yuan
for celebrities, singers, and large-scale theatrical performances.
But the market became flooded with poorly made products and
counterfeits, and after 1995 it began to decline. By 2000, even
the people who lived there had forgotten the village's former
glory.

The township Party secretary, orderly and direct, is a professional military man of around forty. He is in the process of a
large-scale transformation of the clothing market and has plans
to restore its previous economic vibrancy. I ask him why the
clothing market had declined, despite the former importance of

the village. He replied bluntly that it was because of poor management. If you want a large-scale operation, the secretary needs to be a businessman. He must understand advanced management and operational strategies. In addition, they didn't understand the business's basics; they didn't emphasize product quality, for example. His most important work is divided into four parts: transforming the street-level climate, including sewer, electricity, and roadways; improving the efficiency of the government administration by transferring power to a centralized department and simplifying business procedures; identifying core brands and companies; and expanding their scope to attract foreign investment.

The secretary speaks with frank assurance. He's clearly an industrialist who knows how to get things done. He takes us to visit a sweater manufacturing plant. It's owned by a man from Hong Kong, whose ancestral home is in the village. When he returned to visit relatives, they talked him into opening a factory. It's an immense, open building, simple and rudimentary, with electrical fans blowing, the sound of machines whirring and female workers moving about. It's a bustling scene.

I'm more interested in the children in the factory. At the feet of one of the women, a child sleeps amidst the roar of the machines. His face is covered with white bits of wool, and he looks very funny. Another child is attached to his mother's breast, nursing, while both her hands still move busily. A few other children play hide-and-seek and other games, running around the machines. I think neither the factory owner nor the secretary minds this, because it's so common in rural towns. What's more, mothers don't have to leave to find work—they can make a living close to home and still take care of their children. That's a rare thing. Isn't this a better fate than those who have to work in the city, while their children stay in the village or are kept locked up in a rented apartment?

But I can't help asking the factory director: isn't this dangerous? Aren't there other ways to take care of them? The director doesn't think it's very dangerous, although he admits it doesn't conform to standard practices. But if they couldn't bring their children, they most likely wouldn't be able to work. The secretary steps in adroitly. Apparently there are many children like this, and he plans to establish a factory nursery school, where mothers can leave their children. The factory would be like a home. This way, mothers can work without worry, and issues regarding their schooling will be resolved. It's a good idea, but that's still all it is. Funding issues still need to be addressed.

This secretary changed my impression of low-level cadres. In China, there are still some who are working for progress and trying to be good cadres. Perhaps they're just doing it for a promotion, but objectively speaking, they are public-minded and making actual progress. In any case, Chinese rural areas are always lucky to have this kind of functionary.

Next we visit a few model towns, administered by villages and townships, in the southern parts of Rang County. From the county seat, we follow a smooth, paved road, lined on either side by slender, white poplar trees, only as thick as bowls since they were planted after the county secretary's poplar tree development campaign began. As we leave the city, the countryside expands into large fields filled with corn, sweet potatoes, sorghum, and emerald green scallions. I suddenly feel as if I am in the south. We arrive, and I realize that the new model village is complete. There is row upon row of houses, and although they are ordinary, northern-style houses, their height is uniform, and they aren't surrounded by earth, but cement. They have regular sewers, trash depots, and biogas pits. Biogas is something the county has been pushing as energy saving, to the point that those who install them receive a subsidy that covers two-thirds of the cost.

We go into one of the houses. It belongs to an old couple whose son has been working outside the village for a while. They are raising some domestic animals, including two pigs just to increase the gas output. I go see their pigpen and biogas tank, where I am assailed by noxious fumes. I ask them how it's working, and they say they are indeed saving money on coal. It's just that in the summertime the smell is too intense.

After that we visit another village on the main road. It sits very prettily beneath the blue sky. The Party secretary worked personally on this one. It combines Chinese and Western styles, red brick and white walls, arched doors, bedrooms, living rooms, kitchens, bathrooms, all completely functioning. But he has also considered the farmers' practical circumstances. For example, the roofs are flat because they are often used to dry grain. There are also garages, where they can keep their tractors and farming vehicles. Luckily, we find some people playing cards, and I ask them about the villas. They were part of an integrated program, which used community-style leadership in the building process. They have a complete list of facilities: sanitation, a posting board, exercise equipment, and so on. The clearest change is the road. Before it had been a muddy pit when it rained, hard to navigate, with some parts too narrow. Now it's broad and flat and uniform. Everything seems new. Life is no longer muddy.

As we chat, I ask everyone's opinion. As a whole, it seems the farmers are highly satisfied with this integrated program. It's neat, clean, near the main road and the location of their old village.

Maybe there will be business opportunities, and who doesn't want that? But not every family had the money to build a house, and not every family wanted to move from the former village. This includes an elderly man with a grave expression, who sits silently to the side. I ask him about his family, and then I understand his expression. His son and daughter left to work. In a good year, they save 10,000 kuai; in a bad one they can't find work and might even lose money. In order to build this house, the family had spent all its savings and even had to borrow almost 20,000 yuan, while they spent another 40 or 50,000. He's depressed and doesn't know what to do. There are others who built the houses, but no matter what the government did, would not move. This means two villages coexist at the same time, taking up farmland.

I have lunch with the county Party secretary, and he comes off as a bit of a blowhard, like a typical bureaucrat. He wants to show his accomplishments—those incongruous, European-style building features are all his doing. He says he wanted to build something international. Later the villas were adapted so that they would, at the very least, take the villagers' lives into consideration. He discusses the villas proudly, saying he established the village as a benchmark, but when I ask whether the villagers are happy, whether all the details are in place— the sewer, or places for raising animals, or integration with the surroundings, that sort of thing—he speaks scornfully: This is the rural mindset; it's too narrow; they're the ones benefiting from all this.

In talking with different township secretaries, I discover that the Central Committee has established comprehensive, dedicated funding policies for subsidies and management, as well as for farmland irrigation and well construction. The government also administers to places with water pollution and carries out ecological surveys. In addition, the Environmental Protection Office's reach and clout have increased over the past few years. It is for exactly this reason that the paper factory upstream, as well as Rang County's large-scale paper factories and fertilizer plants, will finally all be closed.

The nation is giving increased attention to rural development and is constantly searching for a path that is suitable for the countryside. Yet the strange thing is that rural areas appear stuck in a passive, negative state. There is no true sense of participation in these governmental processes. This is an issue worth considering. The government, cadres, and villagers remain three distinct entities and do not form an organic whole. In good times and bad, the rural government is in constant flux, and the farmers don't know what really belongs to them—including their land. They never had rights before and don't know what they should care about. If the government gives them something, that's good, but if it doesn't, that seems natural, too.

What kind of new life will emerge from these ancient villages, as they fade away? With what attitude, and in what guise, will they arrive at a healthy new life? These are the questions at hand?

Cultural Teahouses

After traveling to many villages I come to realize that Rang County is promoting a project called "Cultural Teahouses" to make villagers a bit more cultured. I find this extremely interesting, for it is closely related to solving the problem of "how the villages can be reborn."

Cultural teahouses are promoted by the county, but they are contracted to individuals, who house them either in their own homes or in a communal building. (They don't build new facilities just for this purpose.) The individuals provide tables, chairs, and tea equipment, while the county government has allocated special funds for bookshelves and books. This is part of the central government's aim to house "distance learning" and other public resources in the teahouses. The government has also bought televisions for distance learning and has provided many different kinds of materials, including every kind of Chinese opera; television dramas from Hong Kong, Taiwan, and the People's Republic of China; and most importantly popular science shows. This allows farmers to relax in the teahouses, chatting, drinking tea, while they also read, watch TV, or study popular science.

On one of those long, hot midsummer afternoons we go check out one of the teahouses. As we arrive in the village, we can see a few kids, stripped completely bare, playing in a manufactured pond. Every once in a while a brave soul dives in or starts a splash fight. It's a boisterous group. As we get closer we see that the so-called pond is only a cement pit, but it has some steps and seems relatively well-maintained, notwithstanding the black oily luster of the water and the trash floating on the surface. To one side a woman is washing clothes and some of those plastic bags used to hold fertilizer. If you look closely at where the water comes from, it appears to be drawn from a well. I imagine it was built to comply with the higher-up's "pool renovation" engineering project (another rural engineering campaign). The water must be changed to stay clean, but it very clearly has not been changed since it was built.

The teahouse and a wide, high platform—a newly built theatrical stage—sit next to the pond. Inside the teahouse, a few people are sitting around watching television, some kind of Hong Kong or Taiwan drama with loud fighting. On the back wall are two bookshelves, with two children reading nearby. A middle-aged farmer, his skin darkened, his air reserved, is also reading intently. On the other side, people are playing cards at two tables.

The man who manages the teahouse looks almost seventy; he trembles as he walks and his head shakes a bit, his back hunched. But when we ask he says he's only fifty-six. I don't usually see men who look this aged, even in rural areas.

He steeps some tea for us and we all sit down. As we chat we find out that he has two grandchildren who live with him. His son works in another county at an electrical transformer substation and his daughter-in-law works somewhere else. His grandchildren are seven and three, and their mother hasn't been back for more than six months. At first they said the elder child would go stay with his father for the summer vacation, but then work got too busy and he had to work the night shift, so he couldn't take care of the child. The teahouse's income comes from sales of tea and card table fees. Each customer pays one kuai for a cup of tea, and more water is free. It's ten kuai to play cards at a table for the afternoon, which comes with free tea. If you fill three or four tables in the morning and afternoon, there's a profit.

We are at the teahouse for two and a half hours and the man reading doesn't move an inch—he's too focused on his book. Around 4:30 he stands up, puts the book back on the shelf, gets on his bicycle, and rides off. There's a hoe and sickle on the back of his bike. I go over to the bookshelf to see what he's been reading: it's *Legend of the Condor Heroes*, the martial arts novel by Jin Yong. The two teenagers read for a while, and then watch TV for a while, and then leave. The Hong Kong/Taiwan dramas are still on; no one had changed the channel. The folks playing cards are still at it. People wander in and out. Most stand over by the tables for a while, and there aren't many people reading. In fact, reading habits are in decline among the people, other than books students need for exams and official texts from Xinhua Bookstore. And that's not even considering the quality of what *is* read.

At one time, there were four privately owned bookshops in Wu. The one that did the best business mostly sold VCDs: two-thirds were from Hong Kong, while a few were traditional Chinese operas or Chinese movies. The other three shops were on the verge of closing. One was called The Hope Book Society. I really liked the name. Three of the four walls were stacked with martial arts fiction, their covers garish and the binding sloppy—typical pirated books. The fourth wall held children's books and educational materials. In the corner there was a small bookcase with a few shelves that held contemporary fiction, foreign literature, self-help books, and books on conspiracy theories, that type of thing. There weren't any books of Tang or Song poetry or any other classical works. The shopkeeper said that middle and high school students rented books most often, along with a few villagers. For the most part, everyone just went straight for the martial arts novels. Even so, business was dwindling, mostly because for the past several years students had been required to stay at school. They were only allowed to go out for two hours on weekend afternoons. The other reason was that the students were often playing computer games during their free time. Very few read. There was only one student who was different from the rest, a male student in the first year of high school. Every week he came to borrow a work of Chinese fiction or a collection of essays, like *White Deer Plain* or *Fortress Besieged*. As I chatted with the owner I learned to my surprise that there was a private book collector in town, a retired private teacher. He had a few thousand books in his home, many of which were the old string-bound editions. When I heard that, I was inspired to go pay him and his library a visit, so I asked the shop owner to look him up. Disappointingly, he discovered that the man had already been dead a year, and his son had sold all of his books as scrap paper. He had taken his father's library, which had filled three rooms, and made it into a building material shop.

We go out to look at the stage. It's high and wide with a cement base reinforced by steel. The roof is made of asbestos sheeting and a steel framework. I ask the village secretary how much it cost; he says around 10,000 yuan. It looked like that was the real cost—the secretaries of several villages had said the same. He also says he doesn't think the stage is very useful; there have only been two performances since it was built. If you want to ask an official or amateur theatrical troop to come and perform, you have to pay. To put on a show for three or four days, you need about 3,000 kuai. In an area where funds aren't easy to come by, this is no small expense. Every household has a television now, with more shows than they could possibly watch, so people want to stay at home. On top of that, there aren't very many people in the village, so the audience is already limited. Still, at weddings and funerals, people do watch movies here, not in the wheat fields like they used to. The village secretary admits that if there were good programming for theater or films they could allow vendors to set up stalls, which would attract people from all around. Then it would be busy. They organized something like that once, but it was too much work. Who has time to arrange that kind of thing?

When we get back to the county seat, I talk with some friends about the teahouses, and they let out a loud laugh. There are lots in the city; you might call them "mah-jongg teahouses." A few don't even bother with books: they get the teahouse permit and use the place as a legal mah-jongg parlor. In Rang City, mah-jongg is a universal pastime. Whether you're a cadre, an office worker, or self- employed, chances are you're a mah-jongg enthusiast. Most people have a fixed set of mah-jongg friends, and after a lunch, if there's nothing else to do, they head over to their regular place and play mah-jongg until midnight. It's like this every day, not only in Rang City, but in most small or medium-sized Chinese cities.

When I talk with Secretary Wei about the teahouse and stage, it's clear that he held high hopes for them. He hoped he could draw support for this platform, including governmental help and public participation. They could improve access to cultural life for rural residents, add a sense of cultural atmosphere, and have a nurturing influence. He could also reintroduce some traditional cultural art forms, including traditional opera, Henan Opera, and Lion Dancing. But the actual results have been less than ideal, and the responses from rural and urban citizens haven't been great. They have even ended up encouraging less positive habits. From an official perspective, some village branch secretaries, county cadres, and various other administrators were only doing it for the sake of appearances; they didn't really organize or supervise them. Some other national educational and cultural measures have not reaped any real benefits either, including the one Qingdao mentioned: "Distance education gives you a television, but they just give it to the larger production team, and there they stay." Some administrative production brigades even have computer rooms that you can use to get on the Internet. There are also training rooms, sewing machines, and well-stocked libraries. Yet, without a single exception, they are all gathering dust. When we would arrive for a visit, the village secretary would run around asking for the person with the keys, who might be in the fields working, or maybe was in town running errands. We would always have to wait for a long time. Most people aren't likely to go to such trouble to borrow a book. The beautiful plans remain castles in the air.

A few popular theater troupes in the county are still frequently invited to sing old pieces at weddings and funerals. But this can't be called a cultural revival. A true cultural revival must be holistic, incorporating lifestyle, customs, and moral views. Only then can a culture be reborn. And yet this is extremely difficult. A culture can be destroyed in less than a dozen years, yet its revival can be nearly impossible. And this is to say nothing of the fact that it exists within the formidable vortex that is modernization.

Listening to the sound of the mah-jongg tiles clicking away in the teahouses and seeing the empty stage in the distance, I think about the countless young people who don't know what path to follow. I see, in their empty expressions, the irretrievable dissolution of a people's culture and lifestyle. The die is cast.

Goodbye, Hometown!

I go alone to the graveyard to say goodbye to Mother.

The village's natural connection to the open plains, the mountain streams and the rivers, means it can always evoke a profound, age-old homesickness. That connection lifts the human gaze upward into the wide world, into the boundless expanse of sky. It allows for unlimited reflection on the soul's source and its final destination.

The earth is eternal. Looking outward from my mother's grave, I see green fields on the left, stretching flat and smooth as far as the eye can see. Farm crops, low and fresh, filled with life. The dusky blue, dimming sky. Clouds at the horizon tinged sunset red. To the right is the broad riverbank and lush forest. Pink silk-tree flowers embroider the treetops and sway in the breeze like tiny dancing fairies. Little, dumpling-like cloud puffs float above. I don't know why, but I suddenly feel that my mother is here with me. She is lying in the earth, but her daughter can feel her, her soul, her spirit. Warmth spreads slowly through my heart. Yes, Mama, I have come to see you. Even though it happens less and less frequently, every time I come, or even when I simply think about this piece of earth where you lie, my heart feels connected to yours, as if you were still watching us closely.

I have never been able to describe the pain of losing my mother as a young child. I can see her lying in bed, watching us go off to school, only able to say "ah, ah" as she wept, unable to hold back her tears. She could not move; she could not speak. She could not express her love, and she was wracked with guilt for bringing this tragedy to our family. She had lost all hope. The sound of her weeping has haunted me for a long time; my weaknesses, self-loathing, sensitivity, and reserve all have their origins within it.

I can't imagine my mother ending up in a box of ashes, especially as I stand here, before her grave. If it weren't for this symbolic burial mound, if she were not physically lying beneath the ground, I couldn't imagine: Is she still watching over me? Is my heart still deeply connected to hers? Every time something important happens in the family, we all must come here, to burn paper money and kowtow. Then we sit beside her grave and tell her about it. Once, when I was young, after my father and brother fought in the middle of the night, my brother ran to the graveyard, a knife in his hand; I followed behind, soaked with fear, not only that my brother might die, but also that my mother would find out what had happened at home. For a moment I really hoped that time would stop forever. To this day I can still remember the sound of my brother shouting and weeping until he went hoarse. He could tell only our mother his sorrows, his helplessness. My brother rolling before her grave, telling her everything, longing for her to hold him, for her to comfort her lonely, wretched boy. I finally understood this time, why, when father's operation succeeded, some of my sisters came home just to tell our mother. For an event to be given its proper significance, she must be told.

Must this age-old way of paying homage become a thing of the past? I remember a friend from the south telling me how they pay homage to relatives at Qingming Festival. They get up early in the morning and go to their relatives' graves, everyone carrying something to eat or drink. They burn paper money, set off firecrackers, and kowtow. Then they eat, talk, chat, and play mah-jongg. They spend the whole day there, only leaving after the sky has grown dark. When I heard this, I felt something both inexpressibly warm and bitter. This kind of remembrance is at once so comforting and so natural. To spend all day with your loved ones, to live with them again as if they were still with you. I have no way of knowing how much rural land has been given over to graveyards, but if heavy-handed methods cause these popular customs to be lost, it will certainly damage our national psyche and character.

The countryside has not been completely transformed and, perhaps some things can still be preserved. Because within it we can still sense the deep emotion and love, the goodness, the generosity, the simplicity and affection of our people. When this is gone, too much will have been lost. Perhaps it is precisely the farmers' and the village's stubborn roots, their sense of identity, their unique ways of life and expressing emotion that will allow them to endure.

In the eyes of the "enlightened" or the "developmentalists," these traits are the mark of the farmers' inferiority. They are an expression of their refusal to accept new ways of life and their cultural backwardness. But isn't the problem in our way of thinking—we who hold power and knowledge? We do not trust our own culture. We want to uproot everything. But we have forgotten what a scholar once said: "Modernization is a classic tragedy. For every benefit it brings, it asks the people to pay with all they hold of value."

I don't know why, but I sense that in the future I will come home less frequently. When one's home exists as a complete memory in one's heart, the desire to return is powerful, and one's love for it is also complete. But these months I've spent penetrating deep beneath the surface, analyzing, excavating, have changed my conception of the village beyond recognition. When love and sorrow are no longer mysterious, and everything is done for utility or expedience, the desire to return is lost. Or perhaps utility has destroyed and profaned the sanctity of those feelings. My feelings for Gramma Wu, Xiao Zhu, and all the others in my hometown, are no longer pure.

Goodbye, hometown.

Goodbye, Mama. Because you are here, I return, and will continue to return until the moment my own life comes to an end.

Afterword

During the last decade, what has changed in Liang Village?

On the nineteenth day of the eleventh lunar month in 2015, my father—who appears in this book as Liang Guangzheng—passed away in the Liang family home. Like my mother, who passed away thirty years earlier, he is buried in a grave behind the village. As far as I'm concerned, this is the greatest change of all. While my father was alive, whenever I returned to Liang Village I felt like a child again: innocent, curious, enthusiastic about every person and thing I happened to encounter, able to completely immerse myself in their stories. With my father gone, along with so many of his peers—Grandpa Ming, Uncle Fu, Uncle Zhong—there's no buffer ahead of me. On the road to the grave, I have become that buffer for others. An even greater sense of responsibility has risen up, seemingly all of a sudden. I feel an even deeper connection to Liang Village, and even more of an obligation to record its continued existence, along with the joys and sorrows of its inhabitants. My mother and father are buried in this little patch of land: it's my source, my past, and now, perhaps, my future.

In the grand arc of history, ten years is a flash. But for one person, or one household, or one village, many things can happen in a decade. Many villagers have passed away: old ones, young ones, some from natural causes, others unexpectedly. All kinds of deaths have played out in Liang Village, each one creating a surge of disruption that subsided almost as quickly as it came, although the scars will always be there. The village is structured in such a way that these deaths become public events. Families get together to discuss, debate and, eventually, decide who should leave to negotiate compensation money and bring home cremated remains of the deceased, or who should take charge of funeral arrangements and putting affairs in order. It's a sign that there's still some kind of cohesion to the village.

I've added it up: in the past ten years, at least a dozen people from Liang Village have died unexpectedly. Some were run over, like my cousin's son Liang Qingfeng and my mother's godson Wang Jiayou, one in Xinjiang, one in Ningbo, both smashed to pieces by speeding trucks. Others were sick and put off getting treated, like a woman of my age called Hualian, who got liver cancer. After finding out how much the treatment would cost, she went straight back to work and carried on working to her very last breath. Then there was the young mother who didn't get her feverish daughter to the doctor in time to save her life. A month later she poisoned herself, and her last words were: "Seeing as you all blame me, I'm going to be with my daughter." Then there was knife enthusiast Qingli, who got into a fight with the village bachelor, Liang Jianhu, and ended up stabbing him to death. Then my father's good friend, the ever irascible Grandpa Ming, who drowned in the water urn of his own home; he was drunk and leaned over to get some water in the middle of the night, only for the jagged opening to sever a major artery in his neck. And then, one quiet afternoon, sixty-five-year-old Mrs. Wang went and hanged herself in a corner of her house. Prior to her death, there had been no big family conflict, no struggle to keep food on the table.

If we look carefully, behind every one of these deaths is a shadow of the times.

Chinese villagers head to the cities for jobs, often on construction sites, where there is minimal safety and little chance of compensation if anything happens. In the case of an accident, a village usually sends a team to the city to help, but even the most knowledgeable village minds end up bamboozled by a deluge of regulations and exemption clauses. It is extremely difficult for injured workers to receive what they should be entitled to. In

Beijing, I am constantly receiving phone calls from fellow villagers who find themselves away from home and caught up in work disputes. Implicated parties often resort to violence, meaning that not only do these villagers lose out on compensation money, they also risk getting beaten up.

The past ten years have seen a rise in suicides among elderly villagers. It has become a very serious problem. Younger villagers leave to find work, sending any children that come along back home for their parents to look after (understandably, given that there is no way they could afford to pay for childcare). Sometimes, one elderly grandparent will be left caring for several children at once, and they feel lonely, exhausted, taken for granted. Sometimes, death seems like the only relief. Although, of course, this is a superficial explanation. To go deeper, it is clear that there is a crisis of elderly care in rural China. In 2009, the government launched a "New Rural Social Endowment Insurance System for the Elderly," which required all villagers to pay 100 RMB a year until the age of sixty, after which they would receive a monthly payout of between 60 and 80 RMB. In 2019, annual contributions were increased to 200 RMB, and the subsequent monthly payouts to 100 RMB (at least, this is the case in Rang County). This is obviously a significant improvement but, in terms of the current cost of living, 100 RMB a month remains barely a drop in the ocean. Fundamentally, the scheme does nothing at all to address the issue of how to provide for elderly villagers.

Even less attention is paid to women's health and fundamental rights. Women in rural areas have always been overlooked. These women, especially those in middle-age, work year-round in extraordinary conditions. While young, most went out to work with their husbands, but since having children many have stayed at home to look after them; others have carried on farming. Women who stay at home are seen as scroungers, as doing nothing to earn their keep—no one is convinced of their worth. Rural women in general suffer greatly from androcentrism. It masquerades as "tradition," "virtue" and even "love," and it keeps women tightly shackled. Take inheritance rights, for example. When a woman's parents pass away, she inherits almost nothing. If she tries to question this, she'll be denounced by everyone around her; not even the law is in her favor. As more villages are demolished and real estate speculation increases, the issue is only becoming more pronounced.

The elderly die, the young grow up, babies are born. Inside a village, death, aging and birth are both private affairs and public ones. The village interior is wide open. Lives come and go but the village endures, much like the big river behind it: always changing, but always there.

If you, the reader of this book—as a stranger, as an outsider— can come to know Liang Guangzheng, Qingli, Grandpa Ming, and can get a sense for their joys and sorrows, perhaps you will start to relate to them. You, like me, might start to believe that they are us, that each person living on this planet is also everyone else.

The past ten years have also brought major changes to local geography.

Behind the village, a man-made river now carries water from south to north (the South-to-North Water Diversion Channel).[1] It is quite the sight to behold, dug deep into the earth, slicing through it like a giant sword. It has ruthlessly superseded the River Tuan, which used to flow nearby; for thousands of years the Tuan nurtured the populations along its banks, but now it is feeble and dried up. This is no exaggeration: the Tuan of my

---

1 The South-to-North Water Diversion Project is one of China's strategic engineering projects, divided into east, west and central routes. The central route originates in the Danjiangkou Reservoir, in the upper reaches of the Han River, and supplies water to Henan, Hebei, Beijing and Tianjin. Situated in Rang County, Henan province, Liang Village is part of the central route. Plans were first conceived in 1956, and work began in 2002. In December 2014, the first phase of the central route was officially declared open.

childhood would regularly swell its banks and flood the village, but decades of incessant sand dredging have decimated the course of the river. Even when the summer rains are at their heaviest, the Tuan remains a trickle.

Construction of the diversion channel has dramatically altered the surrounding villages. Some have had to relocate, leaving the sites their ancestors lived on for generations; some have been cleaved in two, with the enormous, raised river charging straight through the middle; others have shrunk, and now cower into the ground. That last description is not metaphorical, I mean it literally: the new river channel rises several dozen meters above the ground. If you stand on its embankment and survey the villages on either side, they appear squat and indistinct, buried beneath a layer of dust. This kind of overnight transformation can be disturbing to witness. It's not about whether it's right or wrong, it's more that such colossal, breakneck development makes you feel the weight of time. Your own life feels curtailed and insignificant. In a flash, everything you once considered constant is gone, is "the past," even external geographical features. Memories are wrenched up by the roots.

Inside the village, we used to have six ponds of varying sizes, filled with either water or sludge, and they have all vanished. They're filled in now, and houses have been built on top. Because, although we talk of the Chinese countryside as impoverished, and of farmers forced into cities to make ends meet, many of those departed farmers save up a bit of money and build houses in their villages. They're thinking ahead to when they can't work anymore and move back home again. The past decade has seen this tendency arise even among Liang villagers who have been away for years, whose family homes are long gone, who perhaps even have city *hukous* and not a scrap of land left in the village—even they are doing everything in their power to come back and build houses. In Liang Village, the Liang and Han families are both at it. By the embankment in the south of the village, there's an ultra-luxury European-style villa, built by one of the Han kids who left, got rich, and hasn't been back for years. The house is for the whole clan, one floor per household, each with its own bedrooms, kitchen, study and balcony, kitted out with the finest furniture, in the most fashionable designs. On top is a terrace with a grand, domed roof. You can stand up there, enjoying the breeze, gazing at the many turns of the riverbank as it winds into the distance, and the view before you is among the most beautiful the world has to offer. But the rest of the village is crammed with new builds. After all these years of "planning," Liang Village is more of a mess than ever before. "Planning" is a figure of speech: if it works to your advantage, then it's in accordance with planning regulations; otherwise, the regulations don't exist. Just outside the door to my family home, the main road out of the village has been mutilated into a twist of fried dough.

People claim to love Liang Village, and they love to build houses in Liang Village, but anything to do with the public good—I'm talking about roads, building regulations, sanitation, and so on—and these same people get exasperated, sigh, and start angrily blaming officials, or other people. Such things are always someone else's responsibility. Really, it's a question of what will be of most benefit to them. They're out for themselves. In this respect, things now are no different than what the sociologist Fei Xiaotong observed last century, in the '30s and '40s, while writing his book *From the Soil*.[2]

Another trend is that Liang villagers who left for work are starting to come back. These are the ones who have stuck out life in the city for over twenty years and now find themselves entering their fifties, with grandchildren in the picture; while their sons and daughters-in-law continue in the cities, these middle-aged villagers are returning to the countryside in enormous numbers, grandchildren in tow. They're still physically fit

---

2   Fei Xiaotong was a renowned Chinese sociologist. *From the Soil* was published in 1948.

and entirely capable of working—they could be earning their own money and retaining their positions at the head of the family, except that now they have grandchildren to think about, they have to make sacrifices. In this way, subtle changes arise in their standing within the family. They are caring for their grandchildren on behalf on their children but, in order to do so, they've had to leave paid employment. This means they have to rely on their children for money, effectively becoming their dependents. As a result, they are no longer considered the leaders of the family, and this transfer of power leads to all sorts of problems. For example, that of elderly care. In ten years' time, when their grandchildren are grown, these aging villagers will no longer be capable of working and won't have any savings to speak of. If they have dutiful children, fine; if they don't, they will suffer horribly. For an elderly person to be at the mercy of their children's character like this is panic-inducing.

Also among the returnees are younger people with savings. They arrive hoping for opportunities closer to home, which will allow them to raise their children themselves and avoid the fate of being forever separated from their roots. This has been the case for Liang An, who worked as a decorator in Beijing; for Liang Yirong, who calibrated oil pumps in Gansu; for Liang Wanmin, who opened a garment factory in Dongguan; and for Liang Guangliang, who went to work in a Qingdao electroplating factory. All of them came back to Rang County to start over. But business opportunities are not easy to come by, and for some returnees it all ends in disaster. If so, after a year or two back home, they'll pack up their belongings once again and head out to some city or the other to find work.

In terms of land, for the past decade or so, Liang villagers have been "landless farmers." To put it another way, they're the first generation of villagers not to farm. People often ask whether we can still call them farmers if they are no longer farming. But consider the facts: their households are registered in Liang Village, their benefits and social security insurance are different to those of city dwellers, and their children do not have the right to attend school in the city (not even when their parents have been working there for twenty-something years). From this perspective, they're still farmers. It's an identity, not an occupation.

Revenue from farming is next to nothing. In fact, farming often costs more money than it earns. When I was a child, each Liang villager had about 1.4 *mu* of land. Now, as the population has grown, there's barely 0.8 *mu* per capita. A family of six might not even make it to five *mu*. With five *mu* of land and two harvests a year—planting wheat in the winter to harvest in June, then replacing it with cash crops like corn, soy beans, mung beans or tobacco—the total income might just about match the monthly salary of a couple working in the city. This is why so many farmers are reluctant to farm, despite government subsidies (for example a yearly allowance of 180 RMB per *mu*, or specific incentives offering a fixed amount of money for a particular crop).

Since around 2007, large corporations have been moving in on Liang Village. Villagers have been convinced to rent out the three or four hundred *mu* "Northern Mound" in its entirety, at an annual rate of 600 RMB per *mu*. This allows the land to be amalgamated and intensively managed. The government acts as both a support and a guarantor for this process—in other words, the government backs an intensive land management model. Liang villagers have welcomed this with open arms. Why wouldn't they? Prior to this, the land was a burden; they didn't want to farm it, but neither could they leave it idle. The new system means other people managing the land while also paying the villagers rent for it.

In recent years, the Chinese government has implemented a more detailed "land transfer" policy (the time period and mode of implementation vary by county and province). Individual plots of land are merged into single areas and the government then acts as intermediary, ensuring that farmers receive rent payments and that companies find good sites (every local government must meet performance targets). The idea is an integrated system, ensuring the integrity of the economic chain. However, in Liang Village, the government has been exceptionally passive. If a company goes bankrupt, the government is supposed to assume responsibility for paying rent to villagers; in Liang Village, it has failed to do so, and this has led to protracted wrangling. Farmers from Liang and other villages have organized for representatives to petition and file lawsuits, but all these attempts have been blocked. Currently, they're at a stalemate.

There is another, even broader policy, involving the complete relocation of villages in order to optimize commercial flow between farmland and residential areas. Theoretically, residents are free to sell their land if they want to. In practice, they are forced to comply with policies demanding that they abandon their homes and move into custom-built apartment blocks.

However, when I was conducting interviews in Liang Village, every single villager told me the same thing: they would rent you land—even for ten, twenty years—but not sell it to you. "There's no way anyone in my generation is selling land. If I did that, what would be left for my son and grandsons?"

As far as demolition and relocation goes, a few years ago Liang villagers were talking about it, but over the last year or two they've dropped the topic. In other provinces, for example Shandong, it has happened with great fanfare and the social impact has been horrendous, largely due to the lack of adequate housing for villagers to move into. A number of villagers there were "relocated" several years ago, but the promised housing still has not materialized, leaving them out on the streets.

Chinese villages are undergoing their greatest transformation in all their thousands of years of history. Some have vanished, some exist only in name; others are flourishing, and their destinies are inextricably tied to development, political inclination, and the choices made by individuals.

*

One final point I'd like to mention is that this book has stirred up some controversy among Chinese readers, especially academics. The main reason for this is the presence of an "I." Some readers maintain that the first person makes the narration excessively emotional; all the stories and descriptions are "subjective" and therefore insufficiently "real." I gave some thought to these criticisms but, ultimately, when I started to write a second book, *Leaving Liang Village,* I stuck to the same approach.[3] My logic being: Liang Village is my home. When I enter the village, every tree, every house, every person I encounter—they all contain shadows of the past. They are all overlaid with associations. They contain memories, time, vestiges of days gone by. Of course it's emotional. This emotion is part and parcel of "reality," and of what we call "non-fiction." Unreal would be if I deliberately avoided it, and wrote as though completely detached, with no feelings at all. In fact, if we consider it from a reception theory perspective, a reader relates to these two books precisely because of this emotional "I"—because this "I" is also the reader. For readers from outside China, familiar with the literary non-fiction genre, this last point is also key to your understanding and acceptance of the book. Going by this premise, you may have a real understanding of the emotions I write about, and through this you will be able to understand why the book resonated as it did with Chinese readers.

---

3 *Leaving Liang Village* was published in China in 2013, and won awards including that year's Great Books of China Award, Essayist of the Year and the inaugural Prize for Non-Fiction Writing, as well as being named one of the "Top Ten Books of 2013" by Sina.com. If *China in One Village* is about the lives of Liang villagers—the old people left behind at home, the women, the children—and the culture there, the morality, the ponds, the big river, then *Leaving Liang Village* is about those villagers who leave to find work. I spent over a year tracking them down, visiting more than twenty Chinese cities in the process. I wanted to know what they ate, where they lived, how they got about in the city, how they felt about the city they had landed in, and how they felt about the village they had left behind. This is the other side of Liang Village—taken together, *China in One Village* and *Leaving Liang Village* make a complete modern village.

"Liang Village" is not just any village; it's where I come from. I am familiar with its every smile, understand every mysterious twitch of its face, perceive all the loves and hostilities contained therein, now and in times past. I love each and every villager, despite my criticisms, dissatisfactions, and even my complaints. I love them as we love our parents, and our children. This is the main reason I started writing about Liang Village, and it is also the reason I continue to do so. I consider it my duty to keep doing so all my life.[4]

---

4 I am currently working on *Ten Years in Liang Village*. My idea is to write a book about Liang Village every ten years, observing the geographical changes, the altering cultural attitudes, and the villagers as they move through their lives. I'll keep doing it until I, myself, pass on. In this way, over the decades, I hope a truthful "Record of Liang Village" will take shape, which will also be a "Record of Life."